Bay of Danzig

Neustadt Hela

Königsberg

Gdynia Westerplatte
Zoppot
Danzig

Elbing

Dirschau

Marienburg

EAST

PRUSSIA

Deutsch Eylau

CORRIDOR
(Pomerelia)

Bromberg

Mlawa

Thorn

Vistula

L   A   N   D

Warsaw

Warthe

Lodz

Vistula

Gross Wartenberg

Namslau

0   50   100
Miles

0   50   100   150
Kilometers

Upper

Silesia

Cracow

d deFontaine

THE FREE CITY

Danzig and German Foreign Policy 1919–1934

THE FREE CITY

Danzig and German Foreign Policy
1919–1934

by Christoph M. Kimmich

New Haven and London, Yale University Press,
1968

Library of Congress catalog card number: 68–27758

Designed by John O. C. McCrillis,
set in Times Roman type,
and printed in the United States of America by
The Colonial Press Inc., Clinton, Massachusetts.

Distributed in Great Britain, Europe, Asia, and
Africa by Yale University Press Ltd., London; in
Canada by McGill University Press, Montreal; and
in Latin America by Centro Interamericano de Libros
Académicos, Mexico City.

Published with assistance from
the Louis Stern Memorial Fund

for my parents

Preface

The objective of German foreign policy between 1919 and 1933 was the revision of the Treaty of Versailles. Not least among the goals to which the German Republic aspired was the recovery of the eastern territories: West Prussia, Upper Silesia, and Danzig. By virtue of its peculiar status as an enclave of Germans living in an autonomous state beyond the borders of the Reich, Danzig became the means by which Germany intended to effect the return of her lost land. This study, then, is devoted to relations between Germany and the Free City, 1919–34, less for their own sake than for the purpose of examining the history of the Weimar Republic's attempt to revise the borders.

Territorial revisionism, a consistent characteristic of Weimar foreign policy, advanced through three stages of approximately equal duration. In the early years, 1919–25, revision was little more than an express desire of the German government, prompted by sentiment—animosity toward the peace settlement, contempt of Poland, and yearning for the Germans and the land the Reich had lost. In the Stresemann era, 1925–29, sentiment was subsumed under political strategy. Then, in the years after Stresemann's death in 1929, strategy ossified into doctrine: it remained unmodified in national and international situations which were changing rapidly and radically, and was long obsolete in 1933 when Hitler discarded it abruptly and adopted the tactic which culminated in the German-Polish declaration of nonaggression in January 1934. To describe and interpret these stages of territorial revisionism in the Weimar Republic is the purpose of this book.

Acknowledgments

I have great debts. A Fulbright grant enabled me to study at Saint Antony's College, Oxford, from 1961 to 1963 and to work in archives on the continent. The late Johannes Ullrich of the Politisches Archiv, Auswärtiges Amt, Bonn, received me cordially, and his kindness expedited my research. Norman Field of the Library of the European Office of the United Nations, Geneva, put the archives of the League of Nations at my disposal, and the staff of the Bundesarchiv, Koblenz, responded to my requests with characteristic courtesy. In the Library of the Foreign Office, London, I discussed my work with Ronald Wheatley, whose knowledge of Weimar foreign policy and Weimar documents I value. Agnes Headlam-Morley of Saint Hugh's College, Oxford, permitted me to read and cite her father's diary; Andrew and Barbara Foster of Norwich, Vermont, lent me their personal copy of Mr. Foster's thesis on Danzig.

Alan Bullock supervised my work at Oxford. He read my first manuscript with scrupulous care, and his personal example greatly encouraged me during what was, in many respects, a time of beginnings. David Goldey offered me his understanding of interwar history, which clarified my thoughts, and his unrelenting optimism, which sustained my spirits. Rudolph Binion read the manuscript as observantly as if it had been his own, and it has profited from his extraordinary sense for felicitous expression and cogent argument. Gerald Freund's counsel and interest in my work have accompanied me through all the stages of preparation, and it is by his efforts that the book can now be published.

To Fritz Stern I owe my willingness to rewrite my first manuscript. He commented on it and on the revised version, giving me the benefit of his knowledge and of his fine awareness of the complexity of historical situations. His friendship and his confidence in me were an unremitting source of moral support.

My wife Flora worked with me throughout the revision, and in its latter stages we shared the labor equally. The book is, then, to a very large extent our common endeavor.

C.M.K.

January 1968

Contents

CHAPTER 1

The Peace Conference

At the time of the First World War, Danzig deservedly enjoyed the reputation of one of the most beautiful cities on the Baltic. Set back slightly from the sea, it lay in a landscape of fertile flatland, dunes, white beaches, and oak woods extending right to the edge of the water. Its narrow streets, numerous steeples, remaining ramparts, watchtowers, and gates bespoke its medieval origin. The most famous landmark, the Marienkirche, a fine example of fourteenth-century Gothic, rose above the rooftops, its massive outlines visible from a great distance. The church's simple, almost severe exterior of dark red brick enclosed an immense nave of intricate vaulting and ogival arches. The shadow of the Marienkirche fell on Renaissance and Baroque buildings—monuments to the city's prosperity in the sixteenth and seventeenth centuries, when its merchant princes had commissioned Flemish and Italian architects to design and decorate their homes. The patrician houses, reminiscent of Lübeck's, were steep-gabled, with ornamental facades, bay windows, and— peculiar to Danzig—raised stone porches in front of the doors. Here lived the rich and influential, if they had not moved to the residential suburbs of Langfuhr and Oliva or to the villas in the nearby seaside resort of Zoppot. Rows of Wilhelmine buildings, whose architects had sought to emulate the old, enclosed the *Altstadt*. They housed the city's commercial and industrial life.

   Danzig stood guard over the mouth of one of Europe's mighty rivers, the Vistula, which rose near Cracow and flowed some 650 miles through territory inhabited predominantly by Poles. Thus the city, which enjoyed an excellent natural harbor, commanded both sea and river traffic. The port was the source of Danzig's livelihood and, as the half-timbered warehouses showed, had been for centuries. A panorama of piers and docks, bridge and portal cranes, warehouses, granaries, and timber yards stretched along the harbor front, interspersed with the offices of the carrying trade, the brokers, and the shipping agents. More than two million tons of trade passed through the port in 1913. Agricultural products (grain, timber, flour, beet sugar) predominated among the exports; imports consisted primarily of raw materials (coal, iron ore, fertilizers), foodstuffs, and agricultural and industrial machinery. To cope with the trade, the harbor had been improved extensively in the two decades before 1914. Dock railways were laid and the so-called *Kaiserhafen,* a vast area of basins and wharves, was constructed in 1903. In 1899 a well-equipped free port had been opened at the entrance to the harbor. Yet Danzig was by no means a preeminent port: it ranked fifth among German ports in freight turnover and thirteenth among Baltic ports in tonnage of incoming ships.

Danzig's major industry was shipbuilding. Its most famous builder was the Schichau dockyard, which constructed the celebrated liner *Columbus* in 1913. Its Imperial Navy Yard, owned by the government, supplied the German fleet with submarines. Other industries included armaments, chemicals, sugar, beer, and spirits.

The city's language and pattern of life were German. Ninety-six percent of the Danzigers were German, the rest primarily of Polish extraction. Though commerce and industry employed nearly half the population, Prussian civil servants, military officers, and pensioners set the social tone. As the capital of West Prussia, Danzig accommodated the extensive machinery of provincial administration, the offices of taxation and customs and of the railway and postal authorities. A Polytechnical Institute had opened in 1904. Since 1891, the city had been the headquarters of the Seventeenth Army Corps, and a war college had been established in 1894. Danzig's charm, location, and climate encouraged retired officials and soldiers to settle there, and 15 percent of the citizenry was on pension. The populace was by confession about two-thirds Protestant and by political persuasion National Liberal or, to a lesser extent, Conservative— but during the war and thereafter the Catholic Center and Socialist parties were to grow rapidly. German national sentiment—heightened by the Polish presence beyond the city— was universal. Like the other major centers in northeastern Germany, Danzig was middle class and very provincial. The events of the world took place far away: Berlin was a day's trip by rail; Vienna, Saint Petersburg, Paris, and London were beyond reach.

It was this city, pronouncedly and provincially German, which was elevated to independent statehood at the Peace Conference of 1919. Danzig proper, the town of Zoppot, and three rural districts, totaling 1,951 square kilometers and 357,000 inhabitants, became the Free City of Danzig in 1920 so that resurrected Poland might be provided with an outlet to the sea without subjecting the German city to Polish rule.

An outlet to the sea for resurrected Poland had become a pressing issue when the First World War offered the Poles the long awaited opportunity to reconstitute their state, partitioned among Austria, Prussia, and Russia in the eighteenth century. Many Polish patriots had rallied to the national cause. Foremost among them was Roman Dmowski, founder and leader of the National Democratic Party, who sought to win the interest of the western Allies. He was aided by a host of émigré Poles, among them the famous pianist Ignace Paderewski, who forsook his career to devote himself to his country's revival. Polish propaganda abroad was vigorous and emphatic. It insisted that the war be waged not only against William II but also against Frederick the Great. The resurrection of Poland was a prerequisite for peace in Europe; an independent Poland would bar renewed German aggression. Economic and strategic considerations dictated an unimpeded outlet to the Baltic. To survive and flourish, the Polish economy would have to be assured of freedom to trade on international markets. Living between two powerful and hostile neighbors who at any time might join forces to destroy them, the Poles needed secure and unrestricted access to the outside world. If Poland were landlocked, Dmowski argued, she would be "completely dependent upon Germany . . . and thus doomed to gradual destruction." [1]

Polish propaganda found an echo when, in January 1918, Wilson proclaimed his Fourteen Points as Allied war aims. The thirteenth stated that "an independent Polish state should be

1. [Roman Dmowski], *Problems of Central and Eastern Europe* (London, 1917), pp. 72, 74.

erected," comprising "the territories inhabited by indisputably Polish populations . . . assured of a free and secure access to the sea." In June the prime ministers of Britain, France, and Italy endorsed Wilson's proposal for Poland. For the Poles this Allied commitment meant that the future reconstruction of their state was no longer in doubt. What remained uncertain was the delimitation of the frontiers and particularly what was meant by a free and secure access to the sea.

Certainly Danzig seemed the most propitious choice. Its location at the mouth of the Vistula and its command of an extensive rail network made it the natural outlet for the Polish hinterland. Among the German ports on the Baltic, Danzig alone lay near territory populated by Poles, and since Germany had any number of seaports, the loss of Danzig was not likely to interfere with German trade. In October 1918 Dmowski submitted to Wilson a memorandum which summarized the position the Poles were to maintain throughout the Peace Conference: the new Poland should incorporate West Prussia, which included Danzig.[2]

To the French, Danzig's incorporation into Poland—to be sure, with proper guarantees for the German inhabitants— appeared the best solution. The Americans, while not unreceptive to Polish plans, did not commit themselves, and the "Official American Commentary on the Fourteen Points" of October 1918 left the issue unresolved. The British had the strongest reservations. Expressing an unmistakable reluctance to become involved in untenable solutions, the Foreign Office warned in December 1918 that "for the sake of Poland's own future we must firmly oppose exaggerated Polish claims."[3] Balfour, the British foreign secretary, disturbed at the prospect that Poland's access to the sea through a "predominantly German" city might sever East Prussia from the rest of Germany, suggested in October 1918 that the Poles be granted free zones in Danzig harbor and navigational rights on the Vistula.[4]

2. Memorandum by Dmowski, 8 Oct. 1928, in Paul Roth, *Die Entstehung des polnischen Staates* (Berlin, 1926), pp. 133–51.

3. Quoted in Harold Nelson, *Land and Power: British and Allied Policy on Germany's Frontiers 1916–1919* (London, 1963), p. 98.

4. Ibid., p. 64.

A concrete discussion of these possibilities was not broached until the Peace Conference. On 12 February 1919, the Supreme Council (the five Allied heads of state accompanied by their foreign ministers) appointed a Commission on Polish Affairs, also known after its chairman as the Cambon Commission,[5] which was to study and present recommendations on the German-Polish frontier and Poland's access to the sea. The difference between the Commission's proposals and the eventual stipulations in the Treaty of Versailles was the source of Poland's dissatisfaction with the peace settlement.

In the Commission's opinion, Poland's access to the sea would be "free and secure" only if the territory involved were under Polish control. If this meant violating the principle of national self-determination, which had been proclaimed a guiding tenet of the Peace Conference, such a violation was considered legitimate when, as in the case of Danzig, "the national aspirations of a small body of men clash with the vital necessities of a much larger body of men." The Commission therefore recommended that Danzig, both city and port, be given to Poland "in unrestricted ownership." It reasoned that:

a. the legitimate aspirations of the Polish people for an outlet to the sea, as endorsed by Allied statesmen, cannot be fulfilled unless Danzig becomes a Polish port;

b. the so-called Polish corridor to the sea should become a part of the Polish state, because the interests of 1,600,-000 Germans in East Prussia can be adequately protected by securing for them freedom of transit across the corridor, whereas it would be impossible to give an adequate outlet to the inhabitants of the new Polish state (numbering some 25,000,000) if this outlet had to be guaranteed across the territory of an alien and probably hostile power . . . ;

c. the interests of the German commercial population of Danzig will be best served by the development of Danzig as a Polish port;

5. Its chairman was Jules Cambon (France), its other members Isaiah Bowman (United States), Sir William Tyrrell (Great Britain), Pietro

d. with the exception of Danzig itself, every district in the proposed Polish corridor contains a Polish majority;

e. the trade of Danzig port has been deliberately stifled by the policy of the Prussian government, and the removal of the artificial restrictions at present in existence will result in a great increase of population. This additional population will in the natural course of things be composed of Poles, who occupy practically the whole of the hinterland for which Danzig is the only adequate port.[6]

The Cambon Report, submitted to the Supreme Council on 19 March, brought differences on the Polish question into the open and precipitated one of the stormiest sessions of the Conference. All the Allies agreed that Poland was to be resurrected and assured free access to the sea, but they differed on the means by which this promise was to be fulfilled.

Lloyd George opposed Cambon. He strongly questioned the prudence of a report which, if it inspired a treaty the Germans would not sign, might compromise the work of the Conference—or worse, which might compromise the peace if the Germans did consent to sign. His motives for opposing and ultimately modifying the Commission's recommendations were not unmixed. His arguments betray insight, fear, prejudice, and genuine doubt. Fundamental was his concern for the stability of the peace that was to emerge from these deliberations: Germany must find it possible to live with the treaty. Two liabilities would have to be taken into account. The treaty should not drive Germany into revolution; it should present a fair alternative to the incipient anarchy in Europe.[7] Nor should it leave Germany irreconcilable. Obviously, the present distribution of power on the continent

---

della Torretta (Italy), and M. Otchiai (Japan). Their recommendations concerning Danzig were unanimous.

6. Report No. 1 of the Commission on Polish Affairs, Frontier Between Poland and Germany, 12 Mar. 1919, in David Hunter Miller, *My Diary at the Conference of Paris* (New York, 1925–26), *6*, 355–56; H. J. Paton in H. W. V. Temperley, ed., *A History of the Peace Conference of Paris* (Oxford, 1920–24), *6*, 257.

7. David Lloyd George, *The Truth About the Peace Treaty* (London, 1938), *1*, 407–08.

would not endure. Would the vanquished Germans, once they had recovered, abide by a treaty which departed vindictively from the Fourteen Points? Was the proposed arrangement not vindictive? German sentiment would be deeply offended at the loss of Germans to Polish domination.[8] Such offense would never stop seeking relief.

For Lloyd George, a stable peace also presupposed a satisfactory balance of power on the continent. He saw the French search for security as a scheme for French hegemony, and a Poland enlarged at the expense of Germany as part of this plan.[9] France seconded by Poland would dominate Europe. The Germans would not tolerate this situation once they had regained their strength, and to antagonize them also by depriving them of territory was doubly foolhardy. Furthermore, an enlarged Poland would be a weakened Poland. A substantial German minority—and his Welsh background made the British prime minister sensitive to minority issues—would form an "alien and hostile element" within the Polish state and therefore be a source of weakness. "I knew," he wrote in 1938, "that a time would come when Germany would respond to the cry of its exiled people and restore them to the Fatherland by force of arms."[10]

Finally, personal prejudices were not entirely excluded from these considerations. Lloyd George was angry at the Polish lack of moderation. He was no particular friend of the Poles and held a low opinion of their abilities: they "had no idea of organization; . . . no capacity to direct or govern. The premier was a pianist; the president, an idealist without any practical ideas."[11] He would certainly be reluctant to see Danzig, the gateway to the markets of eastern Europe, in the hands of the non-seafaring Poles.

The French did not share Lloyd George's opinions. They had twice been the victims of German invasion; a third conflict

8. Paul Mantoux, *Les délibérations du Conseil des Quatre* (*24 mars— 28 juin 1919*) (Paris, 1955), *1,* 47.

9. Lloyd George, *2,* 990.

10. Ibid., p. 991.

11. *Papers Relating to the Foreign Relations of the United States: The Paris Peace Conference 1919* (Washington, D.C., 1942–47), *4,* 316. (Henceforth FRUS, *Peace Conference.*)

would have to be forestalled. A weak Germany thus became the primary goal of the French peacemakers. Clemenceau argued that the elimination of the German fleet gave security only to Britain and the United States. France needed further protection, especially if the proposed League of Nations proved incapable of ensuring peace.[12]

To a continental country which saw power primarily in territorial terms, a truncated Germany would be a weak Germany. If Poland gained possession of Danzig and its neighboring territory, she would, by French definition, be strong. A strong power at Germany's eastern borders would contain her. Moreover, it was only just that Poland should be indemnified for the partitions and for long German oppression. Clemenceau knew that a Poland enlarged at Germany's expense would defend the status quo and that French support of Polish claims would ensure Poland's loyalty in the future, thus enabling France to dominate the continental balance of power. The French delegation to the Peace Conference endorsed the Cambon Report.

At the Supreme Council's meeting on 27 March, Lloyd George submitted a compromise solution—a free port at Danzig. This found the support of the American president. Thereupon James Headlam-Morley, the English delegation's special adviser on German territorial questions, was directed to confer with Sidney Mezes, the director of the staff of technical experts in the American delegation. Between them they evolved most of the scheme which eventually appeared in the Treaty of Versailles.

The design seems to have come mainly from Headlam-Morley. In February, during the British delegation's preliminary discussions, he had strongly advocated a solution that would make Danzig an autonomous city-state within either Poland or Germany. To assign Danzig to Poland outright would arouse the most bitter animosity, and an arrangement unacceptable to Germany would endanger Polish security. On 3 March he submitted a strongly worded memorandum rejecting the idea of incorporation: "It is not really a matter merely of German sentiment," he wrote, "but of principle." Headlam-Morley thought that if the city could be made autonomous, assured full control of its govern-

12. Mantoux, *1*, 43–45.

ment, and freed of apprehension that it "shall become a subject of Polish national propaganda . . . then we can be sure that the commercial advantages of cooperation with Poland will soon do their work." [13]

That such a solution should have occurred to Headlam-Morley, a historian by training, is not surprising. Danzig's own history suggested the arrangement. As one of the wealthiest and most powerful Hansa towns, Danzig was linked in personal union with the Polish king from the fifteenth to the eighteenth century, and during this period it had reached the height of its prosperity. Much like the free imperial cities in Germany, it enjoyed almost unrestricted sovereignty, exercising virtually independent control over its affairs. It conducted its own foreign relations and maintained its own legations abroad, controlled its secular and ecclesiastical administration, coined money and levied taxes, erected fortifications, raised troops, and kept a fleet under its own colors. It was the sole administrator of harbor and shipping, exacting customs revenues and regulating exports and imports at will. Its relationship with Poland, meanwhile, was mostly amicable and always mutually advantageous. National consolidation in the fifteenth century raised Poland's agricultural productivity and enabled her to export large quantities of grain, while her forests provided a bountiful supply of timber for the world market. In return she imported finished products from the West. Here was an opportunity Danzig was not slow to seize. A monopoly on trade with a fruitful hinterland and membership in the Hanseatic League proved a most profitable combination. As an entrepôt supplying both eastern and western Europe, Danzig enjoyed wealth and importance until the Hanseatic League was dissolved in the seventeenth century and the Thirty Years' War gradually impoverished Poland. Reduced to a third-rate seaport, Danzig fell to Prussia in 1793. Though the late nineteenth century brought improvement, the city never again enjoyed its earlier prosperity and prominence.

13. James W. Headlam-Morley, "Diary of the Work of Sir James Headlam-Morley at the Paris Peace Conference 1919," Unpublished manuscript, pp. 22–23, 42; memorandum by Headlam-Morley, 4 Apr. 1925 (F.O. 12760), The Eastern Frontiers of Germany, Section II: Danzig and the Corridor, p. 5.

Danzig's illustrious past, then, seemed to argue in favor of a free city. But like all historical analogies, this one was flawed. It failed to take into account the nationalist antagonisms which had grown up in the nineteenth century. The harsh policies which the Germans had inflicted on their Polish subjects had poisoned relations between the two peoples. Economic interests would not obliterate national prejudices. The peacemakers, however, assumed that "a union of interests" would lead to "a union of hearts," inasmuch "as neither of the two parties involved can do without the other." [14]

Discussion in the Supreme Council on 1 April showed that both Wilson and Lloyd George favored the scheme. Danzig was to be a free city, with territory large enough to give it breathing space but included within the Polish customs frontier in order to preclude German attempts to strangle the Polish economy. The city was to be sovereign, as Lloyd George told Headlam-Morley, but her foreign relations were to be placed in the hands of Poland to prevent "dangerous intrigues between Danzig and Berlin." A high commissioner of the new League of Nations would be appointed to supervise the arrangement and to settle disputes. The boundaries of the Free City were roughly drawn on a map by Wilson himself; they were then modified slightly by members of the British and American delegations. [15]

The clash between Britain and France had thrown Wilson into the position of umpire, and his decision to support the proposal of a free city had resolved the impasse. His motives can only be inferred. He sympathized with Polish national aspirations and hoped to redress at least partially the wrongs of the eighteenth century. [16] He was aware, however, that the generous settlement which France envisioned for Poland was not altogether in the Polish interest. "The only real interest of France in Poland is in weakening Germany by giving Poland territory to which she has no right," he confided to his advisers. [17] Further-

14. Paton in Temperley, *6*, 260–61.

15. Memorandum by Headlam-Morley, 4 Apr. 1925, pp. 11–12; Headlam-Morley, "Diary," pp. 65–66, 179–82.

16. Paton in Temperley, *6*, 238.

17. Ray S. Baker, *Woodrow Wilson and World Settlement* (New York, 1922), *2*, 60.

more, he was committed to his principles. He knew that the Cambon proposals violated the principle of "indisputably Polish" territory. The ideal solution would have to provide the Poles with the promised access to the sea without extending the new Polish state over territory patently German. "The difficulty," Wilson commented, "was to arrive at a balance between conflicting considerations." [18] And finally, the eventual settlement would have to make due allowance for German interests. Wilson shared Lloyd George's conviction that the Germans at some future date might be willing and able to rescue their countrymen from Polish rule, and the prospect that Germany might refuse, even now, to sign the treaty worried him. The proposal of a free city seemed an excellent compromise to settle the current differences among the Allies. It appeared to obviate the difficulties which Lloyd George predicted in eastern Europe. On an intellectual level it was an appealing reconciliation of the conflicting principles that the Polish state should comprise only Polish territory but nevertheless enjoy free use of a port.

On 3 April, with Clemenceau still beset by grave misgivings but aware that further intransigence might endanger the Conference and his other interests, the Council reviewed the proposed boundaries and approved the creation of a free city. Mezes and Headlam-Morley drafted the final version of the articles, confining it to the broad outlines adequate for the treaty with Germany on the assumption that many details could be left for later settlement on the spot.[19] Thus a compromise was reached which was to satisfy neither Danzigers, nor Germans, nor Poles. Paderewski, having lost a final emotional appeal to the Council, said in resignation: "But Danzig will remain in German hands—consequently, in those of Germany, to which it ultimately will return." [20]

At the same time as they concluded the dispute over Danzig, the Allies agreed on a number of other issues. Like the Danzig problem, most of these were resolved by compromise. Poland received West Prussia, which became her corridor to the sea,

18. FRUS, *Peace Conference, 4,* 417, 418.
19. Memorandum by Headlam-Morley, 4 Apr. 1925, p. 11, 9 May 1919, LN: 4/68/4.
20. Mantoux, *1,* 200.

most of Posen, and parts of Silesia and East Prussia. France had envisioned larger cessions for her protégée but compromised in return for a promised alliance with Britain and the United States and fifteen years' Allied occupation of the Rhineland. This, too, was a concession on France's part, for she had wished to annex the west bank of the Rhine, but Wilson and Lloyd George had been adamant. France had wanted to annex the Saar as well but settled for the right to exploit the land, which would be consigned to international administration. To protect France against future invasion, the German army was to be reduced to 100,000 men. For the sake of his cherished League of Nations, Wilson abandoned his principle that the war should not have been fought for the material enrichment of the victors and permitted Germany's colonies to be divided among Great Britain, France, and Japan. Clemenceau and Lloyd George obliged him to agree to German "reparations" which were in fact also indemnities. These claims against the enemy were justified by a preamble which attributed responsibility for the war to Germany.

The draft of the Allied peace terms was handed to the Germans on 7 May. The English and the Americans were astounded at the harshness of the assembled document; the Germans were thunderstruck. The Germans were all the more aghast because they had anticipated many of these possibilities and for seven months—since October 1918, when they had accepted the Fourteen Points as the basis for an armistice—had been at work on an interpretation of these points, from which they sought to derive proposals, or at least counterproposals, to be advanced at the Peace Conference. When they received the Treaty, they saw their forebodings confirmed and surpassed.

When the Germans had accepted the Fourteen Points in October 1918, both they and the Poles had realized that a settlement in the East as the Poles envisioned it was no longer a speculative but rather a real possibility. The thirteenth point was sufficiently vague to permit the most diverse construals, and the Poles in fact used it to ground their claim that the new Polish state should extend over most of Prussia's eastern provinces (indigenously Polish territory) and include Danzig (outlet to the sea). Now that the Germans had accepted the Fourteen Points, the Polish demands, vocal since Wilson's program had been enunciated in January 1918, were no longer simple Polish extravagance but a danger on Germany's doorstep.

Press and government reacted accordingly. German newspapers of October 1918 denounced the demands as a threat to world peace, a permanent block to German-Polish friendship. In the Reichstag, partisan differences disappeared as party spokesmen vied with one another in aggressively denouncing the idea of territorial cessions in the East. Count Westarp of the Conservatives told the Reichstag on 20 October that Germany would have to insist on the inviolability of the territory of the Reich: Polish claims to Germany's eastern provinces were outrageous. At the other end of the political spectrum, Hugo Haase of the Independent Socialists asserted on 23 October that in the East popular self-determination would have to prevail over linguistic or historical arguments.

That same day a Polish deputy in the Reichstag, Anton Stychel, interpreted the thirteenth point to his colleagues by saying that Poland would have to become a sovereign, independent state with her own seacoast and harbor, and her political and economic independence and territorial invulnerability would have to be guaranteed by treaty. Stychel's speech was sharply censured the following day when the German state secretary, Wilhelm Solf, declared that the demand for Danzig would be in base contradiction to the principles of international justice embodied in the Fourteen Points. In reply, the Polish deputy Wojciech Korfanty submitted that Poland did not desire a foot of German soil but merely, in accord with the thirteenth point, a unified Poland with a secure access to the sea through territory inhabited by Poles—the left bank of the Vistula down to the Hela Peninsula. "As to Danzig, we do not deny it, it is an indubitably German city. If the Peace Conference awards it to Poland, as we hope, then Danzig will merely share the fate of the many minorities and foreign language enclaves which will be unavoidable in the final settlement of the European scene." [21]

To Danzig itself, of course, the implications of the thirteenth

21. *Verhandlungen des Reichstags, Stenographische Berichte*, Bd. 314, pp. 6179, 6190, 6197, 6210, 6255.

point were ominous: the Danzigers knew that the promised access
to the sea would have significant bearing on their future, and they
were aware that the Poles desired the incorporation of the city
into their new state. To a generation reared in the nationalist
tradition of the Second Reich this prospect was doom. When
rumors of annexation reached the Danzig Magistrat, the governing body of the city, its reaction was adamant. On 14 October
it wired the German Ministry of the Interior that Danzig must
never belong to Poland. "The strength of German culture has
created our old Hansa city of Danzig and caused it to grow. It is
German to the core. We demand the right of self-determination.
We want to remain German forever." [22] Hungry and bedraggled
from war, Danzig could not even comfort itself with hopes
for the future. Its fright and anger at the prospect of eventual
annexation to a hostile state were vented in a storm of nationalist
indignation. Protest marches and demonstrations, incidents between Germans and Poles, expressed the city's malaise and compounded it. Throughout the period from October 1918 to the
signing of the Treaty in June 1919, the city was in a state of
near chaos.

The Danzigers were not suffering from hallucinations. The
Poles acted as if eventual annexation were a foregone conclusion.
In the first week of November 1918, Poles began to purchase
property in the city on a large scale. [23] By a decree of 28 November settling the electoral districts for the coming constituent
assembly in Warsaw, Danzig was given five seats. And when
Paderewski, coming from Paris to establish contact with the
new Polish chief of state, Jozef Pilsudski, landed in Danzig on
25 December 1918, he assured the Poles who came to greet
him that Danzig would soon become a Polish city as in olden
times. Polish soldiers, still dressed in their German uniforms,
were exhorted to rally to the Polish banner and join the Polish
war of liberation. [24] In violation of the safe-conduct which the

22. *Frankfurter Zeitung,* 16 Oct. 1918.
23. Regierungspräsident Danzig to Foreign Ministry, 12 Dec. 1918,
PA: WK Nr. 20c, Bd. 49 (ACP 422/443–44).
24. Generalkommando Danzig to Foreign Ministry, 27 Dec. 1918, PA:
WK Nr. 20c, Bd. 49 (ACP 422/435).

German government had granted him,[25] Paderewski went on to Posen, where his visit occasioned an uprising among the local Poles, and to Warsaw, where Pilsudski made him prime minister and foreign minister, thus legitimizing the Parisian Poles' ambitious program for the new Polish state.

It is therefore no surprise to find that the Danzigers sought to influence the decision on their future. The Magistrat filled the German Foreign Ministry with deputations and flooded it with memorandums. Among other things, it urged repeatedly that the implications of the thirteenth point warranted that Danzig be represented in the German peace delegation. These demands struck Berlin as presumptuous, often opportunistic, and narrowly self-centered.[26] For in the meantime Berlin was at work on diplomatic measures to clarify the confusion over the settlement in the East.

The German government apparently tried first to settle the matter directly. A memorandum of the Foreign Ministry, dated 17 October, argued that in recognition of the "new situation" created by the thirteenth point of Wilson's program, it would be best if borders and future relations were settled in direct negotiation with Poland and the results submitted to the Peace Conference. The memorandum suggested that the Polish state (obviously, Congress Poland) be declared sovereign and independent and the German occupation administration dismantled, and that Berlin inform Warsaw that the German troops in Poland were to be withdrawn imminently. Thus the Polish government, if it did not intend to leave the country exposed to Bolshevism, would be obliged to request the retention of German forces. Such a course of action would make the Poles receptive to the wishes of the Reich.[27]

Although Chancellor Max von Baden wisely rejected this

25. Wako Spa to Foreign Ministry, 30 Dec. 1918, PA: WK Nr. 20c, Bd. 49 (ACP 422/466–67).

26. Magistrat Danzig to Foreign Ministry, 7 Jan. and 6 Mar. 1919, PA: WK Nr. 20c, Bd. 51 and 59 respectively (ACP 422/621–23 and ACP 423/306–08); Sahm to Oberpräsident der Provinz Westpreussen, 13 Mar. 1919, PA: WK Nr. 30, Bd. 32 (4080/D924295–96).

27. Vorschläge zur polnischen Frage, 17 Oct. 1918, PA: WK Nr. 20c, Bd. 42 (ACP 421/529–30).

approach, the idea of direct consultation remained alive. On 14 November a Polish *aide mémoire* requesting the dispatch of an official emissary to Warsaw was received positively. The new republican government selected Count Harry Kessler, former liaison officer in Poland and member of the Foreign Ministry. His instructions were to supervise the evacuation of troops from Poland and the Ukraine. Territorial questions were to be referred to the Peace Conference, but discussion of particular accommodations for the Poles was sanctioned. Kessler was prepared to propose, or to accept the proposal, that the Vistula be canalized as far as Warsaw. "A right of way on land, coupled with a railway neutralized and guaranteed by international agreement and a port on the Baltic next to Danzig and under Polish sovereignty" would "complete the arrangement." Kessler arrived in Warsaw on 20 November, firmly resolved that the best scheme would be to open direct negotiations and submit a common plan to the Conference.

Poles at home and abroad, however, bitterly criticized Kessler's presence in Warsaw, and pressures within the Polish cabinet endangered Pilsudski's none too stable position. He was therefore obliged to "suspend" relations with Germany without reaching further settlement. On 16 December, less than a month after his arrival, Kessler left Warsaw.[28]

Kessler's mission has been interpreted as a German attempt to propagate abroad the notion that the Polish government was neutral and thus ineligible to participate in the Peace Conference.[29] It seems plausible, however, to discount such disingenuous intent and regard the mission as Berlin's effort to make the best of a bad situation: by reaching agreement in direct discussions with Pilsudski and offering friendly relations with Germany, the German government sought to circumvent Dmowski's exaggerated claims in Paris. A German Foreign Ministry

28. Harry Kessler, *Germany and Europe* (New Haven, 1923), p. 33; Harry Kessler, *Tagebücher 1918–1937* (Frankfurt/Main, 1961), pp. 30–32, 39, 68–69; Casimir Smogorzewski, *L'union sacrée polonaise: le gouvernement de Varsovie et le 'gouvernement' polonaise de Paris (1918–1919)* (Paris, 1929), p. 30.

29. Smogorzewski, pp. 29–30; Titus Komarnicki, *Rebirth of the Polish Republic: A Study in the Diplomatic History of Europe 1914–1920* (London, 1957), p. 249.

memorandum analyzing the lessons of Kessler's mission offers some corroboration for this interpretation. It concluded that Pilsudski's territorial demands were relatively modest and that real opposition came from the Polish National Democrats in Paris, who pursued the territorial program of a Poland "from sea to sea"—from the Baltic in the north to the Black Sea in the southeast. It was therefore in Germany's interest to strengthen Pilsudski and not to create undue difficulties for his government, in particular not to stand in the way of Polish territorial claims toward Russia.[30]

While attempting to deal directly with Poland, Berlin of course did not neglect preparation for the expected peace negotiations. In November 1918 the Friedenskommission, or Friko for short, a special agency responsible directly to the foreign minister, had been created. Headed by Count Johann von Bernstorff, a former ambassador to Washington, the Friko established offices in Berlin and staffed them with civil servants who were to put information pertinent to the negotiations at the disposal of the delegation which would meet with the Allies. The Friko was instructed to base its proposals for Poland on Wilson's thirteenth point, his statement to Congress on 11 February 1918 that "every territorial settlement involved in this war must be made in the interest and for the benefit of the populations concerned, and not as a part of any mere adjustment or compromise of claims among rival states," and his observation on 4 July 1918 that "the settlement of every question, whether of territory, of sovereignty, of economic arrangement, or of political relationship, [must rest] upon the basis of the free acceptance of that settlement by the people immediately concerned, and not upon the basis of the material interest or advantage of any other nation or people which may desire a different settlement for the sake of its own exterior influence or mastery." [31]

30. Memorandum by Hatzfeld (Foreign Ministry), 29 Dec. 1918, PA: WK Nr. 20c, Bd. 49 (ACP 422/445–47); Kessler, *Germany and Europe*, p. 33, comes to the same conclusion. That Pilsudski was not entirely unamenable is visible in the dispatch from the German mission in Warsaw, reprinted in the *Frankfurter Zeitung*, 21 Dec. 1918.

31. FRUS 1918, Supplement I, *1*, 112; Baker, *3*, 45–46.

Thus charged, the Friko set to work. It held meetings, questioned experts, and assembled statistics in the quest, among other things, for a proper answer on Poland's access to the sea. Among those whose opinions were solicited was Heinrich Sahm, lord mayor of Danzig, whose concern with the issue was immediate. Sahm represented the Prussian civil service's tradition of scrupulous conscientiousness and loyalty to the state. A man of action rather than of contemplation, clearheaded and decisive, though not rash, he was endowed with a keen political intelligence. In February 1919 in his inaugural address as lord mayor he had warned the Poles: "Hands off Danzig." This became his guiding principle. He was later made the first president of the Senate of the Free City, an office he held for ten years. Sahm was largely responsible for Danzig's official attitude toward its new status. It was his policy which the city pursued during the 1920s.

Sahm's evaluation of the situation was harshly realistic. Germany must adhere loyally and correctly to Wilson's principles. If Germany and Danzig made reservations which put Poland's free access to the sea in doubt, then Danzig could not invoke the right of self-determination and remain within the Reich: the Allies would award the city to Poland. Principles could not be made the object of petty bargaining; sacrifices were necessary. Sahm therefore called for plans to allow the Polish economy the widest possible freedom of development. Poland was to receive a firmly based legal right, a so-called state servitude, at which even the most suspicious enemy could not cavil. This right was to include a free port under unrestricted Polish administration and Polish customs regulations, a German guarantee that the Vistula, also under Polish administration, would be kept navigable between Danzig and Warsaw, and Polish tariff sovereignty over several German railway lines to Danzig. The guarantees and assurances would have to be framed in such a way as to preclude any interference, now or later, from Germany.[32]

Sahm's plan provoked bitter controversy. Major opposition

32. Geschäftsstelle für die Friedensverhandlungen, *Entwurf von Bestimmungen für den Friedensvertrag über den Zugang Polens zum Meer* (Berlin, 1919).

came from Germany's indignant eastern provinces. The plan was deemed basely egotistical, even treacherous to them, a subterfuge meant to ensure Danzig a monopoly of Polish sea trade. The merchants of Königsberg protested that the adoption of these recommendations and their execution would mean the economic ruin of their city. At a meeting on 15 April 1919, to which Danzig had not been invited, representatives of Königsberg explained to the Foreign Ministry that the adoption of the plan would entail worse consequences than if Danzig were forfeited. Whatever happened, they said, Königsberg would lose and Danzig profit, but Sahm's plan would make the loss more grievous. To soothe ruffled tempers, officials of the Foreign Ministry agreed that Sahm's memorial would not serve as a suitable basis for negotiations after all.[33]

The clash of opinions is pathetic, almost eerie. The Königsbergers, and the Friko in agreeing with them, awarded their priorities in a fashion grotesquely incommensurate to the situation confronting them, a situation which Sahm knew intimately and understood. Their claim that Sahm's suggestions were the very maximum and not the minimum concessions he had envisioned betrays a resolute refusal even to attempt to understand what he had said. Instead they let a squabble about economic gain occlude their vision of valid possibility and brutal alternatives. Like the German government, they were confident that documented proof of West Prussia's, and thereby Danzig's, German nationality would preclude removal from the Reich, that sweeping concessions to Poland were prodigal.

On 22 April the Foreign Ministry drew up the final draft of its guidelines for the German peace delegation. It stressed that the basis for the treaty was Wilson's program, binding on both Germany and the Allies. It consigned the interpretation of the thirteenth point to an impartial body which would decide what territory was indisputably Polish. Plebiscites would be permissible, but these were not to be sanctioned in West

33. Chamber of Commerce, Königsberg, to Foreign Ministry, 8 Apr. 1919, BA: R 43 I/1; Preussisches Finanzministerium to Ministry of Finance, 19 Apr. 1919, PA: WK Nr. 30, Bd. 42 (4097/D925875-81); Chamber of Commerce, Königsberg, to Foreign Ministry, 26 Apr. 1919, BA: R 43 I/1348.

Prussia, lest East Prussia become detached from the rest of
the Reich. An outlet to the sea would be provided, not by way
of a corridor, but at one or several free ports on the Baltic,
to which transit privileges and reciprocal agreements on rail
and river traffic would guarantee ready access.[34] The Germans
were of course not ignorant of the advantages afforded them
in the arrangements they put forward. There is, however, no
good reason to doubt that they sincerely believed these arrangements would satisfy Poland's needs. They understood Poland's
access to the sea in strictly legal, not territorial, terms.

When the draft of the Allied treaty was received on 7 May,
the entire staff of the Friedenskommission, in the midst of
general German dismay, set about the grim task of persuading
the Allies to modify their stance. Clemenceau's admonition
that criticism of the fundamental principles would find no hear-
ing and only practical suggestions would be considered may
have cast a shadow of hopelessness over these efforts, but it
did not deter the Germans from arguing that they had been
shamefully deceived. They still hoped that the painstaking
commentary which they had prepared would convince the
Allies, especially the American president on whom everything
was staked, of this violation and of the de facto impossibility
of putting certain articles into practice. They believed that
counterproposals would be entertained, and they hoped that, if
these were received in a spirit of willingness to negotiate, a
fair concord might be concluded. Berlin was not fully aware
of the antecedent struggle at Paris which precluded any far-
reaching alterations.

The Magistrat of Danzig presented its own suggestions. In the
event that all hope of remaining within the Reich had disappeared, its memorial read, it recommended that the Free
City be expanded to include the adjoining towns of Hela,
Dirschau, and Neustadt, that Danzig be made a member of
the League, that the post of high commissioner be removed or
at least its tenure limited to the time which would elapse before
the Free City could be established, that full sovereignty explicitly
be granted the Free City, and that the Treaty adopt specific

34. Neufassung der Richtlinien für die deutschen Friedensunterhändler,
22 Apr. 1919, BA: R 43 I/2.

changes which would make the city's privileges more precise.[35]

The official German observations delivered to the Allies on 29 May repudiated the Treaty on the twofold ground that it represented a violation of the promise of a just peace and was impossible to execute. The German suggestions were less realistic than those of Danzig and consisted of a sterile repetition of familiar arguments. The Danzig settlement stood "in direct opposition to all assurances given in the declarations of President Wilson" and would lead "to violent opposition and a continuous state of war in the East." The economic arrangements had been constructed to make "this purely German territory Polish," whereas Poland's access to the sea could be provided without cession of territorial, railway, or fluvial sovereignty. Germany offered free ports and agreements on rail and river transit but demanded that "Danzig and its environs remain within the Reich."

Neither an impotent Reich nor a distressed Danzig could alter the terms. Clemenceau asserted that there was "no other possible way to create a free and secure access to the sea." Danzig was being restored to "a position similar to that which it held for so many centuries." [36] On 16 June the Allies threatened to renew hostilities if the Germans did not accept the Treaty within seven days. The German government acquiesced, and its delegation to the Conference resigned in protest. On 28 June the new German plenipotentiaries signed the Treaty, which stated that Germany renounced her right over the territory of Danzig in favor of the Allies (Article 100), who agreed to establish Danzig as a free city within the boundaries they had designated. The Free City was to be placed under the protection of the League (Article 102), which would appoint a high commissioner to help in drawing up a constitution, guaranteed by the League. The high commissioner was to be the court of the first instance for differences arising between Danzig and Poland from the Treaty and subsequent agreements (Article 103). The Allies would negotiate a convention between the two

35. Gemeinsame Sitzung des Magistrats und des Vorsteheramts der Kaufmannschaft zu Danzig am 16. Mai 1919, PA: Deutsche Friedensdelegation Versailles, Pol 8s (4662H/E214578–81).

36. Temperley, 2, 292–93.

with the object of placing Danzig within Polish customs frontiers and ensuring Poland a free and secure access to the sea, of forbidding discrimination against the Poles in the city, and of providing that Poland undertake the conduct of the city's foreign relations (Article 104). When the Treaty came into force, German residents of Danzig would lose their German nationality and become nationals of Danzig (Article 105), unless they chose German citizenship and emigrated (Article 106). The property of the Reich or Prussia in Danzig was to pass to the Allies, who would transfer it to the Free City or to Poland as they saw fit (Article 107). Danzig was to bear its fair share of the financial liabilities which the peace settlement imposed on the Reich (Article 108).

In the course of the German government's deliberations on the thirteenth point, Danzig, an integral part of Prussia, fell into the province of the Foreign Ministry. The city, which had remained prominent in the minds of the ministers throughout the preparations for the peace negotiations, attained symbolic status at the Conference. To the Foreign Ministry—and in this it faithfully reflected public opinion throughout Germany—Danzig was a poignant reminder of a bitter disappointment. These associations contributed in no small measure to official German thinking and future policy toward the Free City.

CHAPTER 2

Danzig and Berlin, 1919–1920

When the Treaty of Versailles came into force on 10 January 1920, sovereignty over Danzig passed into the hands of the Allies. Although no Allied representative was present to take charge, the transfer proceeded smoothly. Authority was exercised by the municipal government—the Magistrat with Sahm at its head—in conjunction with several members of the erstwhile provincial administration. Various new agencies were established to replace or supplement the old Prussian ones. Prussia agreed to advance the funds necessary to maintain administrative and communications services for the rest of that fiscal year. German laws effective at the time were retained, and the local branch of the Reichsbank remained open to supply the city with credit and currency.[1] The German and Prussian authorities solemnly pledged to keep alive the common cultural heritage and the community of interests and traditions.[2]

The official Allied administrator, Sir Reginald Tower, a senior member of the British foreign service, arrived in Danzig early in February. A bachelor of proud bearing and independent turn of mind, Tower had been British minister in Munich before the war and was familiar with the German language and the German scene. He had been appointed "to discharge the obligations devolving upon the Allies from the Peace Treaty in regard to Danzig," in particular to settle relations between Poland and Danzig. He was responsible solely to the Conference of Ambassadors, an agency set up in Paris to supervise the execution of the Treaty.[3] To maintain order, Tower was supplied

1. Simons (Versailles) to Foreign Ministry, 10 Jan. 1920, PA: F.P. Danzig a, Bd. 2; Erlass des Preussischen Finanzministeriums, 21 June 1920, PA: Fi 1, Danzig, Bd. 1; Reichsbank-Direktorium to Foreign Ministry, 18 Nov. 1919, PA: F.P. Danzig a, Bd. 2, and F.W. 44.

2. Aufruf an die abgetretenen Gebiete, *Sonderausgabe zum Amtsblatt der Regierung zu Danzig,* 13 Jan. 1920.

3. Curzon to Tower, 31 Jan. 1920, LN: 4/2932/4; Tower to Curzon, 20 Feb. 1920, *Documents on British Foreign Policy* (DBFP), 1st series, *11,* no. 199.

with two Allied battalions under General Richard Haking, which stayed in Danzig from February until November 1920. On 13 February, Tower was also designated high commissioner of the League of Nations. In this capacity he was to collaborate with the Danzigers in drafting a constitution, which the League had to approve before the Free City could formally come into existence.

Because Tower came from a country which had thwarted Poland's acquisition of Danzig, the Danzigers welcomed his appointment and the Poles did not. Both were convinced that he represented British interests and that he wished to pave the way for British trade in eastern Europe.[4] Tower showed great dedication in his search for an equitable reconciliation of conflicting national interests and in his attempt to provide the future state with sound foundations. That his task was difficult amid Danzig-Polish animosities—and that he may have found it thankless upon occasion—is not surprising.

Tower learned to his satisfaction that most of the administrative ties between Danzig and Germany had been severed. On 13 February he accepted control of the city from Danzig's former Regierungspräsident, Lothar Foerster, who had been commissioned by Berlin to transfer the city to Allied administration and adjust with the Danzigers matters affecting justice, customs, railways, and the port. Several days later, on 17 February, the Allied Frontier Delimitation Commission arrived to settle the boundaries, which were to become effective upon the approval of the constitution.

To carry out the actual administration, Tower established a Council of State (Staatsrat), composed of municipal officials and the directors of the port, customs, railway, and postal services. Virtually without assistance and Allied directive, the Staatsrat, under Sahm, took over the former Prussian administration, reorganized it, and adjusted it to the requirements of the new state. It also dealt with the daily affairs of the city: the maintenance of order, economic provisioning, and the regulation of trade passing through the harbor. Rarely did Tower have occasion to

4. Ernst Ziehm, *Aus meiner politischen Arbeit in Danzig 1914–1939* (Marburg/Lahn, 1960), p. 40.

intervene in its activities—usually only when mediation between the Staatsrat and Poland was required.

Leaving the Staatsrat to administer the city, Tower turned his attention to more pressing duties. He set out to negotiate a convention between Danzig and Poland which, coming into force with the establishment of the Free City, would define and implement the prerogatives of the respective parties in accordance with the broad outlines of the Treaty of Versailles. It was soon obvious that the negotiations would not be easy. Cooperation and harmony between Danzigers and Poles were prerequisites to success—and absent. In a report to the Conference of Ambassadors, Tower summed up his first impressions:

> Those representing the German element in Danzig are straining every nerve to circumvent the provisions of the Peace Treaty with regard to the Poles, and are inclined to misread willfully the wording of Article 104. . . . There is an exaggerated confidence on the part of the Poles that the provisions relating to Danzig in the Peace Treaty were framed exclusively for the benefit of Poland, in other words, that Poland was to exercise full administration in Danzig with the sole exception of purely local matters from the very day that the Peace Treaty came into effect.[5]

Both Danzigers and Poles were bitter at the prospect of a free city, and each party to the negotiations was bent on turning what it saw as an unfortunate situation to its own profit. Neither was interested in compromise.

At the first meeting on 26 May, each delegation submitted a draft for the Convention. The Polish draft aimed at converting Danzig into a Polish city in all but name. It foresaw Polish control of the harbor, customs, and communication services; the introduction of Polish legislation and currency; and a permanent Polish garrison and naval base in the city. From the Poles' point of view, this arrangement was the sole means of assuring their free and secure access to the sea, which the Allies had promised but failed to provide. The Danzig draft, inspired by the desire

5. Tower to Conference of Ambassadors, 25 Feb. 1920, LN: 4/3270/3270.

to curtail Polish influence and establish a completely independent city, called for the explicit recognition of the sovereignty of the new state; combined administration of harbor, railway, and river; and joint ownership of communications services.[6] In Danzig's opinion, the treaty accorded the Poles "an opportunity, and nothing more, for the development of Polish foreign trade through the Free City of Danzig." [7]

The lines were clearly drawn. Severed from Germany, Danzig was determined to make no concessions which might threaten its sovereign independence. The Danzigers were ever mindful that the Poles were disproportionately more powerful than they, and they sought in absolute sovereignty the means whereby Polish claims and privileges could be effectively denied. The goal was autonomy, less for autonomy's sake, than for the sake of eventual return to Germany.[8]

Poland sought a Convention which would enable her to use her economic rights in Danzig to gain political advantages and reduce the city's stipulated autonomy. Her motives are not difficult to discern. Virtual possession of Danzig would constitute a decided triumph for the prestige of the government in Warsaw —Polish public opinion in the press and popular politicians clamored for the reversal of the loss suffered at Paris. Moreover, the arguments cited by Polish propaganda during the war and at Paris were still valid: the Poles were apprehensive lest their access to the sea be subject to curtailment, especially in times of emergency. Unless they were in control, communications through Danzig were precarious. The British ambassador in Warsaw noted the Polish tendency to see in the Danziger "not a harmless citizen of a Free City given over solely to the peaceful paths of commerce, but rather a representative of militant Germany, the old enemy, seeking to throttle [Poland's] free access to the sea and to the markets of the world." [9]

6. *Amtliche Urkunden zum Vertrage zwischen der Freien Stadt Danzig und der Republik Polen* (Danzig, 1920), pp. 21–53.

7. Excerpts from Notes of a Meeting of the Conference of Ambassadors Held at the Quai d'Orsay, 29 Apr. 1920, LN: 4/21121/8528.

8. Heinrich Sahm, *Erinnerungen aus meinen Danziger Jahren 1919–1930* (Marburg/Lahn, 1958), p. 174.

9. Rumbold to Curzon, 29 Mar. 1920, DBFP, 1st series, *11*, no. 240.

Events in the summer of 1920 demonstrated that the Poles were reckoning not simply with hypothetical possibilities. The Russo-Polish War had turned against Poland, and her very existence was in doubt. Urgently in need of war matériel, she had purchased large consignments abroad to be delivered by way of Danzig. When the shipments arrived in July, the Danzig dockers, sympathetic to Soviet Russia, refused to unload. Entreaties by Sahm and Tower had no effect; the strikers did not relent. To make matters worse, in mid-August, when the Russians were approaching Warsaw, the Danzigers, following an example set by the Reichstag in July, asked Tower to declare the city neutral. Had Tower acceded to this request, the city could have prohibited the transport of munitions through its territory. Tower, however, withheld his consent, and when the French and British governments decided to order their troops to unload the ships, the dockers returned to work at the end of August.[10] By then their strike had hampered the Polish military effort. The Poles' misgivings seemed confirmed. Their difficulties with the city were, to their minds, not a local clash, but a conflict of international proportions: the strike and the proposed declaration of neutrality were outward manifestations of German *revanchisme*.[11]

Tower knew that the Versailles articles, because of their vagueness, were dangerous. He understood that an interpretation which weakened the status of the Free City exposed Danzig to Polish annexation. He counseled moderation to the Poles on the premise "that the Convention should not go any further in the way of concessions towards Poland than is compatible with the position of Danzig as a Free City." [12] As a result, the negotiations led to collisions not only between the negotiating parties but between Tower himself and the Poles.[13] When it became

10. Foerster to Foreign Ministry, 29 July 1920, PA: Po 3, Danzig, Bd. 1; Tower to Curzon, 12, 18, 26, 31 Aug. 1920, DBFP, 1st series, *11,* nos. 427, 456, 489, 502.

11. *Rzeczpospolita,* 28 Aug. 1920, PA: Po 3, Danzig, Bd. 1.

12. Memorandum by Colban (League Secretariat), 2 Jan. 1920, LN: 4/2623/4.

13. Tower to Conference of Ambassadors, 19 Apr. 1920, LN: 4/4030/3270.

evident that the two contradictory interpretations of the Treaty could not be reconciled, Tower referred the whole matter to the Conference of Ambassadors.

Meanwhile, Tower encountered difficulties over the constitution for Danzig. The Danzigers had already done some preliminary work. In the summer of 1919 the Magistrat had sent delegations to Hamburg, Lübeck, and Bremen to study their constitutions. It then appointed a drafting committee in which all political parties were represented. Working independently, Sahm submitted a draft in September 1919, the Socialists in October. A Constituent Assembly, in which Socialists and Nationalists predominated, was elected in May 1920. When it convened on 14 June, it turned to discussion of the drafts at hand. The form of the government was the primary subject of dispute. Sahm proposed a type of Magistrat with twelve-year tenure for its members; the Socialists desired a purely parliamentary system. The Assembly reached no agreement, despite Tower's prodding. Finally, when Tower established a deadline after which the matter would be referred to Paris, the non-Socialist members of the Assembly reached a compromise which was adopted on 11 August 1920 over the opposition of the Socialists and the Polish delegates.[14]

The Constitution of Danzig was modeled, especially in its sections on basic rights and privileges, on that of Weimar, the most noteworthy difference being that it lacked a counterpart to Article 48, which allowed for the suspension of the bill of rights and rule by emergency decree. Essentially democratic, the Constitution stipulated that sovereignty rested with the people. They were represented by 120 deputies in the Volkstag, elected every four years by "universal, equal, direct and secret suffrage of all citizens, of either sex over twenty years of age, in accordance with the principle of proportional representation." Its legislative functions, modeled on those of the Reichstag, consisted primarily in initiating, debating, and passing laws. The Volkstag was also responsible for choosing the Senate, at once upper house and cabinet, which was the supreme power in the state. The Senate was composed of a president, a vice-president, seven principal and thirteen parliamentary senators. The principal senators, including the president, held office for four years and presided

14. Ziehm, pp. 42–45.

over different administrative departments. The parliamentary senators' tenure in office depended upon the confidence of the Volkstag. The Senate directed government policy. In it was vested executive authority to promulgate laws, conduct the administration, draft the budget, determine revenues and expenditures, and name public servants. The president of the Senate acted, in practice though not in theory, as head of state. The second half of the Constitution was an elaborate bill of rights in which the inviolability of person and property, freedom of speech, creed, and assembly were guaranteed. German was to be the official language, but Polish-speaking Danzigers were assured the use of their language in education, internal administration, and before the law courts. Danzig's special ties to the League came to the fore in several articles. The Constitution could be amended by a two-thirds majority of the Volkstag, but only with the consent of the League. And the Free City was not, without express permission from the League, to "serve as a military or naval base, erect fortifications, or authorize the manufacture of munitions or war material on its territory." [15]

The Constitution made little mention of the Republic of Poland. It was the Convention, drafted under the auspices of the Conference of Ambassadors and signed by Danzig on 9 November 1920 and by Poland nine days later, which regulated the respective rights and obligations of the two states toward one another. It defined, in a manner generally favorable to Danzig, the privileges Poland was to enjoy in the Free City, notably free and secure access to the Baltic. Its primary importance lay therefore in the domain of commerce. It created a customs union between the two states, subject to Polish legislation and tariffs, and stipulated that revenues be divided according to a prearranged formula. The customs service itself was staffed by Danzig officials and under Danzig administration, subject to Polish inspection. The port, waterways, and railways serving the port were placed under the control and administration of a Harbor Board, to be staffed equally by Danzigers and Poles, with a neutral chairman. The other railways, with the exception of streetcars and some lines serving primarily the needs of the city, were given to the

15. League of Nations, *Official Journal* (LNOJ), Special Supplement, no. 7, July 1922.

control and administration of Poland, which was to defray the costs and receive the profits. Poland was accorded the right to establish postal and telegraphic services from the port to Poland and from Poland abroad via the harbor. Danzig guaranteed the civil liberties of the Polish minority in the city with assurances similar to those which Poland gave her own minorities (Article 33). The Convention also clarified Poland's right and obligation to conduct Danzig's foreign relations. To facilitate communication with Warsaw, Poland was to have a diplomatic representative, the commissioner general, in Danzig, but there was no provision for the diplomatic representation of Danzig in Warsaw. Finally, the Convention stipulated explicitly that all disputes affecting relations between Danzigers and Poles, whether relevant to the present document or to subsequent agreements, be adjudged by the high commissioner of the League, who, in turn, might refer the issues to Geneva (Article 39).[16]

The Warsaw Agreement, concluded in October 1921, regulated in detail the general provisions of the Convention. It defined in particular the complicated structure of the economic and customs unions, giving Poland the right to prescribe policy but safeguarding Danzig by means of various exceptions and privileges.[17] Even this detailed accord, however, could not bring absolute clarity to an arrangement of such complexity.

On 15 November 1920 Danzig was formally declared a free city. The Allied administration was dismantled and Tower relinquished his post. Two days later, the Council of the League of Nations accepted the Constitution of Danzig in its essentials. At the same session it approved a report by the Danzig *rapporteur,* Viscount Kikujiro Ishii, which outlined the responsibilities of the League toward the Free City. The Ishii Report stressed that the League was to guarantee the Constitution so as to ensure internal independence and to protect the territorial integrity and political autonomy of the city against all external aggression.[18]

16. Georg Crusen, *Der Pariser Vertrag vom 9. November 1920* (Danzig, 1936).

17. Hermann Lewinski and Richard Wagner, eds., *Danziger Staats- und Völkerrecht* (Danzig, 1927), pp. 442–547.

18. LN: 20/48/98 (I).

The Council further resolved on 22 June 1921 that Poland was "especially fitted" to be called upon to uphold internal order if disturbances threatened her secure access to the sea. The possibility that the high commissioner might call for Polish troops haunted the Danzigers throughout the interwar period.

The high commissioner was the presence of the League in Danzig and the link between the League and the city. He exercised no control or supervision over Danzig's internal affairs except insofar as these might endanger the Constitution guaranteed by the League. He bore responsibility solely to the League.[19] His chief function was mediation, or even arbitration, between Danzig and Poland. His unofficial conciliatory influence constituted probably the most practical part of his activities. Both Danzig and Poland had the right to appeal his decisions to the League Council, whose verdict was final. (There was no specific provision in any of the documents for dealing with the parties should they refuse to accept a verdict of the Council.) Danzig-Polish conflicts before the League would be in the hands of a rapporteur, usually a member of the Council, whom officials of the League's Secretariat assisted in drawing up his reports and recommendations. The Secretariat in fact exercised considerable influence on the life of the Free City: it provided information and advice to the high commissioners, played an occasional mediatory role between warring parties in Geneva, and saw that the obligations of the League were fulfilled.

When the Free City had been thus established, the Danzig Constituent Assembly declared itself the first Volkstag and elected a Senate with Sahm as its president. Sahm's inaugural address emphasized Danzig's trust in the League as the protector and guarantor of its existence and autonomy and Danzig's determination to adhere to the treaties, which, it hoped, would be the basis of good relations with Poland. The city, he added, was bound to Germany by blood, language, and culture; its foremost duty was to maintain forever its German character.

Temporary High Commissioner Bernardo Attolico, an official of the League Secretariat who succeeded Tower in Danzig, put the matter slightly differently in a report to Geneva. He saw Danzig

19. Memorandum by the Secretary General on the Duties and Functions of the High Commissioner, February 1920, LN: C.D. 3.

as an "avowed anti-Polish community," not in the least elated at
the prospect of being "the *débouché* and the emporium of Poland." One might mollify these sentiments by creating a "Danzig
spirit." Such a spirit, however, could be generated only if the
Danzigers gained confidence in the future of the Polish Republic,
overcame their fears of Polish annexation, and decided that
severance from Germany was to their advantage.[20] The tone of
Attolico's text was not optimistic.

In their reluctance to accommodate themselves to the new
political order dictated from Versailles, the Danzigers exhibited
a spirit prevalent throughout Germany. When the Treaty had
become public on 8 May 1919, a cry of protest had burst from
both the public and the press. The leading article of the *Frankfurter Zeitung* bore the headline "unacceptable demands," and
the paper carried as its supplement a map of Germany to illus-
trate "the sacrifices our enemies desire." The territorial losses
were in fact the most sensational aspect of the Treaty, and
among these the losses in the East lay closest to the German
heart. The cession of Alsace-Lorraine, also lamented, had been
forecast in the Fourteen Points and came as no surprise, whereas
the public was unprepared for the expropriation of West Prussia
and Danzig. East Prussia, ancient realm of the Teutonic Knights
and birthplace of Prussian glory, was to be separated from the
Reich by Polish territory reaching to the sea, and Danzig, cradle
of German culture, was to become a separate state. To reach
East Prussia or Danzig, one would have to cross Polish territory, and the Corridor was to become an ineluctable reminder of
Versailles over which, almost physically, one kept stumbling.
Propagandists of all persuasions elaborated upon the losses: a
political, cultural, and economic organism had been damaged,
in the East lay its "bleeding borders," an "open wound in the
body politic." By implication, the wound would have to be
closed—through restoration.

The fervor and the unanimity of the clamor against the Treaty
cannot be explained solely as a reaction to some putative injustice; it was far too vindictive. Its origins were psychological.
The war, carried on despite tremendous losses, had been

20. Attolico to League Council, 23 Feb. 1921, LN: M 21/4/29.

justified as the means by which Germany would acquire a place second to none in Europe. Promises of fame and triumph had engendered an enthusiasm among the populace which enabled it to bear great sacrifices. In return, the people expected extensive territorial annexation, especially in the East. And now the country not only had failed to gain land, but had lost land—and much more: its glorious army and its honor. Enormous expectation became enormous disappointment. The loss was the more grievous because the public acknowledged neither that Germany had lost the war fairly on the battlefield nor that her war aims had been wicked and required expiation.

It was insult added to injury that Poland should receive these territories. Animosities between Germans and Poles had become virulent during the Second Reich, and for the Germans of the Weimar Republic they were no less so. In the Bismarck era, Poles were thought to constitute a menace to the security of the Reich, and the German government pursued harsh measures meant to limit their activity and control their numbers in Prussia's eastern provinces. These measures succeeded merely in arousing Polish opposition and stimulating nationalist agitation. When this became obvious, Berlin was caught in a dilemma. The government had staked so much on its policy that retreat to a moderate position was impossible: the issue had become a matter of prestige. To save face, the Germans embraced a doctrine which justified the greatest severity and replaced reality as a basis for action: official and private propaganda affirmed the Germans' racial superiority and championed the cause of German culture among the benighted Slavs. To a mentality which placed the Pole beneath contempt, the settlement at Versailles was an outrage. It exacerbated the Germans' animus against their eastern neighbors and thus precluded conciliation.[21]

The government's reaction to the Treaty was remarkably similar to that of the press and public. In the Reichstag debate on 12 May all parties protested the Treaty, and the deputies made emphatic and impassioned reference to the eastern provinces Germany was to lose. On 23 July Foreign Minister Her-

21. Martin Broszat, *200 Jahre deutsche Polenpolitik* (Munich, 1963), pp. 96–131.

mann Müller (Socialist) told the Constituent Assembly at
Weimar that, while the German government would seek to ful-
fill the Treaty to the best of its abilities, it "would leave no
doubt" of its revisionist intentions.[22] Müller knew that the parties backed him. While in domestic affairs agreement among
Socialists, Democrats, and Nationalists was unattainable, they
were at one in their conviction that the new eastern frontiers
could not endure. All agreed that the point of departure and
the essence of Germany's external policy was to be the revision
of the territorial settlement of 1919. As the Democratic Party
congress was to put it:

> We shall never accept the dictate of force as permanent
> legal order. We shall never recognize the separation of Ger-
> mans from the fatherland. We shall never relinquish the
> principle of self-determination, and, basing ourselves on
> this principle, we shall strive for the unification of all Ger-
> mans.[23]

In the government, then, as in the Foreign Ministry, revision of
the Treaty of Versailles was the main object of foreign policy.

At the moment, however, the government could do little in
pursuit of a policy urged upon it, as it were, by public accla-
mation. Military ventures were unthinkable, a diplomatic show
of force equally out of the question, and the hope of a fair hear-
ing, either before the forum of world opinion or among the
ruling powers in Europe, had just been extinguished. The only
possibility which remained open was to take small measures
within the latitude the Treaty allowed.

A prerequisite of future revisionist claims was the retention
of *Deutschtum*—of German inhabitants, property, and culture
—in the lost territories. The obvious method was to supply
assistance wherever German interests were threatened. Danzig
was a particularly promising object for such solicitude. Its relative independence meant that Berlin could address itself directly,

22. *Verhandlungen der verfassunggebenden Deutschen Nationalver-
sammlung, Stenographische Berichte,* Bd. 328, p. 1853.
23. Programm der Deutschen Demokratischen Partei, December 1919,
in Wilhelm Treue, ed., *Deutsche Parteiprogramme 1864–1951* (Göttingen, 1954), p. 123.

if secretly, to a sympathetic government, whereas contact with the German minority in Poland was necessarily directed to scattered individuals exposed to Polish reprisals. Furthermore, Berlin believed that, by maintaining Danzig's resistance, it could reinforce the resolve of the Germans in the Corridor and those cut off from the rest of the Reich in East Prussia.[24] Above all, the Foreign Ministry was convinced that, if it could establish the validity of its claim to Danzig, this validity would perforce extend to the Corridor. For the Germans saw Danzig and the Corridor as an indissoluble geographic and economic unit: the coveted landbridge to East Prussia.

In the middle of July 1919 the minister of the interior, who retained competence over Danzig as long as it remained within the Reich, personally called all the ministries of his government, the Prussian prime minister, and several Prussian ministers to a conference. "The government of the Reich," the invitation read, "finds it of the utmost importance that, before the Peace Treaty comes into effect and dissolves all connection between Danzig and its environs and the rest of Germany, the retention of political, economic, and cultural contacts be discussed exhaustively with representatives of the future free city." [25]

The projected meeting took place on 23 July. That it should have stood under the aegis of the Reich, rather than of the Prussian authorities, indicates that Danzig was a matter no longer of local but of national concern. That the minister of the interior, Eduard David (Socialist), should have chaired the meeting himself further enhanced Danzig's status. The conference, which, to judge by the emphatic phrasing of the invitation and its grandiose list of recipients, was intended to produce a broad plan for future relations with Danzig, was endowed with the prestige of top-level deliberation.

There was, however, a curious discrepancy between the level on which the meeting was convoked and the level on which it was conducted. Only after the discussion was underway did Lord Mayor Sahm gain the floor to deliver his prepared remarks,

24. Dirksen (Danzig) to Foreign Ministry, 8 Dec. 1924, PA: Sch 16, Danzig W, Bd. 2.

25. Ministry of the Interior to Foreign Ministry, 17 July 1919, PA: AA Weimar, IV.13 (4665H/E219752–53).

obviously meant as a preliminary address. He assured those present that Danzig's administration and the predominant part of the population thought it their sacred duty to make their new state a bulwark of Deutschtum and to contribute thereby to the morale of the Germans in West and East Prussia. They wished therefore that their relations with Germany be as close as Allied interest in the city, the presence of the high commissioner, and the Polish conduct of the city's external relations would permit.

The discussion then returned to the practical plane. The Finance Ministry suggested a convention which would allow Danzig to retain the German mark, only to add that, until the German currency became stable, such a convention was impracticable. The Prussian Ministry of Finance assured German pensioners in the city that their funds would continue automatically until the German law prohibiting pension payments to foreign nationals could be rewritten in their favor. The Ministry of Labor pointed out that Danzig, in its own interest, should retain German insurance programs, for the future city-state would be too small to support its own industrial, employment, and health insurance corporations. It also hoped that Danzig's public works would remain within the general framework of the German economy. Similarly, the Prussian Ministry of Justice thought it would be mutually advantageous if Danzig retained German law and legal institutions.

The Danzigers were then given an opportunity to state the needs for which the discussion had yielded no provisions. They requested that their Polytechnic Institute, an effective organ for the propagation of Deutschtum, be placed on the same academic level as its German counterparts. They hoped that German funds for the Institute and the city's libraries and museums would be forthcoming, and that the Reich would supply raw materials and fuel to their city, which faced impoverishment because its declining exports failed to cover the cost of its indispensable imports.

Summing up, Minister David promised that the problems raised at the meeting would be forwarded to the proper ministries. The Reich would use all admissible means to maintain Danzig economically. The government, he concluded, had the warmest interest in Danzig's welfare and its preservation as a German city. The Danzigers in the meantime should preserve a healthy optimism. He cherished the hope that current hardship would engender the strength necessary to overcome difficulty.[26]

The meeting is a revealing commentary on the state of German policy toward Danzig in the summer of 1919. The Germans had intended to initiate action on Danzig before the Treaty came into effect and hampered their efforts; they wished also to assure Danzig of Germany's concern for its well-being, securing thereby Danzig's loyalty and ensuring its receptivity to plans from Berlin. But the meeting was premature. No one really knew yet how the Treaty's provisions for Danzig should be interpreted. Thus no one commanded information on which a comprehensive program to rectify the situation could be founded. The suggestions which the ministries brought forth were therefore singularly unimaginative, confined to the obvious within each particular sphere of competence, and directed purely at retention of existing arrangements. Germany's plans for Danzig went little beyond her fundamental interest in pursuing intimate relations with the Free City and preserving Deutschtum in the lost territories. The German ministers were unwilling to initiate action. Their remarks were prompted more by sentiment than by resolve.

Nor were the Danzigers better prepared. Their remarks were sublimely general and their requests trivially particular. Their minds were wholly occupied by attempts to find remedies for immediate needs, and a comprehensive scheme designed to anticipate future difficulties was as remote from them as from the Germans.

The immediate results of the July meeting were few, for Germany's primary concerns lay elsewhere. The government was preoccupied with the staggering task of executing the Treaty. Negotiations, conferences, memorandums, and countless man-hours were devoted to preparing for the transfer of the German colonies and reducing the armed forces. The territories slated for separation were to be ceded in the spring of 1920, and the

26. Aufzeichnung über die Besprechung, betr. den künftigen Freistaat Danzig, 23 July 1919, PA: F.P. Danzig a, Bd. 1.

efforts of all competent personnel were required to disentangle and cut their administrative, juridical, and financial ties to the Reich. The regulation of reparations loomed large among the liabilities of the future. The young German republic sought to establish itself and gain firm footing amid a chaotic civil situation. The promulgation of the constitution entailed extensive and intricate new legislation. Postwar inflation necessitated the imposition of economic controls and tax increases. Factories closed for want of raw materials, unemployment figures soared, and breadlines lengthened. Strikes and street demonstrations contributed to the national uproar.

Action on Danzig was hampered also by confusion over the city's new status. The Foreign Ministry, which exercised jurisdiction over those arrangements which would prepare Danzig for separation from the Reich, found that the various government offices and the Prussian ministries balked at its directives. They feared that exceptional treatment of Danzig, legally a foreign country, would create an embarrassing precedent for Germany's other external relations. Disputes about the proper interpretation of the Treaty's stipulations led to delays and, worse, to the occasional countermanding of earlier accords and assurances. The stated goal of supporting Deutschtum in Danzig was at times vitiated by sheer ignorance of and contradictions between the measures proposed by different ministries.[27] Such disunity of German purpose became a minor theme in relations with Danzig. And while the ministries quarreled among themselves, each pursuing its own interests, Danzig barraged the competent authorities with requests and reminders and waited for relief.

Early in December 1919, Sahm, exasperated at Berlin's unresponsiveness, requested that the entire complex of questions relevant to Danzig be brought under unified control. He urged that the problems of the future state be discussed in their entirety in an interministerial conference so that all would be aware of Danzig's difficulties, especially of the uncertainties of its "national" future. The Poles were acquiring industrial and residential property at such a rate that Germany would be

27. Sahm to Ministry of the Interior, 6 Sept. 1919, PA: F.P. Danzig f.

obliged to lend active support to housing and industrial schemes for German Danzigers. The public treasury was depleted: 8,000 unemployed persons drew a weekly relief of 250,000 marks, a sum which the city alone could not raise. Final settlement was also needed on welfare payments to disabled veterans and the next of kin of war casualties and on pensions for retired officials remaining in Danzig.[28]

In a closed discussion preceding a meeting with the Danzigers on 3 January, the German ministries aired their reservations and objections. If Danzig found a generous response, one might expect similarly immoderate requests from the other territories to be ceded; the subsidies must be offered as loans, not as outright grants; Berlin was responsible for pensions but not for social welfare, and the two should be distinguished; to extend unemployment benefits to foreign countries was illegal; it was unlikely that the Reich could afford to pay development subsidies and building-cost allowances to Danzig. Only State Secretary Edgar von Haniel of the Foreign Ministry pursued a clear aim, pleading for generosity lest the Danzigers conclude that Germany had lost interest in their city.[29]

But the picture was little changed at the subsequent conference. The chancellor, Gustav Bauer (Socialist), claimed that both the Reich and Prussia were willing enough to help, but that the financial situation precluded far-reaching commitments. He did not want to make promises which could not be kept. Of course Germany was not withdrawing from her responsibilities for the welfare of invalids, war widows, and orphans, but the matter was exceedingly difficult. To commit the German government to pension payments to people about to lose their German citizenship could set a costly precedent. Perhaps advances and loans without interest could meet the present difficulty. As for Danzig's other wishes, they would be treated with consideration. The city, he urged, should not depart from the Reich embittered.[30] Bauer's generalities were designed as much

28. Sahm to Chancellery, 8 Dec. 1919, PA: F.P. Danzig a, Bd. 2.
29. Chefbesprechung zur Besprechung mit Danzig, 3 Jan. 1920, BA: R 43 I/374.
30. Besprechung mit Vertretern des künftigen Freistaats Danzig in der Reichskanzlei, 3 Jan. 1920, PA: Po 2B, Danzig.

to hide the lack of unity among the ministers as to stress the difficult position in which the Reich itself was caught.

Berlin did, however, respond to Danzig's most pressing needs. In September 1919 Sahm drew the attention of the Ministry of the Interior to the near bankruptcy of the government industries in Danzig—the Imperial Navy Yard, the artillery arsenal, and the ordnance factory. If these industries, which employed some 7,000 workers, were shut down, he claimed, the 25,000 persons affected would probably emigrate to the Reich, and it was likely that in the division of the state property in Danzig (Article 107 of the Versailles Treaty) the works would be awarded to Poland. If the German government failed to give support, it would "forfeit the great mission of Deutschtum from the very start." [31]

At a meeting in the Foreign Ministry on 22 September the retention of German workers was held imperative for political and economic reasons. Mass dismissals would damage the German cause and encourage Bolshevist agitation. With financial support from Berlin—either direct subsidies or continued payment of wages—Danzig would be able to take over the factories in trusteeship. If it could operate them on a sound economic basis, its chances of gaining permanent possession would be considerably improved. On 8 October Danzig received the works in trusteeship. It was obliged to pay salaries and wages, but a loan of five million marks was supplied without interest or date of amortization in order to stimulate productivity and ensure the employment and livelihood of thousands of German Danzigers.[32] Simultaneously, at the urging of the Foreign Ministry, lucrative government contracts went to the shipyards.[33]

In September and again in December 1920, the municipality of Danzig received loans totaling 85 million marks for continued upkeep of the factories, which held contracts from both the German and the Polish governments but lacked working capital. The credit, produced at the behest of the Foreign Ministry, was

31. Sahm to Ministry of the Interior, 6 Sept. 1919, PA: F.P. Danzig f.

32. Memorandum by the Foreign Ministry, 23 Sept. 1919, PA: F.P. Danzig a, Bd. 1; Ministry of Finance to Magistrat Danzig, 8 Oct. 1919, PA: F.R. Danzig Staatseigentum.

33. Ministry of Reconstruction to Danziger Werft, 27 Nov. 1920, PA: Sch 4, Danzig Geh., Bd. 1 (K215/K054956).

extended through the Danzig Darlehenskasse, a bank loosely connected with the Reichsbank, and thus did not appear to come directly from the Reich.[34]

Danzig's economic situation deteriorated to the point of crisis when the Treaty became effective in January 1920. The city was cut off from German markets and supplies without finding compensatory trade elsewhere. Traffic with Poland was minimal, for Poland had nothing to export and her currency was fluctuating. After the Russo-Polish War broke out in the spring of 1920, trade with Poland came to a standstill. Danzig, which had received direct and indirect government subsidies when it had belonged to the German economy (its income had never matched its expenditure),[35] was now expected to feed its population and occupation forces, pay relief to the war workers who had moved to the city between 1914 and 1918 and were now unemployed, and procure foreign contracts for its industry at a time when every country was placing orders with domestic enterprises.[36]

Negotiations to alleviate these hardships of the transition had begun in Berlin early in 1920. Repeated conferences led to an agreement signed on 13 March 1920 and known as the March Agreement. Its full details were not made known to Tower, who gave it his reluctant approval after attempts to secure Polish supplies had proved unsuccessful.[37] By its provisions, Germany accorded privileged economic treatment to Danzig, which remained nominally under Germany's foreign trade regulations but was treated in fact like a domestic market. Domestic prices would be charged, export prohibitions would not be applied, and neither export duties nor minimum export prices would be exacted. Germany would supply Danzig with quantities of flour,

34. Memorandums, 18 Dec. 1920 and 14 Mar. 1921, PA: Fi 2, Danzig Geh., Bd. 1 (K207/K049925–7 and K049965–70).

35. Ernst Volkmann, "Die Finanzprobleme des Freistaates," *Deutsche Wirtschaftszeitung* (2 Feb. 1928), p. 106.

36. Hanns Bauer and Walter Millack, eds., *Danzigs Handel in Vergangenheit und Gegenwart* (Danzig, 1925), pp. 161–62; Denkschrift by Foerster, 10 June 1920, PA: Deutsche Friedensdelegation Versailles, Pol 8s.

37. Aufzeichnung über die Besprechung am 11. Februar 1920, PA: F.W. 44c; Tower to Conference of Ambassadors, 12 Mar. 1920, LN: 4/3525/3525.

potatoes, meat, and similar staple commodities, with finished products for its own consumption, and with raw materials and unfinished products for its industry.[38]

Negotiations for Berlin's third major contribution to Danzig's welfare were initiated in the fall of 1919, when the departure of many civil servants caused the city to turn to the Reich for personnel. The Foreign Ministry was wholly amenable to meeting this need, for it had a stated interest in the retention of German officials in Danzig, who would reinforce pro-German sentiment in the future Free City and countervail Polish encroachments. A solid core of German civil servants was a highly effective means of promoting and strengthening Deutschtum.[39]

This was not the first time that Germany had dealt with the uncertainties confronting civil servants in the eastern provinces. At its meeting of 26 July 1919, the Prussian cabinet had guaranteed these officials employment in Germany and reimbursement of any losses if they continued to occupy their posts until the fate of the provinces had been determined. These privileges had been extended also to officials in Danzig, but now the Magistrat pleaded that the arrangement be broadened to enable the city to retain its civil servants permanently.[40] Prompted by the Foreign Ministry, the Prussian government announced that the German civil servants, including teachers and professors, in Danzig's employ as of April 1921 would be officially on leave of absence from Germany until April 1925, when they would have the option of returning with their status and rights intact. Even these limitations fell when, in 1921, Prussia amended the agreement to include persons who might enter Danzig service after 1921 and permitted all officials to assume posts in Germany whenever they wished.[41] Danzig agreed to extend to its civil servants the same employee benefits they enjoyed in the Reich. Thus no disadvantages accrued to them.[42] Danzig legitimized its

38. Bestimmungen über den deutschen Warenverkehr im Osten, 25 Aug. 1920, PA: H 11 Nr. 3, Danzig, Bd. 1.
39. Foreign Ministry to Preussisches Staatsministerium, 20 Nov. 1919, PA: F.P. Danzig g.
40. Staatsrat Danzig to Foerster, 26 Apr. 1920, PA: Po 2B, Danzig.
41. Ministry of Finance to Chancellery, 18 July 1925, BA: R 43 I/376.
42. Runderlass des Preussischen Staatsministeriums, 10 June 1920, BA: R 43 I/374.

acquisition and retention of German officials by providing legally that upon appointment they automatically became citizens also of the Free City. These arrangements permitted an unimpeded flow of officials between Germany and Danzig throughout the interwar period.

Assistance to the government industries, the March Agreement, and the convention on civil servants were all measures taken in response to Danzig's specific demands. Each was occasioned by an emergency which threatened to undermine Germany's claim to the Free City. Because the measures initiated came only in response to Danzig's pressing needs of the moment, one may conclude that Germany lacked a program for the accomplishment of her aims. These aims, however, even if the means by which they were to be accomplished had never been systematically described, were clearly enunciated. Berlin sought to maintain Deutschtum in Danzig. The Treaty of Versailles stipulated that Danzig would have to become a free city, but the Germans were determined that this new status should alter Danzig as little as possible. Germany's ultimate objective was of course revision of the Treaty and recovery of the lost territories in the East. But for the moment she had no plan even for the immediate aim of preserving Danzig's German character.

Sahm and his colleagues had no compunctions about approaching Berlin for help. They were willing to commit themselves openly to the political aims of the Reich. In so doing, they forfeited any hopes of pursuing an independent policy which their government, or subsequent governments, might entertain. Berlin was buying Danzig. Under these circumstances, which persisted throughout the interwar period, no "spirit of Danzig," which Attolico had cherished, could possibly germinate. Any group—such as the handful of merchants who, enticed with the prospect of Danzig's becoming the port for thirty million Poles, traveled unofficially to Warsaw as early as November 1919 to discuss the mutual advantages of such a situation—[43] was submerged by the tide of popular sentiment and

43. Memorandum by William Klawitter, Spring 1926, PA: Stresemann Nachlass, Bd. 350 (7414H/H175419–38).

government policy. The hopes of the peacemakers—that the Danzigers would remember their past, in which their city had been similarly autonomous, and develop a sort of neo-Hanseatic patriotism—were pure illusion.

CHAPTER 3

Danzig Alone, 1920–1925

In the first five years after the Peace Conference, the Germans could take no action toward revision of the territorial settlement in the East. The Weimar Republic waged a battle for survival. Struggling with the task of postwar recovery while seeking a place for itself in the changed international society, the republican government found cooperation and sympathy neither at home nor abroad. While it fended off attacks from the left and the right at home, it sought in conferences abroad to reduce reparations. When it resorted to dilatory tactics, the French, by occupying several German cities in 1921, forced the Germans to accept the Allied reparations bill. To pay the debt, the government printed money indiscriminately, and inflation ensued. The climax came in 1923. The Germans defaulted on their payments, and the French occupied the Ruhr. Civil war broke out as the left attempted a coup in Saxony and Thuringia, the right in Bavaria, and separatists in the Rhineland proclaimed secession. Berlin undertook to finance a general strike against the French in the Ruhr, and the currency collapsed. The situation was too chaotic to encourage, or even permit, a policy of territorial revision. Only ultranationalist fringe groups still discussed the matter.

Relations between Germany and Danzig had changed after the establishment of the Free City. The year 1919–20 had been a period of innovation. Berlin had made its contribution to the form Danzig was going to take and certain precedents had been set: the preservation of the status quo in Danzig and the obstruction of all Polish encroachments. If the city were maintained as German as possible and were never obliged to concede rights to Poland, Germany could be sure of its loyalty when she pressed her revisionist claims. Now that the Free City was an established fact and the foundations for a loyal and cooperative Danzig laid, the flow of memorandums and proposals abated and the frequent meetings ceased. In these first five years, 1920–25, relations remained unobtrusive and stable.

But while Danzig was not in the forefront of German concerns, it was not forgotten. The link was maintained by a German consul, after 1921 a consul general, in Danzig, who transmitted communications and information about the city to the Eastern Department of the Foreign Ministry. Berlin of course continued to meet the city's pressing needs, and among these economic needs were primary. On the surface Danzig appeared to be prospering. Foreign investors came in swarms, expecting that Danzig, as in centuries past, would become a clearinghouse for exchange between eastern and western Europe. Vast quantities of Allied goods shipped to a destitute Poland in 1920 and 1921 inflated the trade figures speciously. The city's own trade, however, was modest, and it was obvious that the situation would worsen when the customs and economic unions of Danzig and Poland came into effect in the spring of 1922 and permanently closed the customs frontiers with Germany. Danzig's trade with Germany would be impeded by high duties, and the Polish markets that opened would not be able to absorb the city's products. The Polish economy was in a precarious state. In 1921 approximately two-thirds of the Polish population drew its living from agriculture, much of which was still at a low level of productivity. The industrial sector of the economy was in three different stages of development owing to the partition, and its readaptation and coordination were slow. Items for export were few, and inflation of the currency made trade difficult. The Polish tariff, which was to be applicable to Danzig, would raise the prices of consumer articles, raw materials, and half-finished products from abroad. The projected change was serious, for the Free City, unable to support itself industrially or agriculturally, had to import over half its consumer goods, and local farming and manufacturing were not productive enough to pay for these purchases.[1] The total cost for Danzig would be immense: it could not pay the higher prices for its imported raw materials and half-finished products, maintain its wage level (considerably higher than that of the Poles), and market its

1. Confidential report by Haking, Economic Conditions of Danzig, 6 May 1921, LN: 4/12600/3525.

consequently very expensive manufactures abroad without special concessions for its trade.

In November 1921 Danzig had turned to Berlin for new arrangements to offset the March Agreement which would lapse when Danzig entered the customs union with Poland. At a meeting with representatives of the Foreign Ministry and the Ministry of Economics on 21 November, the Senate requested that the old system continue unabated and even be expanded, allowing Danzig to reexport to Poland. The Germans were not eager to oblige. They pointed out that, while they were aware of the hardships which Danzig faced and the danger of polonization, they also had responsibilities toward the German economy. Complaints from Königsberg about Germany's privileged treatment of Danzig were increasingly bitter. Germany wished to retain a restrictive trade policy toward Poland and would have to insist on full assurance that any goods exported to Danzig were destined solely for home consumption. Since Danzig's economic union with Poland would make it impossible to trace the ultimate destination of German goods sent to the Free City, further supplies at preferential rates would have to be regulated by a quota system covering Danzig's own needs.[2] Such a scheme coincided with privileges which the Warsaw Agreement of 1921, recognizing that Danzig's standard of living was higher than Poland's, had assured the Free City. Article 212 gave Danzig the right to import, at a low tariff and independent of Polish trade restrictions, certain specified commodities for domestic consumption—the so-called Danzig contingents. Concurrently the city was granted the right to export its industrial and agricultural products irrespective of Polish export restrictions. The Poles were not permitted to check or question the import quotas selected but were to be notified of them quarterly.

The upshot of a series of discussions in Berlin was that, although economic preferences were an imposition on a none too healthy German economy, continued support should be given for the sake of Danzig's Deutschtum. Agreement was reached in February 1922. Certain quotas were to be established and

2. Protokoll der Besprechung im Auswärtigen Amt am 21. November 1921 über deutsch-danziger Wirtschaftsbeziehungen, PA: Handakten Direktoren: Dirksen, Minderheiten in Polen.

distributed among Danzig importers by a distribution agency in the Free City. The products for export to Danzig fell into two categories: such items as chemicals, pharmaceuticals, textiles, rubber, and construction materials were to be exported to Danzig at domestic prices; such goods as precious metals, iron and steel products, machinery, and furniture were to be exported at higher than inland but lower than minimum export prices. Danzig was also granted the right to export to Germany without having to pay German import fees or adhere to import restrictions.[3] Clearly, though the Warsaw Agreement provided legal bases for such transactions, the new German-Danzig agreement went far beyond the spirit of the law.

Berlin responded with similar beneficence to specific requests from Danzig. The Reichsbahn and the Ministry of War offered contracts to Danzig factories; freight charges across the Corridor were partially reimbursed; North German Lloyd had its first large postwar liner, a 32,500-ton sister ship to the *Columbus* of 1913, built at the Schichau shipyard in Danzig during 1922–23. In response to news that the Polish government was buying up all available business property on the Danzig harbor front, the Foreign Ministry urged large German industrial concerns to open branch offices in the Free City or to buy an interest in established, but weak, Danzig enterprises.[4]

Germany also responded to the financial needs of the Free City. Its financial problems were many, for it had to help defray the cost of the High Commissariat, the Harbor Board, which administered the port, and the customs administration. As an independent state, it was obliged to maintain numerous agencies and services which had rested in Berlin before the war —the per capita cost of government (102.32 marks) was one of the highest in Europe. Danzig had to pay its share of the German national debt and of the reparations imposed on Germany, and it had to buy from the Reich the state property

3. Ergebnis der Diskussion im Auswärtigen Amt am 16. Februar 1922, betr. deutsch-danziger Wirtschaftsbeziehungen, PA: H 11 Nr. 1, Danzig, Bd. 1; Aufzeichnung Dr. Naumanns über Wirtschaftsbeziehungen zu Danzig und Memel, 28 Nov. 1922, PA: ibid., Bd. 2; Foreign Ministry to Finance Ministry, 29 Mar. 1922, PA: H 11 Nr. 3, Danzig Geh., Bd. 1.

4. Foreign Ministry to Ministry of Trade, 4 Mar. 1922, and memorandum by Dirksen, 9 Jan. 1922, PA: Po 3, Danzig, Bd. 2.

awarded the city after the war. It owed money to the Conference of Ambassadors for the Allied occupation and administration in 1920 as well as for the surveying of its frontiers. But its revenues were low. According to the Warsaw Agreement (Article 206) it received roughly 8 percent of the total customs revenues collected in the port of Danzig and at the Polish frontiers, which, given the current imports into Poland (some four million tons in 1922), was little. The same economic ebb reduced income from taxation and the various fees connected with the port. Furthermore, because its currency was German, Danzig suffered the inflation and bankruptcy which overtook the Reich.[5]

In December 1920 the Reichsbank had provided the Free City with a loan of 50 million marks and had agreed to retain its branch office in the city to discount promissory notes and issue loans.[6] In February 1921 the Free City asked that the Reichsbank discount Danzig treasury bonds for 500 million marks to meet state expenses.[7] Ernst Volkmann, Danzig's senator of finance, presented the case in Berlin. Without some liquid funds by the end of the month, he claimed, the city and municipality could not pay for the provisioning of the population, provide the salaries and wages of the shipyard workers or of their own employees, or meet welfare expenditures. A paralysis of the economy would be unavoidable. Danzig's only other alternative was to turn to Poland, where aid would probably be forthcoming, but the conditions odious.

Volkmann's woeful tale found a sympathetic reception. The directors of the Reichsbank agreed that a refusal from Germany would be tantamount to abandoning Danzig to Polish influence. However, since the sum was vast and the transaction political, the Reichsbank demanded that the German government supply a secret guarantee of the loan.[8] Thus the cabinet decided that,

5. Rapport du Comité Financier, 15 Mar. 1922, LN: C.220.1922.I.

6. Reichsbank-Direktorium to Chancellery, 29 Dec. 1920, PA: Reichsminister, 55, Bd. 1 (3015H/D597803–07).

7. Reichsbank Danzig to Reichsbank-Direktorium, 16 Feb. 1921, PA: Fi 2, Danzig Geh., Bd. 1 (K207/K049959–62).

8. Reichsbank-Direktorium to Foreign Ministry, 19 Mar. 1929, PA: Fi 2, Danzig Geh., Bd. 1 (K207/K049928–30).

while Danzig should be permitted to discount its treasury bonds with the Reichsbank, the amount of the transaction should be reduced and its exact determination left to the Finance Ministry. The finance minister voiced doubts at the wisdom of this undertaking and urged that sentimental factors be excluded and a bankrupt Danzig be presented to the Allies as a blatant example of the failure of the Peace Treaty, but under the persuasion of the Foreign Ministry he eventually gave his consent. He guaranteed 150 million marks to cover the needs of municipal Danzig and 100 million for the Free City.[9] On 22 September the Reichsbank raised Danzig's discount credit on short-term, non-interest-bearing bonds by 100 million marks to 230 million. It also decided to honor an unspecified number of treasury bonds distributed by the Senate with values up to 1,000 marks. It accepted as collateral a mortgage on forests and property owned by the Free City, and the mortgage was put in the hands of a trustworthy third party of whom no foreign power was likely to become suspicious.[10]

Even these massive loans could not solve the difficulties created by continuous inflation, and after considerable hesitation, Danzig adopted its own currency, the gulden, in October 1923 —shortly before Germany reformed her monetary system. In February 1924, the Bank of Danzig, a bank of emission, was established with capital of 300,000 pounds sterling, and the gulden was based on the pound ($£1 = 25$ gulden).

Cultural as well as financial considerations played a role in Germany's decision to support Danzig's pensioners. Danzig had been assured in July 1919 that the pensions to its citizens would continue to be paid. However, when the Peace Treaty came into effect, according Germany the right to suspend pension payments in the ceded territories pending a financial settlement with the new authorities, the Finance Ministry declared that it would continue payment only until December 1921 and that, more-

9. Aufzeichnung über die Chefbesprechung am 21. März 1921 and Reichsbank-Direktorium to Ministry of Finance, 9 Aug. 1921, PA: Fi 2, Danzig Geh., Bd. 1 (K207/K049934 and K049971–72).

10. Reichsbank-Direktorium to Foreign Ministry, 22 Sept. 1922, PA: Fi 1, Danzig, Bd. 1.

over, Danzig would have to contribute 25 percent of whatever increases were decreed. The decision pleased neither Danzig nor the Foreign Ministry. To forestall large-scale emigration, provisional ordinances were adopted in November 1921. Pensions in Danzig and Germany were to be equal, and Germany would pay 60 percent, Danzig 40 percent, of the total sum of pensions in the Free City. This scheme assured Danzig an annual subvention of six million marks. The Foreign Ministry persuaded the Finance Ministry of Germany's financial interest in preventing a major exodus of German pensioners from Danzig to the Reich, where the Finance Ministry would have to pay 100 percent of the pensions. To conceal the arrangement, Danzig nominally accepted the entire burden and disbursed the money; it was reimbursed secretly by Prussia and the Reich.[11]

Germany's aid to Danzig during 1920–25, although as munificent as during 1919–20, was no longer unconditional. In the year before the Free City was established, Berlin had responded to Danzig's most urgent appeals with unqualified crash programs. Now it compromised between its own financial liabilities and its vested interest in Danzig's welfare. For Germany's economic situation had deteriorated sharply since 1919, whereas Danzig had enhanced at least its potential for economic expansion. The Free City was now an economic unit with Poland, and Berlin thought Danzig would do well to exploit this arrangement, if for no other reason than to attenuate its demands on the Reich.[12] Moreover, Germany found, once she had assured herself of the Free City's loyalty, that she could exploit the resolve of the Danzigers. Leading merchants, such as William Klawitter, the president of the Chamber of Commerce, were committed to keeping Danzig's commerce German even if it meant sacrifices and contradicted economic logic. Danzig's Senate, as the Foreign Ministry well knew, was reliably German, and its policy and Germany's were the same. The German consul in Danzig reported that the Senate fully realized that it was engaged, not in Danzig economic politics, but in German politics

11. Ministry of Finance, Runderlass, 9 Jan. 1922, BA: R 43 I/375.
12. Thermann (Danzig) to Foreign Ministry, 29 June 1925, PA: Gesandtschaft Warschau, P 15, Danzig, Bd. 2.

and that it considered this a patriotic duty despite the sacrifices involved for Danzig.[13]

The free exchange of civil servants made it possible to keep Danzig's administration staffed with Germans. Whenever retirement or resignation left gaps, replacements were recruited from the Reich. To find a native Danziger in the higher echelons of the Danzig civil service, especially during the 1920s, was rare. The principal senators were almost without exception not Danzigers (President Sahm came from Pomerania, Finance Senator Ernst Volkmann from the Ruhr, Interior Senator Willibald Wiercinski from Dresden), as were the chief of police, the chief justice, and the president of the Bank of Danzig. Not only the bureaucracy was staffed with Germans, but the academic and ecclesiastical offices as well. Loyalty to Germany was thus native to the entire ruling elite of the Free City. Policy was made and carried out by men of German birth and training, and to expect them to pursue an independent Danzig policy was unreasonable.

The structure of the Danzig administration was as German as its staff. The civil service was organized on the German model to the point of interchangeability. Justice, taxation, education— all were practiced as in the Reich. The Constitution stipulated that all German laws were to remain in force (Article 116), and subsequent legislation imitated German precedents. The trade unions remained German in structure and hierarchy and were governed by their German counterparts.

There was extraordinary parallelism, too, between the political life of Germany and that of Danzig. The political parties in the Free City were, with some minor exceptions (notably the Polish Party), nothing more or less than small copies of those in the Weimar Republic, of which they felt themselves a part. Party labels and platforms were the same, and the parties drew support from the same elements in the population. As in the Reichstag, the Nationalists, later joined by the National Socialists, stood at one extreme, the Socialists and Communists at the other. Between them were the Democrats and Centrists (and the Poles). Election trends generally followed those of

13. Ibid.; memorandum by Dirksen, 31 Aug. 1922, PA: Po 1, Danzig, Bd. 2.

the Reich. The Socialists, who had enjoyed a plurality in 1920, declined in 1923–24, while the Nationalists and Communists rose sharply; they returned with roughly a third of the popular vote in 1927–28, dropped to a quarter in 1930, and thenceforth gave way to Nationalists and National Socialists. Throughout, the Center Party remained constant.

Of course, Danzig's political life was not a perfect replica of a larger prototype. The relationship with Poland was uppermost in Danzig's politics and appeared prominently and consistently in the platforms, legislation, and policy of all parties. The Nationalist-Conservative coalition which dominated the Senate and Volkstag almost continuously between 1920 and 1933 pursued a line utterly intransigent and hostile toward Poland. The Socialists, who led a coalition in the Volkstag in 1923 and again in 1928–30, tended on the whole to be more conciliatory toward the Poles, seeking cooperation to boost the economy of the Free City. But the nationalism of Nationalists and Socialists alike far exceeded that of their respective parties in the Reich.

Whatever its composition, every Senate defined the city's relationship with Poland as purely economic and opposed Poland's efforts to extend her power in Danzig.[14] The city was convinced that while it prospered and benefited from the Polish economy, it was entitled to lead a politically and culturally untrammeled existence. This was a remarkable misconception: Poland would never permit an alien state to exercise an entirely uncontrollable influence over Polish maritime trade. Danzig's attitude, however, was not incompatible with German policy: Berlin was pleased if Danzig could benefit commercially from its peculiar status without compromising itself politically.

Of course the fate of the Free City was not determined by Danzig's policies alone. The Poles, who, contrary to their expectations, had been deprived of the city at Versailles and in 1920 had failed to win approval of their draft for the Convention, never ceased to entertain hopes of incorporating the city into the Polish state. Germany was aware of Poland's designs on Danzig—so much so that all Polish gestures were construed as sinister measures toward polonization—but she believed that

14. Memorandum by the Danzig Senate on Danzig-Polish relations, 11 Jan. 1923, LN: C.60.M.22.1923.I.

the League of Nations could block Polish measures which neither Danzig nor Berlin could prevent or forestall.

Danzig and Berlin shared the conviction that the League had a stake in seeing the status of the Free City preserved. Sahm strove hard, "with undeniable skill and great stubbornness," to keep the League involved and turn it into a "bulwark against the Polish danger." [15] Because at this early stage Geneva still believed that, as soon as the practical arrangements between Danzig and Poland had been satisfactorily instituted, the antagonisms would be superseded by common economic interests, it received Sahm cordially. Great Britain's evident interest in the Free City strengthened German trust in the League.[16] High commissioners such as Tower and Haking—who, after relinquishing the command of the occupation troops, held the post during 1921–23—enjoyed Danzig's respect, and the Germans and Danzigers believed that under their care Danzig was in good hands.

The role of the League was particularly important to Germans and Danzigers in the conflict over the Free City's sovereignty, which the Danzigers asserted and the Poles denied. Berlin valued Danzig's sovereignty for "the protection it afforded until the (inevitable) reunification with Germany." [17] The controversy over sovereignty persisted throughout the Free City's history.[18] No agreement ever emerged on whether sovereignty was vested in Warsaw, Geneva, or Danzig; there was no precedent for the city's status and no parallel anywhere in international law. That there would be controversy was predictable from the beginning. The Allied peacemakers had created the League, the Polish Republic, and the Free City and had established a unique, if

15. Consulate Geneva to Foreign Ministry, 23 Jan. 1922, PA: Referat Völkerbund: 16. Ratstagung (L782/L229288–96).

16. Foreign Ministry to Foerster, 29 Jan. 1921, PA: Po 11 Nr. 1, Danzig Geh., Bd. 1 (K213/K053220–23).

17. Aschmann (Geneva) to Foreign Ministry, 15 Nov. 1924, PA: Gesandtschaft Warschau, P 15, Danzig, Bd. 1.

18. Andrew Foster, "The Free City of Danzig: A Study in Politics and Economics," Unpublished master's thesis (University of Pennsylvania, 1935), pp. 66–74; John Brown Mason, "The Status of the Free City of Danzig Under International Law," *The Rocky Mountain Law Review* (1933), pp. 85–99.

rather ill-defined, relationship among them. It was clear that the triangular juridical responsibility which bound them together endowed each with certain rights and obligations, but it was far from clear wherein these rights and obligations lay.

The Danzigers argued that the Allies in calling Danzig the "Free City" had meant it to be sovereign, and that the League had affirmed this intention by accepting the Constitution, whose provisions gave the city the necessary characteristics of a state. To justify themselves as an independent, sovereign, and equal, if small, member of the family of nations, they also appealed to various treaties and rights, including the high commissioner's famous decision of 1924, which had concluded that "Danzig is a state in the international sense of the word and is entitled to the use of expressions denoting that fact." [19] Finally, they sought to affirm their city's sovereignty by exercising unrestrained authority within their walls, especially against any actual or imagined encroachments on Poland's part. They stressed their liberty to determine the city's nature by laws on alien registration and on the acquisition of citizenship and property.

Of course the fact that the League had assumed the protection of Danzig and had guaranteed its Constitution put certain restrictions on the city's sovereignty. The presence of the high commissioner was a constant reminder that the court of last instance lay in Geneva, and although the Danzig government never hesitated to call upon the high commissioner to adjudge its grievances, neither the League nor its representative was popular in the city. The high commissioner correctly reported to the League in 1929 that "it was impossible for [the Danzigers] to adapt themselves to the Geneva ideal of international peace and cooperation." [20] Poland, too, restricted Danzig's sovereignty. Polish conduct of the city's foreign relations, the Polish administration of railways and equal participation in the control of the harbor, the very fact that the Free City had been created to give Poland an access to the sea—all were cited as proof of Poland's powers over it.

What mattered of course, all legal interpretations and their

19. *Entscheidungen des Hohen Kommissars des Völkerbundes in der Freien Stadt Danzig, 1924* (Danzig, 1925), p. 70.
20. Report of the High Commissioner, 10 May 1929, LN: C.221.1929.I.

ramifications notwithstanding, was that Danzig was "small, weak and circumscribed," [21] Geneva far away, Germany impotent, and Poland close enough and strong enough to pose a constant threat. Danzig's sole defense against Polish pressure was insistence on its sovereign, and thus inviolable, character. An internationally accepted sovereign status meant that Danzig could count on support from nations which were committed to the League and had an interest in preserving European peace. Danzig rightly perceived that the sovereignty dispute was not merely theoretical: its solution in favor of Poland would give the Poles a legal right to take measures contrary to the city's interests as the Danzigers saw them.

The Free City experienced its first major political crisis in the spring of 1923. Like all subsequent crises with Poland, this one entailed an attack on and attempt to diminish Danzig's sovereignty and was accompanied by economic aggression. It did not strike out of the blue. Since the establishment of the Free City, Danzig and Poland had been involved in a succession of disputes. The interpretation and implementation of the Convention, which governed the economic relations between the two states, had led to quarrels. When these could not be settled in negotiations, they were submitted to Haking, who, like Tower, was sympathetic to Danzig. Half of the 66 decisions rendered by the high commissioners between 1921 and 1934 were reached before the end of 1923. Danzig-Polish conflicts appeared before almost every session of the League Council.

The Poles found the protracted debates in Geneva both unprofitable and demeaning. Unprofitable because the League, though competent to adjust the legal and technical difficulties between Danzig and Poland, was unable to correct the political animosities which were the root of the quarrels. Demeaning because, in her eagerness to establish herself in the dignity of her newly recovered statehood, Poland felt humiliated when her squabbles with a mere city became a public spectacle. She believed that these confrontations tarnished her international image, and this in turn had domestic repercussions. The opposition parties exploited the government's embarrassment, and Danzig became an internal issue as well.

Public embarrassment intensified the government's private

21. *Entscheidungen . . . 1924*, p. 68.

frustration at being obliged to consign all overseas trade to a port over which it exercised virtually no control. The Danzigers were not loath to capitalize on their commercial windfall, and they could cite the Convention to their advantage. The Poles, who enjoyed only limited rights of surveillance, suspected, moreover, that the Danzigers were defrauding them. Thus the agreements of 1920 and 1921, which the Poles had accepted reluctantly, became all the more onerous. And quite aside from the psychological moment of the arrangement with Danzig, Poland's security was endangered: as long as her outlet to the sea was not territorial but depended on the goodwill of Germans and their respect for treaties, as a Polish commissioner general was to observe, her economic and political independence was threatened.[22]

The crisis in Danzig emerged during the uneasy weeks which followed France's occupation of the Ruhr in January 1923 and Lithuania's almost simultaneous seizure of Memel. The Germans and the Danzigers speculated that the Poles might choose this moment, when the major powers were distracted, to change Danzig's status radically. The memory of Poland's annexation of Vilna in 1920 was in the minds of many.

On 22 February Sahm sought to calm anxious Danzig by deprecating rumors that the Poles would imitate the Memel coup. He told the Volkstag that the Polish commissioner general had assured him that Poland contemplated no hostile acts.[23] However, in an address to the Polish deputies in the Volkstag on 27 February, the commissioner general struck a different note. Poland was dissatisfied: her rights under the Versailles Treaty were far from realized, the common customs union existed more in theory than in practice, and the Harbor Board exhibited a pro-Danzig attitude, for its decisions were contrary to Polish legislation. In short, Poland's access to the sea, the primary reason for the creation of the Free City, was still not assured. It would, he concluded ominously, be very much in the interest of the city if its Senate adopted a more equitable policy.[24]

22. Henryk Strasburger, *Sprawa Gdańska* (Warsaw, 1937), pp. 17, 57–59, quoted in *Ostland Berichte* (1937), pp. 12, 23–24.
23. Sahm, *Erinnerungen,* p. 73.
24. Polish News Agency, 27 Feb. 1923, PA: Po 1, Danzig, Bd. 3.

The Polish press in Danzig took this opportunity to attack the Senate, and the Polish deputies in the Volkstag, who represented some 3 percent of the city's population, denounced Danzig's German leadership and German citizenry. The party's newspaper carried an open letter to the new high commissioner, Mervyn MacDonnell, who had arrived on 3 February 1923 from the British civil service in Egypt to replace Haking, whose term had expired. The letter accused the Senate of a stubbornly anti-Polish policy which violated the Treaty and tended to obstruct Poland's economic, social, and cultural rights by every feasible means.[25]

That some tentative plans were afoot seemed beyond doubt. Reports of Polish troop movements poured into the German Foreign Ministry, word reached Berlin that the nationalists in the Polish Sejm had urged the government to send its military into East Prussia and Silesia, and the German ambassador in Moscow claimed to know on good authority that the Poles were planning to attack Danzig with French consent.[26] Marshal Foch's projected visit to the Polish capital in May lent credibility to the speculations. On a visit to Poznań, Prime Minister Wladyslaw Sikorski warned that Danzig was no more than a free city and that its whole future depended on Poland; Warsaw did not intend to remain complaisant. Inflammatory articles, demonstrations in Danzig and Poland, aggressive resolutions in the Sejm, all pursued the same argument. Threats to apply to Danzig the trade restrictions effective in Poland should the Danzigers persist in evading Polish import-export regulations sent a team of negotiators hurrying to Warsaw.[27]

The Danzig Senate sought to dispel the fears of the populace. It ascribed the verbal assaults to the needs of Sikorski's cab-

25. *Gazeta Gdańska,* 1 Apr. 1923, PA: Po 3, Danzig Geh., Bd. 1 (K212/K051892–96).

26. Christian Höltje, *Die Weimarer Republik und das Ostlocarno-Problem 1919–1934* (Würzburg, 1958), p. 38; Embassy Moscow to Foreign Ministry, 27 Mar. 1923, PA: Reichsminister, 55, Bd. 1 (3015H/D597819).

27. Liedke (Danzig) to Foreign Ministry, 14 and 21 Apr. 1923, PA: Po 3, Danzig Geh., Bd. 1 (K212/K051887–91 and K051901–04); Legation Warsaw to Foreign Ministry, 18 May 1923, PA: Gesandtschaft Warschau, P 15, Danzig, Bd. 1.

inet, which was supported largely by the left and obliged to justify itself to the right.[28] The explanation had substance. A cabinet crisis was brewing in Warsaw, and the Sikorski government sought to divert attention from domestic difficulties and to deflate the nationalists' charge that it was lenient toward Danzig. The Senate also thought that the Polish pugnaciousness was meant to influence the new high commissioner and to prepare the way for a request that the League reinterpret relations between Poland and Danzig.[29] The Polish government was vexed with what it considered Danzig's recalcitrance, as officials intimated to MacDonnell, and it was frustrated at Danzig's obstruction of plans to establish Polish commercial and industrial agencies in the Free City and to promote an influx of Poles. The German consul in Danzig reported that Warsaw looked upon the accumulation of foreign capital in Danzig—German banks, industries, and shipping agencies—with displeasure.[30]

The situation became acute late in April. Speaking at Kartuzy near Danzig, Polish President Stanislaw Wojciechowski declared that for three years Poland had tried to win Danzig's cooperation by concessions and goodwill, but that this period was now over. Danzig did not desire cooperation but thought merely to utilize Polish labor and raw materials, exploiting the Polish Republic for the benefit of its own industry and commerce. One must stop the flow of lifeblood into Danzig until Danzig entered into loyal collaboration and recognized Poland as a major power with legal rights in the Free City.[31] Further amplification came from Trampczynski, the marshal of the Polish Senate, who declared in an interview in Poznań that strong medicine was the only cure. He advocated redistribution of customs revenues, Polish police in the port, and Polish customs officials.[32] These threats produced near panic in Danzig, which feared an imminent coup de main—especially after the Poles, on a transparent pretext, broke off negotiations for the abroga-

28. Sahm, pp. 81–82; Legation Warsaw to Foreign Ministry, 18 Apr. 1923, PA: Po 2, Polen Geh., Bd. 4 (K170/K024838–41).

29. Liedke (Danzig) to Foreign Ministry, 14 Apr. 1923, PA: Po 3, Danzig Geh., Bd. 1 (K212/K051887–91); Sahm, p. 80.

30. Liedke to Foreign Ministry, ibid.

31. *Dziennik Poznanski,* 1 May 1923, PA: Po 3, Danzig, Bd. 3.

32. *Danziger Neueste Nachrichten,* 30 Apr. 1923.

tion of certain restrictions they had imposed upon Danzig when, earlier in April, the Danzigers had refused to entrust the port to a Polish customs administration.[33]

Then it became apparent that the worst was over. Speaking before the Sejm Committee on Foreign Affairs in mid-May, Aleksander Skrzynski, the foreign minister, rejected a forcible solution of the difficulties with Danzig. He promised that Poland would use diplomatic means to rectify her grievances. Her relationship with the Free City should be governed by the Treaty, which the Convention, unwarrantedly favorable to German interests in Danzig, could not legally supersede.[34] Ten days later, the Sikorski government fell, and Poland descended into a state of political confusion from which she did not emerge until Pilsudski's coup d'état in May 1926.

At its July meeting, the Council of the League put an end to the crisis in Danzig. It rejected Poland's contention that the high commissioner had no authority to intervene in matters arising from Polish domestic legislation, such as customs policy, and resolved that the high commissioner himself should determine whether a dispute fell within his competence (Article 103 of the Versailles Treaty), whereupon either party to the dispute might appeal to the League (Article 39 of the Convention). When the Polish delegate moved that the Convention be abrogated because it contradicted the spirit of the Treaty, on which the legality of all subsequent agreements rested, Lord Robert Cecil asked him pointedly whether the Poles had signed the Convention and, if so, whether they intended to keep agreements they had endorsed. That ended the discussion.[35]

The German consul in Danzig, Herbert von Dirksen, of second-generation bourgeois nobility and richly endowed with the prejudices of his class, observed jubilantly that the Polish harassment had had the very opposite of the intended effect.[36]

33. Legation Warsaw to Foreign Ministry, 10 May 1923, PA: Reichsminister, 55, Bd. 1 (3015H/D597823).

34. Legation Warsaw to Foreign Ministry, 17 May 1923, PA: Reichsminister, 10, Bd. 2 (2945H/D570928).

35. Sahm, pp. 85–86; Consulate Geneva to Foreign Ministry, 14 July 1923, PA: Referat Völkerbund: 25. Ratstagung (L784/L229351–71); LNOJ (1923), pp. 1000–01, 1005–06.

36. Dirksen to Foreign Ministry, 11 July 1923, PA: Po 1, Danzig, Bd. 3.

But neither he nor the Foreign Ministry regarded the events of the spring and summer of 1923 as an unmixed triumph. The Poles had attacked Danzig on its most sensitive spot. The city's economic survival depended upon Polish forbearance. If the Poles curtailed Danzig's trade with the hinterland, withdrew their contracts from Danzig's industry, and diverted Polish traffic from the port, the city would be seriously debilitated. Intimidated at such a prospect, Danzig might be persuaded to accede to Polish wishes, rewrite old agreements and negotiate new ones, whereby the city would be opened to Polish infiltration and ultimately lost to the Germans.[37] Dirksen's report that Poland's tactics had convinced certain influential Danzigers, among them Commerce Senator Julius Jewelowski, that concessions would be the best foundation for maintaining the city's independence and German character lent substance to the Foreign Ministry's misgivings. Jewelowski, head of the party of negotiators who had gone to Warsaw during the crisis, believed that in a tranquil political climate Danzig's economy would flourish. As long as the city prospered, it would be politically secure. Thus he did not share Sahm's hostility toward Polish presence in the city. A handful of Danzig merchants also demurred, but not for political reasons. They were unwilling to submit to penury for the sake of national ideals.[38] This dissent among the Danzigers troubled the Foreign Ministry throughout the Weimar period.

The fears of 1923 were revived when, in January 1925, a Polish measure aimed again at Danzig's precarious sovereignty caused great concern among the public and in the press and threw the city's vulnerability into high relief. The incident which triggered the furore was, in itself, trivial. In order to facilitate Poland's communications with the port at Danzig and abroad, the Convention of 1920 had recognized Poland's title "to establish in the port of Danzig a post, telegraph, and telephone service communicating directly with Poland" and her right to acquire the necessary buildings (Articles 29–31). On the morn-

---

37. Liedke (Danzig) to Foreign Ministry, 21 Apr. 1923, and Dirksen to Foreign Ministry, 19 June 1923, PA: Po 3, Danzig Geh., Bd. 1 (K212/K051901–04 and K051936–38).

38. Dirksen to Foreign Ministry, 8 May 1923, PA: Po 3, Danzig Geh., Bd. 1 (K212/K051914–15); Sahm, pp. 59, 82, 96.

ing of 5 January the Danzigers discovered that Polish letterboxes had appeared at various street corners overnight, each labeled in Polish and German, ONLY FOR LETTERS TO POLAND. The Polish post office on the Heveliusplatz was opened to the public, and Polish mailcarriers began their rounds. The same day, the Senate received a note from the Polish commissioner general, dated 3 January, announcing the extension of Polish postal services. There was an outburst of indignation from the citizens of Danzig, and the next night the Polish eagle on the boxes— for the moment a symbol of the dreaded polonization of the city—was daubed red, white, and black, the old German imperial colors.

Two complaints reached the High Commissariat simultaneously: the Senate contested Poland's right to expand her postal services, and the commissioner general, Henryk Strasburger, demanded compensation and apologies for defacement of state property. At the same time, Strasburger, whose strong opinions on the position the Free City should occupy within the Polish economy had intimidated the Danzigers when he had arrived the previous year, coldly notified the Senate that Poland reserved the right to take measures for the protection of Polish property in the city if the Danzig police proved incapable of maintaining order.[39] The Senate, which saw the vandalism as no more than minor damage to property, expressed its regrets and appealed to the public to keep the peace in the interest of Danzig. But tempers were not mollified; the Polish press denounced the outrageous insult to Poland and attacked Danzig in tones unprecedented in the German consul's experience.[40]

On 11 January, Strasburger, apparently backed by his government, refused to comply with High Commissioner MacDonnell's request to restore the *status quo ante* as a measure against the recurrence of untoward incidents. He threatened to institute repressive measures against the Free City if MacDonnell authorized the Senate to remove the boxes.[41] An echo came from

39. Dirksen to Foreign Ministry, 9 Jan. 1925, PA: Reichsminister, 55, Bd. 1 (3015H/D597849 and D597852–53).

40. Dirksen to Foreign Ministry, 9 Jan. 1925, PA: Reichsminister, 55, Bd. 1 (3015H/D597850–51); Sahm, pp. 100–01.

41. Dirksen to Foreign Ministry, 14 Jan. 1925, PA: Reichsminister, 55, Bd. 1 (3015H/D597861–63).

Warsaw, where Stanislaw Thugutt, a member of the cabinet, spoke of the possibility of economic reprisals and a thorough revision of the Danzig-Polish relationship.[42] The Polish press accused the High Commissioner of unprincipled partiality and of overstepping his authority and demanded his recall.[43] Mac-Donnell, clearly out of his depth, wrote Erik Colban, who as head of the League's section for administrative commissions was competent for Danzig, to come and advise him.

Sahm sought to calm the Danzigers with assurances of his confidence in the League and a display of personal composure. In private he was much less composed. He told Colban that an excited citizenry was pressing the Senate to act and that he could give him no assurance that further incidents would not occur. The matter was urgent, he stressed, and the League would have to take decisive action.[44] In the Senate, Sahm described the incident as a Polish fait accompli, aimed at casting doubt on the Senate's unlimited authority within the city and at reducing Danzig's postal revenues.

Although the issue was ambiguous, Danzig's legal position was the stronger. In 1922 High Commissioner Haking had rendered two decisions on postal affairs, which concluded, first, that the Polish postal service was limited to the port and, second, that the service should be extended only to the Polish authorities in the Free City and to Polish mail going or coming from abroad. It was not to duplicate Danzig's services or to be open to Poles resident in Danzig. On the strength of these precedents, MacDonnell decided on 2 February 1925 that a Polish postal service outside the port was inadmissible and that the mailboxes would have to be removed.[45] The Polish government appealed to Geneva.

The German Foreign Ministry believed that Poland intended not only to challenge the sovereignty of the city but also to jeopardize the authority of the high commissioner. The League,

42. Foreign Ministry to Embassy London, 15 Jan. 1925, PA: Reichs-minister, 55, Bd. 1 (3015H/D597864).

43. Dirksen to Foreign Ministry, 16 Jan. 1925, Reichsminister, 55, Bd. 1 (3015H/D597869).

44. Sahm, pp. 102–03; Record of Conversation Between Sahm and Colban, 16 Jan. 1925, LN: 4/41756/20994.

45. *Entscheidungen . . . 1925* (Danzig, 1926), pp. 4–19.

should it deny MacDonnell the right to implement his decision, would undercut the power of his office, and Danzig would be left at Poland's mercy. The Foreign Ministry requested its consul in Geneva to put the case thus to members and officials of the League and instructed its missions in the countries represented in the League Council to influence the press.[46]

At its meeting on 13 March, which followed a closed session of the members, the Council did not back MacDonnell—the only instance in which the League disavowed the decision of a high commissioner. It agreed to leave matters as they stood until the Permanent Court of International Justice at the Hague could render an advisory opinion. On 11 June the Council examined the Court's opinion that, though the postal services were to be confined to the area of the port, "there is nothing in the texts of the international agreements [regarding Danzig] which suggests any limitation of the use of the postal services to Polish authorities and offices."[47] In accepting these conclusions, the Council acknowledged the Polish viewpoint and denied the relevance of Haking's second decision. In September 1925 the Council adopted the report of a commission of experts who had been sent to Danzig to delimit the port for the purposes of the postal service. The port was held to be that large area of Danzig in which all the establishments adjunct to sea transportation and trade were concentrated. Danzig's opinion that the port consisted of the waterways and the technical facilities in the harbor was rejected. The decision, over Sahm's vehement remonstrances, had fallen in Poland's favor.[48]

For the German Foreign Ministry and its consul in Danzig the mailbox episode and its outcome were an occasion for stocktaking. Poland had succeeded in humiliating Danzig and impinging upon its sovereignty. She had won the conflict by presenting the world with a fait accompli and then disregarding

46. Memorandum by Schubert (Foreign Ministry), 26 Jan. 1925, PA: Po 3, Danzig, Bd. 8

47. Permanent Court of International Justice, Collection of Advisory Opinions, series B, no. 11, pp. 37, 41.

48. LNOJ (1925), pp. 1371–77; Sahm, p. 108. Nor were the Polish mailboxes outside the agreed limitations of the port removed. See Ian F. D. Morrow, *The Peace Settlement in the German Polish Borderlands* (London, 1936), p. 89n.

outright the High Commissioner's request. The League, more-over, had in effect approved this course of action. Poland would no doubt employ such tactics again.[49] As in the political crisis of 1923, the Poles had threatened, and then applied, economic reprisals. Danzig had been boycotted: the Polish press campaigned against the purchase of Danzig goods, Polish merchants were discouraged from attending the Danzig industrial fair, the supply of Polish raw sugar to Danzig's refineries had been curtailed,[50] and, as Sahm was to complain, Polish firms had cancelled contracts on the ground that they could not act "contrary to the direction given by the Polish government." [51] The Polish government obviously hoped that Danzig would de-cline into economic misery. It hoped, ultimately, that the League, once it had been convinced that Danzig as an independent state was not economically viable, would let the city fall to Poland.

The Germans found furthermore that the League had made a poor showing. MacDonnell was weak. Unlike Haking, who had promoted support for his decisions in Geneva, MacDonnell remained passive in Council sessions, believing that once he had arrived at a decision, his job was done.[52] The Danzig rapporteur J. M. Quiñones de León, Spanish ambassador in Paris, was ignorant of and indifferent to the city's difficulties and was known to sympathize with the French in questions of eastern Europe. He had succeeded Viscount Ishii in April 1923, and since then he had been implicated in one unfavorable decision after another.[53] Finally, Colban felt Danzig-Polish differences

49. Liedke (Danzig) to Foreign Ministry, 25 Sept. 1925, PA: Po 3, Danzig, Bd. 1.

50. Thermann (Danzig) to Foreign Ministry, 23 Apr. 1925, PA: H 11 Nr. 1, Danzig, Bd. 3.

51. Sahm to High Commissioner, 14 Feb. 1925, LN: 4/42944/3525.

52. Liedke (Danzig) to Foreign Ministry, 25 Mar. 1925, PA: Po 3, Danzig Geh., Bd. 1 (K212/K052048–59).

53. During Quiñones' tenure, the Poles received broad concessions to rent installations in the harbor, Polish employees were accepted by the Harbor Board, and the Polish language was admitted in the Board's deliberations; the Danzigers' right to deport undesirable aliens was restricted and their freedom to submit issues to Geneva diminished. Poland received the Westerplatte promontory in the harbor as the site for a munitions depot. See below, p. 98. Memorandum by Thermann (Danzig), 1 Mar. 1926, PA: Po 3, Danzig, Bd. 13.

to be largely Danzig's fault and thought it the responsibility of
the League, not to modify the Versailles settlement and thus
eliminate friction, but to encourage Danzig to draw closer to
and join Poland by developing the commercial interests which
they shared.[54]

The Germans were dissatisfied not only with the persons to
whom the League had entrusted responsibility for Danzig but
with the League itself. In 1924 the consul in Danzig had commented on the Council's "lack of interest" in issues affecting
the Free City, and the German minister at Berne had called
its attitude toward Danzig "sharply negative." [55] To the consul
it seemed that the League was willing to sacrifice small states
to the interests of the larger powers within its membership.
"As a direct consequence of the close relationship between the
Danzig question and the problem of the eastern borders," it
felt itself behoven not to let its deliberations about the mailbox
affair "sharpen unnecessarily the conflict between England and
France or irritate prematurely those who have a vested interest
in Franco-Polish friendship." [56] The forum at Geneva apparently
harbored too many conflicting interests to evolve a consistent
and firmly protective policy toward Danzig, a policy clearly
representative of and responsive to the city's needs and welfare.
Danzig's needs would elicit satisfactory response from the
Council only if they were represented as the interests of a
major power.

In the Free City, too, the mailbox affair had had serious
repercussions. A political reaction had followed the crisis of
1923, and the Socialists, known for their conciliatory attitude,
controlled the Volkstag between June and December of that
year. The reaction in 1925 was even stronger. A vote of no
confidence toppled the parliamentary senators, and in August
a coalition of Socialists, Centrists, and left-wing liberals formed

54. Consulate Geneva to Foreign Ministry, 27 Jan. 1925, PA: Referat
Völkerbund: Deutschland-Polen-Danzig, Bd. 1.

55. Liedke (Danzig) to Foreign Ministry, 30 Dec. 1924, PA: Gesandtschaft Warschau, P 15, Danzig, Bd. 1; Müller to Foreign Ministry,
26 Mar. 1924, PA: Referat Völkerbund: 28. Ratstagung (L784/L229427–
51).

56. Liedke (Danzig) to Foreign Ministry, 25 Mar. 1925, PA: Po 3,
Danzig Geh., Bd. 1 (K212/K052048–59).

the new government. The new coalition stated as the first point of its official program that it sought cordial terms with Poland and, while it would watch over the independence of the city and the maintenance of all treaties, would abstain from any "provocative nationalist gestures." [57] To the German consul, "a government which is prepared to improve the relationship with Poland by all means and at almost any price" was a serious threat to Germany's policy. He described the atmosphere as "gloomy" and stressed that divergent views on Poland were fostering tension within the ranks of the commercial and political world.[58] After the mailbox episode it was obvious to the Germans that Danzig's intransigence was not sufficient to preserve the status quo.

57. Thermann (Danzig) to Foreign Ministry, 7 Aug. 1925, PA: Gesandtschaft Warschau, P 15, Danzig, Bd. 2.
58. Thermann (Danzig) to Foreign Ministry, 4 Sept. 1925, PA: H 11 Nr. 1, Danzig, Bd. 3; Thermann to Dirksen, 11 Dec. 1925, PA: Handakten Direktoren: Dirksen, Polen, Bd. 10 (5462H/E367824–27).

CHAPTER 4

Stresemann, 1925–1929

Germany's postwar difficulties culminated in 1923, and thereafter the crises abated. Under Gustav Stresemann's chancellorship the government abandoned the general strike in the Ruhr and reformed the currency. In April 1924 the Dawes Plan made reparations practicable, and even profitable, for Germany. Economic recovery began. The relief of civilian misery brought with it a moderation of extremist agitation, and civil strife subsided. Relative stability engendered confidence in the government, and the republic emerged considerably strengthened. The Dawes Plan also affected Germany's external affairs: the regulation of the Treaty settlement had reached a certain plateau, and Germany was no longer wholly preoccupied with parrying new and unexpected blows. Sanctions gave way to negotiations. The years of immobility came to an end.

Stresemann, who during his brief chancellorship had initiated many of these changes, benefited from them after he became foreign minister in November 1923. They opened to him opportunities and possibilities unavailable to his predecessors and allowed him to maintain in foreign policy a continuity of style and aim unique during the Weimar period.

Stresemann was an exceedingly complex personality; no judgment on him will ever be final. He combined within himself elements of conservatism and liberalism, monarchism and republicanism. Much of his character had been shaped in the days of imperial rule (he was born in 1878 and had entered political life in 1907), but his career in Weimar politics, which saw him in high office for six years and brought him into contact with all the leading European statesmen of his time, endowed him with immense responsibility for the fate of his country, which he did not fail to recognize. He never quite lost his nostalgia for imperial Germany. But his reason endorsed the republic, in which too much was at stake for him to remain committed to the past.

Stresemann handled foreign affairs with consummate skill. Combining foresight with expediency, he was a formidable negotiator. He was flexible but not averse to intransigence when he believed it would be effective. Quick to detect motives and weaknesses, he was adroit at putting others in his service. Indisputably he was a diplomatic tactician of the first order. He knew that his diplomacy would have to achieve its objectives without the benefit of military force, sustained only by the prestige of his country. Yet he was not without a streak of romanticism, and his sober assessments of Germany's possibilities often blended with utopian visions in curious flights of fancy.[1]

Stresemann fully recognized the extent to which domestic opinion could influence the formulation and conduct of foreign policy. He solicited support from the various political parties, maintained his parliamentary connections, and kept close contact with the Reichstag's standing committee on foreign affairs. He knew the value of intimate conversation, and it was here that he was at his best and most persuasive. He also availed himself of the press: he held news conferences frequently, cultivated the friendship of journalists, and wrote anonymous articles for various German newspapers. To assuage the more impatient of his countrymen and to assure himself of the nationalists' support, he often resorted to their aggressive tone. Stresemann has been depicted as the "good European" and as the "precursor to Hitler." Both portraits are overdrawn. He was a patriotic statesman. His service as foreign minister in six cabinets under three chancellors drew support chiefly from the Socialists, the Democrats, and the Center Party, opposition primarily from the Nationalists and National Socialists, and ambivalent support from his own People's Party.

Stresemann's diplomacy was devoted to the one primary objective the German government had pursued since 1919: the revision of the Treaty of Versailles. Under Stresemann, however, Germany abandoned her policy of studied recalcitrance toward the Treaty and pursued a course of conciliation. The Dawes Plan, which he negotiated in London in early August

1. Theodor Eschenburg, *Die improvisierte Demokratie* (Munich, 1963), p. 145.

1924 and pushed through the Reichstag late the same month, marked the beginning of the new policy. Previously the government had insisted that it could not possibly pay reparations, and the paroxysms of the economy seemed to bear out its pronouncement. Now the government had entered into an arrangement which made reparations feasible, and it proceeded to meet the payments. Its reward was release from isolation and a general relaxation of international tension. Locarno was the second step. The ultimate effect of the new policy was that Germany could pursue revisionism more actively and more systematically than in the years when she had been bent solely on proclaiming that the Treaty was outrageous.

The Locarno Treaties, signed in October 1925, were Stresemann's first major diplomatic victory. When he had offered the security pact the previous February, his purpose had been primarily defensive. He had sought to ward off what appeared to be renewed sanctions against Germany and deepening isolation. In the fall of 1924 the League Council endorsed a French proposal that it establish permanent inspection stations in the demilitarized Rhineland. In the German government the proposal raised the fear that the Rhineland would eventually be neutralized and therefore easy prey to separatism. These anxieties deepened when on 5 January 1925 the Allies, at France's behest, announced that, because of certain violations of the disarmament stipulations, they would extend the occupation of the Rhineland beyond the schedule established in the Treaty. Stresemann saw a clear link between disarmament and eventual evacuation: he believed that the proposed inspection stations and extended occupation stemmed from France's failure to find adequate guarantees that she was secure from renewed German aggression. These measures, then, had a common origin with a rumored Anglo-French-Belgian alliance, of which Stresemann had learned late in 1924 and which of course would have dashed any hopes he might have entertained of winning for Germany a position of equality among the major European powers.[2]

To obviate these measures, Stresemann offered to recognize the present Franco-German border and to guarantee the de-

2. Gustav Stresemann, *Vermächtnis. Der Nachlass in drei Bänden*, ed. Henry Bernhard (Berlin, 1932–33), *2*, 90–91.

militarization of the Rhineland. It was a momentous step. Germany was willing to renounce her claims to Alsace-Lorraine and Eupen-Malmédy as the necessary price for French security. She hoped that by allaying France's apprehensions she could escape sanctions and ostracism and gain latitude for initiatives in foreign policy.

In the main part of Stresemann's pact, the Treaty of Mutual Guarantee, Britain, France, Belgium, Germany, and Italy guaranteed collectively and severally the maintenance of the territorial status quo on Germany's western frontier (Article I) and agreed to settle all disputes over the area by peaceful means (Article III). Germany and Belgium, and again Germany and France, contracted to resort to war only in self-defense or in pursuance of League decisions (Article II).[3] In appended arbitration treaties Germany and Poland, and again Germany and Czechoslovakia, committed themselves to peaceful settlement of all disputes. Finally, Germany complied with the Allies' demand that she give warrant of her good faith by joining the League. She entered as a permanent member of the Council in September 1926, and the Locarno Treaties became binding.[4]

Of course as soon as the German pact proposals became public—French newspapers broke the story late in February 1925—speculation ensued. In Germany and abroad the proposed treaty was interpreted as Germany's prelude to opening the question of her eastern borders.[5] It was conjectured that Germany was freeing herself from French harassment in the West so that she could address herself single-mindedly to the East. By removing France's fear of German invasion, moreover, Germany was eliminating France's stake in the Franco-Polish treaty of mutual defense against German attack, concluded in 1921: the French would no longer be motivated to protect Poland unconditionally from German encroachment.

Stresemann sought to discourage such speculation lest it stir up opposition in France. In a sharply worded telegram he in-

3. Specifically, of decisions based on Article 15, paragraph 7, and Article 16 of the Covenant, which together defined the obligations of member states in case of international aggression.

4. League of Nations, *Treaty Series, 54,* 290–363.

5. *Frankfurter Zeitung,* 4 Mar. 1925; London *Times,* 5 Mar. 1925.

structed the German consul in Geneva to deny firmly all reports
that the proposed security pact was simply a means by which
Germany intended to open the eastern question. The ambassadors in London and Paris were requested to make similar
denials.[6]

Stresemann's protestations were made in good faith. Though
he never denied that his pact was relevant to the eastern borders,
its purpose, nevertheless, was not imminent revision. At this
time the Foreign Ministry had no concrete plans for an active
policy of territorial revision. The first written evidence of Germany's intentions in the East dates from 21 March 1925, some
six weeks after Stresemann had submitted his proposals for a
pact to the French. Doubtless, revisionism had been the subject
of extensive oral discussion within the Foreign Ministry ever
since the Treaty of Versailles had been signed, but only at this
late date did a ranking official feel moved to record his rumina-
tions. Furthermore, the thoughts on the matter were set down at
this time, not because any plans had ripened, but only in response to external stimulation.

On 18 March 1925 Sahm visited the Foreign Ministry on his
way back from Geneva and described to Dirksen, formerly
consul in Danzig and now deputy director of the Eastern
Department, the rumors about revision circulating in Geneva,
to which he apparently lent credence. He inquired whether the
German government might not indeed open the Corridor question at this time. Dirksen expressed astonishment at Sahm's
importunateness.[7] Three days later, stressing that his suggestions
were purely conjectural and could be realized only at some
unknown point in the future, Dirksen urged in a top secret
memorandum that the diplomatic missions receive correct information on Germany's objectives, which he then proceeded
to outline as he saw them.

Dirksen's observations on Germany's strategy for revision of

6. Stresemann to Consulate Geneva, 9 Mar. 1925, PA: Reichsminister,
55, Bd. 1 (3015H/D597919); Stresemann to Embassy Paris, 5 Feb. 1925,
in Alfred Anderle, *Die deutsche Rapallo-Politik* ([East] Berlin, 1962),
p. 116; Sthamer (London) to Foreign Ministry, 21 May 1925, PA:
Po 3, Danzig Geh., Bd. 1 (K212/K052079–81).

7. Memorandum by Dirksen, 18 Mar. 1925, PA: Staatssekretär, Po,
Bd. 2 (4569H/E168896–98).

the eastern borders are evidence that policy was still in the early stages of planning.[8] Negotiations for Locarno, however, were already underway. The assumption that Stresemann's proposals were designed only to raise the eastern question was therefore fallacious. Locarno stood in a much larger context.

The aim and general effect of the Locarno Treaties was détente in Europe. By giving the other parties to the pact satisfactory assurance that her intentions were pacific, Germany recovered freedom of movement. She then proceeded to challenge the Treaty of Versailles. She addressed herself to reparations, the occupation of the Rhineland, parity in the reduction of armaments, and the revision of the eastern frontier. The eastern boundaries, then, were one problem among many. Certainly Germany concluded the Locarno Treaties with the East in mind, but she did not conclude them exclusively for the sake of the East nor for the purpose of broaching the question imminently.

From Stresemann's point of view, the security pact was designed, not to open the eastern question, but to leave it open. The very clear differentiation which the pact made between Germany's western and eastern borders served a specific purpose. The Germans refused to guarantee the eastern borders. Throughout the long and difficult negotiations for the pact, they stubbornly parried all French attempts to extend to the eastern frontier a settlement analogous to the agreement which Germany offered in the West. They restricted themselves to the assurance that all differences arising between Germany and Poland would be settled by arbitration. Thus the pact, which pledged the preservation of Germany's western boundaries, did not block the adoption of a policy designed to achieve alterations in the East.[9]

On 30 June 1925 Stresemann dispatched to the principal diplomatic missions a directive which expanded on the views put forth by Dirksen in March and clarified the alterations which Germany envisaged for the East.[10] It defined Germany's territorial demands as the return of Danzig and the Corridor as

8. Aufzeichnung über die Aufrollung der Korridorfrage, 21 Mar. 1925, PA: Staatssekretär, Po, Bd. 1 (4568H/E168384–85).

9. *Vermächtnis, 2,* 281–82.

10. Stresemann to Missions, 30 June 1925, PA: Staatssekretär, O, Bd. 4 (4556H/E149414–34).

far south as a line cutting Filehne-Czarnikau-Kolmar-Bromberg-Thorn-Deutsch Eylau.[11] Upper Silesia would also have to be returned. In their own best interest, the Germans would have to give up all claims to Posen, for "the German standpoint will be immensely burdened if we also strove for the return of ethnographically indubitably Polish territory."

The idea, mooted in British circles, of fusing Danzig and the Corridor into an autonomous state was discarded as risky, since it would neither constitute a firm connection between Germany and East Prussia nor assure the ultimate return of the Corridor to the Reich. Moreover, such an amalgamation increased the danger of Danzig's becoming polonized, for it would add to the almost entirely German population of the Free City an equal number of Poles. A plebiscite in the Corridor was rejected as hazardous, since Polish de-germanization had altered the balance of population. The plebiscite in Upper Silesia in 1922, Stresemann recalled, had split the area.

Germany did not wish to eliminate Poland: "a new partition of Poland such as in 1793 or 1795 would never be an objective of German policy." The Poles would be granted compensation. The Germans here drew on the views which Sahm had argued before the Friko in 1919 and which had been revived and enlarged upon in British diplomatic circles in the spring of 1925.[12] Poland would receive a free port in Danzig, internationally guaranteed rights to tariff-exempt rail and river traffic, liberal transit privileges through German territory to the Baltic—rights analogous to those presently accorded Germany in the Corridor. Poland might conceivably secure another access to the sea by means of "corridor rights" to Memel; speculation even touched on a possible exchange of corridors, whereby Poland would be entitled to Lithuanian territory, though Stresemann warned that this idea would have to be handled cautiously.

11. Dirksen, in November 1925, was to be more precise: the Germans wanted Danzig, the Corridor, eastern Upper Silesia, parts of central Silesia (the districts of Gross Wartenberg, Namslau, and Guhrau), and a slight modification of the Posen borders. See Aufzeichnung über Fragen der deutschen Polenpolitik, 16 Nov. 1925, PA: Staatssekretär, Po, Bd. 1 (4569H/E168406–15).

12. Edgar D'Abernon, *An Ambassador of Peace, 1920–1926* (London, 1929–30), *3*, 149–50.

In his directive Stresemann conceded that Poland could not be expected to surrender her present corridor voluntarily and that for the moment the precise means of return were still unknown. Obviously Poland would have to be reduced to a state of derangement sufficient to make her acquiesce in territorial concessions in return for relief. She would have to be pressed. Military measures were clearly out of the question. In a sound evaluation of German strength, Stresemann had observed that "bragging and saber rattling without a saber" made no sense, and to his ambassador in London he wrote that the solution of the frontier problem would come about solely by "peaceful means." [13] Whether such a pacific orientation was a matter of preference or merely dictated by circumstances must remain a moot question. His papers give no answer. Stresemann once remarked that Germany's military impotence defined "the limits, nature, and method of German foreign policy," [14] and it seems unlikely that he even weighed the possibility of war.

In June 1925 Stresemann had speculated that of all possible parties, Russia was the most likely to inflict the necessary pressure on Poland in a conflict over their common borders. "A solution of the Corridor question without cooperation between Germany and Russia is hardly conceivable." [15] Writing in August 1925, Dirksen thought that of the "practical possibilities of altering the eastern borders" a Russo-Polish war was the most promising. In such a conflict Germany could not remain passive. Should Russia be victorious and the Polish government forced to withdraw to Cracow, "German policy will hardly let slip such an opportunity to regain the territories which had been wrested away." [16]

After Locarno such speculations took a new direction. Stresemann did not turn away from Russia altogether, for he believed that Germany should not restrict herself to a one-sided western

13. Stresemann to the Kaiser, 10 Oct. 1925, PA: Stresemann Nachlass, Bd. 261 (7118H/H145901–04); Stresemann to Sthamer (London), 19 Apr. 1926, PA: Stresemann Nachlass, Bd. 350 (7414H/H175393–99).
14. *Vermächtnis, 2,* 172.
15. Stresemann to Missions, 30 June 1925, n. 10.
16. Quoted in Jürgen Spenz, *Die diplomatische Vorgeschichte des Beitritts Deutschlands zum Völkerbund 1924–1926* (Göttingen, 1966), p. 192.

orientation. The conclusion of the Berlin Treaty with Russia in April 1926 indicated that the tie, established at Rapallo in 1922, would remain. As long as Russia and Germany were on a good footing, a threat would hang over Poland. Furthermore, as long as Germany retained Russia's amity, she would not be obliged to court the friendship of the western powers solely on their terms. But Russian collaboration in regaining the lost territory, for all its appealing simplicity, was of limited value. In a memorandum which surveyed the arguments relevant to establishing a policy, Erich Zechlin of the Eastern Department offered the opinion that the Russians would never tolerate a Polish corridor through Lithuania and that France would never countenance the return of the present corridor to Germany after a victorious Russian war, especially if Germany resorted to arms.[17] Stresemann realized that a military solution was the logical conclusion of dependence on Russia. Germany, however, was no candidate for military ventures.

As reliance on Russia diminished, reliance on the western powers waxed. The internal speculations of the Foreign Ministry on the subject were very much influenced by Locarno. When Britain refused to concur with France in demanding guarantees for the German-Polish borders, the Germans regarded her as sympathetic to their cause. Whereas in June 1925 Stresemann had found it "conceivable" that the "Anglo-Saxon powers" might apply some economic pressure on Poland if the idea gained ground that certain sacrifices by the Poles would promote general peace, in April 1926 he advanced the view that "the cooperation of Britain is an indispensable prerequisite."[18] But even if the existing boundaries discomfited them, Zechlin observed later, the British would never adopt "all our justified claims." They would not risk alienating France, and their very traditions would make intervention on the continent unlikely. Germany could not act without Britain, but Zechlin doubted that Germany could rely chiefly upon her. That left France, and she, thought Zechlin, held the key. If Germany could promote the present détente and win her confidence, France would concede that

17. Bemerkungen über die Lösung der östlichen Grenzfragen, 19 Nov. 1926, PA: Staatssekretär, Po, Bd. 2 (4569H/E168868–77).
18. Stresemann to Missions, 30 June 1925, n. 10.

Germany's claims to the eastern territories were reasonable and present no further obstacle to retrocession.[19] In October 1926 Stresemann told the Foreign Affairs Committee of the Reichstag that "when the time comes in which it will be possible to debate the eastern question in any form, it must be clearly recognized in Germany that this question can be settled only in concert with France." [20]

Anglo-French assistance and the neutrality of Russia in the modification of Poland's borders became constants in the Foreign Ministry's speculations and in the speeches of the Foreign Minister. The time would come when circumstances in Poland— civil strife, economic depression, or small wars—would permit concerted intervention. By accommodation and adjustment, an international conference would secure a settlement which would benefit Germany and not be unpropitious to Poland, e.g. the economic rehabilitation of a debilitated Poland for a price.[21]

A revisionist policy designed to achieve its ends by interna-tional action required an extensive propaganda campaign. The German campaign, begun in 1919, swelled to unprecedented proportions after Locarno. Fully cognizant of the value of propaganda, which Stresemann called "one of the most im-portant tasks of German policy," [22] the government maintained its own agency, the Reichszentrale für Heimatdienst, founded in 1917, and channeled money through the Foreign Ministry, which cooperated with the Ministry of the Interior and the Prussian Ministry of the Interior in encouraging the production of propaganda material. It is impossible to estimate exactly how much the government spent on propaganda—probably little in comparison to the sums spent today—but between 1926 and

19. Bemerkungen über die Lösung der östlichen Grenzfragen, 19 Nov. 1926, PA: Staatssekretär, Po, Bd. 2 (4569H/E168868–77).

20. *Vermächtnis, 3,* 38.

21. This policy was touched on in Stresemann to Sthamer, 19 Apr. 1926, n. 13, and becomes explicit in Dirksen to Rauscher, 15 June 1926, PA: Handakten Direktoren: Wallroth, Polen, Politik (5265H/E321190–92). For an abortive attempt to institute this policy when Poland appeared to have reached a state of sufficient debilitation in 1925–26, see below, pp. 156–59.

22. Stresemann to Missions, 30 June 1925, n. 10.

1929 the Foreign Ministry received 18 to 26 million marks a year
for that purpose.[23] Additional money came from industry and the
Deutsche Städtetag, an association of the governments of the
major German cities, which distributed its Deutschtum fund—
some 73,000 marks in 1928—after consultation with the government ministries.[24]

The entire output, prodigious in quantity, variable in quality,
reflected the view that

> Germany must convince the world of her good cause. She
> should never become tired of proving the injustice, the
> absurdity, the disaster and the danger of the Polish Corri-
> dor, and the justice, the historical necessity, and the
> creative character of the German revisionist claim.[25]

The campaign served a double purpose. It sought on the one
hand to mobilize world opinion, especially in Britain, France,
and the United States, and on the other to promote domestic
interest in the eastern boundaries, so that the government could
rely on public support of, or at least acquiescence in, revisionism.
The campaign, then, was conducted on several levels, according
to the audience to which its appeal was directed.

The bulk of the material was overt propaganda which private
and semiofficial organizations turned out for consumption by
the general public at home and abroad. It was mostly cheap
throwaway literature for broad circulation—pamphlets, broad-
sides, posters, handbills—which used exaggerated claims, quota-
tions out of context, and misrepresentations of fact in strident
appeals to emotion and prejudice. The German minority in
Poland was said to be "terrorized"; the Danzigers were "stran-
gled" economically and "polonized" socially; Danzigers and
East Prussians were the object of a Polish "plot" to seize and
incorporate them; Danzig was the "powderkeg of Europe." The
texts were reminiscent in tone and method of the worst anti-
Polish propaganda of the Wilhelmine period, which defamed

23. Henry Bretton, *Stresemann and the Revision of Versailles* (Stanford, 1953), pp. 157–59.

24. Aufzeichnung über die Besprechung auf dem Deutschen Städtetag,
January 1929, PA: Po 25, Danzig Geh. (L1580/L479912–15).

25. Arnold Zelle, *100 Korridor-Thesen* (Berlin, 1933), p. 33.

Polish society, disparaged Polish economy, derided Polish politics, and sneered at Polish culture.

The literature for popular consumption could also be more subtle, more sophisticated. Expensive volumes of glossy photographs in elaborate layouts made an impression very different from that of the lurid handbills. They were designed to please—and persuade—a more cultivated reading public. Their appearance exuded respectability and serious concern; their content was literate and seemingly reasonable. Such works concentrated on describing the creation of the Free City, its relations with Poland, its importance as a Baltic port. A favorite stratagem was to suggest a fictitious corridor (e.g. for Canada through the United States to the Atlantic or for Switzerland through Italy to the Adriatic) in order to make the "intolerable conditions" in the East more vivid. The smooth relationship between Yugoslavia and Greece, where the Yugoslavs had a free port at Salonika under binational administration and a railway line of their own, was held up as a model for a new Danzig settlement. So was the arrangement whereby Czechoslovakia leased free zones in the port of Hamburg.[26]

The Foreign Ministry sponsored much of the popular propaganda. It commissioned authors and publicists to write books and pamphlets and submitted advance orders for the publications, which it then distributed abroad. It authorized the consulate in Danzig to subsidize the local Staatsarchiv's propaganda and refutations of Polish propaganda, which it then had published.[27] It gave money to the Danziger Heimatdienst for the series *Material zum Problem Danzig* and *Danziger Schriften für Politik und Wirtschaft* and paid for translations into English and French. It also sought extant articles and books favorable

26. Examples are symposia such as Friedrich Heiss and A. Hillen Ziegfeld, eds., *Kampf um Preussenland* (Berlin, 1931) and *Deutschland und der Korridor* (Berlin, 1933), in the Volk und Reich Verlag, founded 1925, which specialized in such publications; Karl von Loesch and Max Boehm, eds., *Die grenz- und volkspolitischen Folgen des Friedensschlusses* (Berlin, 1930); journals such as *Ostland* (1920–28) and *Volk und Reich* (1925–44).

27. Walter Recke, *Polens Zugang zum Meer* (Danzig, 1930); Erich Keyser, *Der Kampf um die Weichsel* (Berlin, 1926) and *Der Weichselkorridor im Urteil des Auslandes* (Berlin, 1931).

to Danzig, preferably by foreign authors, and bought copies
for international and internal distribution. Its files fairly bristle
with propaganda projects and literature pertaining to Danzig.

The Foreign Ministry also put the so-called Deutschtumsorganisationen in its service. These agencies devoted themselves
to the fate of German enclaves around the world and lavished
special attention on the *Grenz- und Auslandsdeutsche,* Germans
in borderlands and foreign countries. Prominent among them
were the Verein für das Deutschtum im Ausland in Berlin and
the Deutsches Auslandsinstitut in Stuttgart, whose board of directors included representatives of the government. The Deutscher Schutzbund für das Grenz- und Auslandsdeutschtum,
founded in 1919 and headed by Karl von Loesch during the
Weimar period, was a federation of various agencies dealing
with Germans abroad. Its Eastern Committee grouped together
the associations concerned with the eastern borderlands (Deutscher Ostbund, Reichsbund der Danziger, and the like). All
these organizations set out to strengthen the bonds between
Germany and her nationals abroad, helping to preserve German
culture and the German way of life among the emigrants. They
sponsored festivals and touring exhibits, lectures on German life
and culture, youth and student group excursions, and the publica-
tion of lavishly illustrated books on history and culture, calen-
dars, regular journals (*Volk und Heimat, Der Auslandsdeutsche*),
and polemical pamphlets. Each received considerable financial
support, not only from the Foreign Ministry, but from the
Ministry of the Interior.[28]

Propaganda on a more erudite level was addressed to the
members of the professions which influence public opinion:
journalists, teachers, students, politicians, and prominent busi-
nessmen. The Wirtschaftspolitische Gesellschaft, founded in 1922
and headed by Margarete Gärtner, was an ostensibly independent
organization that in fact received its support largely from the
German government and from industry. It sought to inform
citizens of Great Britain and the United States of the consequences of the Versailles Treaty and to enlist their sympathy
for German grievances. It distributed information to foreign

28. Aufzeichnung über die Deutschtumsorganisationen, March 1928,
PA: Po 25, Polen, Bd. 8 (L682/L215556–78); unsigned memorandum,
25 Mar. 1929, BA: R 43 I/548.

authors who wanted to write pertinent books and sponsored trips through the Corridor to Danzig. Margarete Gärtner, who led these tours, was not displeased if her charges were subjected to rigorous Polish customs examinations and circumstantial changing of trains at the Corridor. In Danzig she impressed upon them the indisputably German character of the city and the hardships of its present unnatural circumstances. And she crowned the trip with a sumptuous reception at a private East Prussian country estate.[29]

The trips to Danzig were thought to have reached maximum efficacy when the travelers felt moved to write of their experiences. Official encouragement of proper literature did not stop at indirect inducement, however. The Foreign Ministry directed its Eastern Department to gather and document useful material on the history, politics, economic consequences, and possible solution of the eastern problem, which was then made available to foreign authors.[30] It approached journalists, teachers, and students with projects of an apparently academic nature and gave money to publishing houses for the promotion of selected studies.[31]

The government extended contracts and subventions to the

29. Margarete Gärtner, *Botschafterin des guten Willens* (Bonn, 1955), passim. Sir Robert Donald, René Martel, and Robert Tourly solicited and received information from the Gesellschaft. Lord Londonderry, Robert Boothby, and Dorothy Woodman of the Union for Democratic Control made the trip to Danzig. In 1931 William H. Dawson made the trip, and the information he gathered from this experience and from Gärtner herself was published as *Germany Under the Treaty* (London, 1933).

30. Foreign Ministry to Embassy London, 9 Jan. 1927, PA: Po 2, Polen Geh., Bd. 12 (K170/K026916–71).

31. Books thus subsidized were Karl Josef Kaufmann, *Das deutsche Westpreussen* (Berlin, Deutsche Rundschau, 1926); Paul Roth, *Die Entstehung des polnischen Staates* (Berlin, Liebmann, 1926); Walter Recke, *Die polnische Frage als Problem der europäischen Politik* (Berlin, Stilke, 1927); Robert Tourly, *Le conflit de demain: Berlin-Varsovie-Dantzig* (Paris, Delpeuch, 1928), also published in German; Robert Donald, *The Polish Corridor and Its Consequences* (London, Butterworth, 1929); René Martel, *Les frontières orientales de l'Allemagne* (Paris, 1929), also published in German and English; O. d'Etchegoyen, *Pologne, Pologne* (Paris, 1926), also published in German. Memorandum: Zur Frage der polnischen Propaganda, 4 Jan. 1929, PA: Handakten Direktoren: Dirksen, Minderheiten in Polen.

various *Ostinstitute,* which were thus enlisted in the service
of politics. The Deutschtum department of the Ministry of the
Interior appropriated special funds for the promotion of eastern
studies at universities and private research centers, describing
these projects as "research preparatory to the revision of the
Versailles Treaty." At a meeting held at the Ministry in 1927,
the chairman of the Leipzig Stiftung für deutsche Volks- und
Kulturbodenforschung inquired whether the projects financed by
the Ministry were to be "serious studies or propaganda pieces."
The candid ministerial reply was that "the bleeding eastern
borders should be depicted in an authoritative study as drastically—and as quickly—as possible." [32] Geography, history, economics, statistics—all were pressed into service. Aside from
the Stiftung in Leipzig, government contracts went to the
Osteuropa-Institut in Breslau, the Institut für ostdeutsche Wirtschaft at the University in Königsberg, which published several
monograph series, the Institut für Grenz- und Auslandsstudien
in Berlin, under M. H. Boehm, and the Ostland Institut in Danzig, a vigorous propaganda mill.

On a third level propaganda was direct conversation among
diplomats. Stresemann and Carl von Schubert, state secretary in
the Foreign Ministry from 1924 to 1930, tried to persuade the
ambassadors accredited in Berlin of the reasonableness of German wishes for revision.[33] In June 1925 Stresemann wrote his
diplomats that they were to stress in private conversation the
untenability of the eastern borders and the desirability of their
revision "in the interest of universal peace." The ambassadors
and ministers were to point out that the territories lost in the
East were German land, populated and governed by Germans
for centuries. The present arrangement was highly unsatisfactory:
the Poles were taking measures to de-germanize the area and
had applied undue pressure on Danzig. An access to the sea
was in fact not a matter of life and death for Poland—only
five to ten percent of her trade went by sea. Danzig, furthermore,
was languishing in the customs union with Poland and subject

32. Quoted in Broszat, *Polenpolitik,* p. 179.
33. D'Abernon, *3,* 87–88, 101; Aufzeichnung für eine Unterhaltung
mit Lord D'Abernon betr. Polenpolitik, 29 Dec. 1925, PA: Staatssekretär,
Po, Bd. 1 (4569H/E168456–65).

now to the chaos of the Polish economy. The Corridor was a stumbling block to Poles and Germans alike, for both West and East Prussia were in decay. If the eastern borders could be revised as Germany desired, then "as far as she was concerned, there would remain no obstacle to good German-Polish relations, and one of the greatest threats to European peace, the German-Polish friction, would have been removed as adequately as lay within the limits of human endeavor." The diplomats were to make explicit, however, that Germany had no desire to broach the question of the borders at the moment. She intended only that her wishes be known and accurately understood.[34]

The League represented another, and somewhat more elevated, outlet for German propaganda. From the forum at Geneva, Germany could plead her case before the public; privately she could clarify her standpoint to representatives of all the major European governments. The Germans set out to demonstrate both the difficulties which the Treaty of Versailles created in the East and the injustices perpetrated by the Poles. They pressed their point most pertinently by presenting grievances concerning the German minorities in Poland and seconding the complaints which Danzig brought to Geneva. In both instances Germany's concern went beyond the defense of fellow Germans: support for Danzig and the minorities was given for ulterior purposes, as the head of the Foreign Ministry's Legal Department observed, "namely in the interest of territorial revision." [35]

In the sessions in which Danzig appeared on the agenda— and there were many—German support was loud and clear. Both in the Council and privately members of the German delegation stressed Germany's interest in Danzig's difficulties and the blame Poland had to bear for these. They responded to Polish propaganda with German counterpropaganda. Germany encouraged the Danzigers to bring their grievances to Geneva, and the exact procedure of presentation was often

34. Stresemann to Missions, 30 June 1925, n. 10; Stresemann to Sthamer, 19 Apr. 1926, n. 13, and appendixes to this letter, Aufzeichnung über die wirtschaftliche und politische Sanierung Polens, PA: Stresemann Nachlass, Bd. 350 (7414H/H175400–16).

35. Memorandum by Gaus (Foreign Ministry), 19 Apr. 1930, PA: Staatssekretär, Poda, Bd. 2 (4570H/E169545–49).

previously agreed upon, so that the appeal before the Council was a well-rehearsed performance. The Germans used similar tactics with the minorities in Poland. These were encouraged to petition the League for redress of grievances. The Foreign Ministry virtually hired certain individuals, to whom it also gave legal advice, to deluge the Council with complaints and charges against the Poles, and the volume of letters of petition to the League on behalf of the German minorities in Poland reached ludicrous proportions after 1926.

Thus Germany neglected nothing in her effort to establish her claims by means of propaganda. From the tawdry handbill to the confidential diplomatic conversation, the message was the same. Since she could not realize her aims in the East on her own initiative, she was obliged to depend on persuasion.

While Germany sought the friendship of the western powers, waited for distress to overtake the Polish state, and pressed her propaganda campaign, she continued to lend Danzig assistance. In the mid-1920s, the preservation of Danzig required a greater effort than before. The improvement which the Dawes Plan effected in Germany's economy had no counterpart in the Free City. Superficially, as in 1921, its economy appeared to thrive. The volume of goods handled in the port surpassed pre-war figures in 1924 (2,374,557 tons as opposed to 2,112,101 in 1913) and continued to grow until in 1928 it reached 8,615,682 tons. Marine traffic increased proportionately: 3,340 ships cleared the port in 1924, 6,183 in 1928. In 1913 Danzig had ranked fifth among German ports in total freight turnover; in the years 1926 to 1933 it was second only to Hamburg. However, while freight tonnage in 1928 exceeded that of 1924 by 260 percent, the value of the goods increased by only 1.2 percent. After 1925 coal represented more than 60 percent of total exports through the port of Danzig, climbing in 1928 as high as 79 percent but only 4 percent of this volume was bought and sold by Danzig merchants. A minimal quantity of the chief imports—ores, scrap metal, fertilizers—went through their hands. Danzig's trade had fallen to Polish syndicates and Polish merchants.[36]

36. Thermann (Danzig) to Foreign Ministry, 16 Apr. 1930, PA:

The year 1925 was critical. When her economy went into recession and the zloty fell, Poland curtailed imports and sought to supply her needs solely by domestic manufacture. She erected exchange regulations, levied indirect taxes, and decreed monopolies on such goods as tobacco and spirits, which, compounded by the trade war that broke out between Germany and Poland, seriously obstructed Danzig's markets. Capricious Polish tariff legislation made it difficult for Danzig to anticipate the course of its commerce and to plan for the expansion of its economy. Danzig's farmers, already hurt by a crop failure in 1925, were troubled by competition from cheap Polish agricultural produce. By the end of the year, 58 percent of the firms on register in October 1925 were in liquidation or receivership, notices of sheriff's auctions filled the newspapers, and unemployment stood at 17,374.[37] The following years brought some improvement, but the city remained in distress. Its manufacture and trade continued to drop. Unemployment reached a low of 7,695 in August 1928 but soon returned to its usual level of about 15,-000—10 percent of the labor force.

Inevitably these economic difficulties affected the finances of the Free City. The high cost of administering the tiny state, which in 1929 accounted for 53 percent of the budget, had more than doubled the burden of taxes since 1914. Yet high taxes did not keep the state solvent. Revenues declined as taxable income diminished, and the taxes of an impoverished agriculture and an insolvent industry remained unpaid. Income from customs, expected to be the city's chief source of revenue, dropped from 23 million gulden in 1924 to 17.5 million in 1925, to 11.4 in 1926, and rose again only slowly thereafter. Since the cost of the Danzig customs administration was 7.6 million gulden, its net profits were low. The budget, which had shown a surplus of 9,767,023 in 1924, reflected at the end of the fiscal year 1925

Sch 16A, Danzig Geh., Bd. 1 (K219/K058695–728); statistics in *Collection of Documents Regarding the Application Submitted by the Government of the Free City of Danzig to the High Commissioner of the League of Nations, Danzig, for a Decision in the Matter of Danzig-Gdingen* (Danzig, 1930), pp. 80–96.

37. Kabinettsvorlage, 13 Jan. 1926, PA: Handakten Direktoren: Dirksen, Polen, Bd. 10 (5462H/E367851–60); Runderlass by Zechlin, 10 Aug. 1926, PA: Fi 1, Danzig, Bd. 2.

a deficit of 14,040,002 and of 9,733,209 a year later.[38] Just
as the Foreign Ministry feared, economic distress bred internal
opposition. In August 1925, as in 1919, a delegation of merchants went to Warsaw to discuss mutually advantageous arrangements with the Poles, and in the same month the Volkstag
chose a Socialist-Liberal coalition of senators.[39]

In despair at their economic distress, members of the Danzig
Senate and Chamber of Commerce had turned to the German
consul in February 1925. Their appeal was worded to touch a
raw nerve in the Foreign Ministry:

> A Polish Danzig means that the Corridor, which Germany
> hopes to revise, will be disposed of in a manner unfavorable
> to the Reich. It is not to be assumed that the Allies and the
> League will abrogate the Corridor to Germany's advantage,
> if Danzig, the ganglion of the Corridor, has fallen into the
> hands of the Poles. The Corridor, after all, is generally
> known, not as the Polish Corridor, but as the Danzig
> Corridor, since the economic and cultural center of this
> area lies, not in surrounding Pomerelia, but in . . . Dan-
> zig.[40]

The consul, Edmund von Thermann, who had succeeded
Dirksen in 1925 and who retained the post until 1933, turned
immediately to Berlin, but there the response was discouraging.
Ministerial obstructionism was at work, and the Foreign Ministry found that other ministries challenged its priorities.

In September 1925 Dirksen, in exasperation, proposed a new
course of action. He suggested that Danzig draw up a comprehensive memorandum outlining its difficulties and needs,
which the Foreign Ministry could then submit to the cabinet.
If the cabinet approved an aid program for Danzig, the other
ministries would have to concur.[41] This was a new departure:
henceforth the Foreign Ministry was willing to entertain a broad

38. Zuschuss des Reiches zu den Danziger Ausgaben, PA: Fi 3, Danzig
Geh., Bd. 1 (K208/K050306–24); LNOJ (1926), pp. 1450–67.

39. Memorandum by William Klawitter, Spring 1926, PA: Stresemann
Nachlass, Bd. 350 (7414H/H175419–38).

40. Das politische Problem Danzig, February 1925, PA: H 13, Danzig
Geh., Bd. 1 (K211/K051750–57).

41. Dirksen to Thermann, 4 Sept. 1925, and Dirksen to Volkmann,

scheme of assistance; its previous method of dealing with emergencies as they arose had been abandoned.

The Danzig memorandum, which Sahm and some of his close colleagues had drawn up privately for reasons of security, painted in heavy strokes the economic troubles of the Free City. Merchants, farmers, and industrialists were impoverished, and the city could not help them. If local enterprise was not to collapse, Danzig would have to gain outside help. It needed long-term credits to finance production, a profitable outlet for its industry and agriculture, which meant preferential treatment of its exports to Germany, and, specifically for industry, contracts and rights to passive finishing trade, whereby Germany would supply Danzig firms with duty-free raw or partly finished materials, which they would process and market either locally or in the Reich.[42]

The Foreign Ministry placed the request on the cabinet's agenda and sought support from the other ministries. These, however, raised grave doubts. The lucrative passive finishing trade, the Ministry of Economics observed, was restricted by the official *Veredelungsordnung,* which stipulated that non-Germans might engage in it only if the product in question were produced in insufficient quantity or quality in the Reich. The Finance Ministry objected to customs preferences for Danzig on the ground that, although Article 108 of the *Reichsabgabenordnung* of December 1919 provided for the duty-free import of goods, this concession might be extended only if the regular duties caused undue hardship to the German importer or the German economy. Altogether the reaction in informal interministerial sessions was not auspicious.[43]

---

9 Sept. 1925, PA: Handakten Direktoren: Dirksen, Polen, Bd. 16 (5462H/E369535–37 and E369539–42).

42. Denkschrift des Danziger Senats über die Wirtschaftsnot in Danzig, PA: Wi 1, Danzig Geh., Bd. 1. The League's bilingual *Official Journal* renders *passiver Veredelungsverkehr* as *trafic passif de finissage* and "passive finishing trade."

43. Aufzeichnung über die Besprechung in der Reichskanzlei am 22. Dezember 1925, betr. Unterstützungsaktion für Danzig, PA: Wi 1, Danzig Geh., Bd. 1; Memorandum by Drubba (Foreign Ministry), 4 Jan. 1926, PA: Handakten Direktoren: Dirksen, Hilfsaktion Danzig (5462H/ E367841–50).

At the cabinet meeting on 1 February 1926, at which Stresemann himself pleaded Danzig's case, it was agreed that a credit
of ten million marks should be extended to Danzig through the
Prussian State Bank. But even the unanimity of the cabinet
decision could not check the opposition. The Finance Ministry
reduced the sum by half and the Prussian State Bank set a
discount rate of 7.75 percent. It also insisted that the Senate
underwrite the loan.[44] With a heavy heart the Danzigers accepted the result of their appeal.

Ministerial obstructionism, apparent in 1919–20 when the
German government was still improvising procedures which
would take Danzig's new status into account, had not disappeared. It was in fact so strong that it had prompted the Foreign
Ministry to take a comprehensive statement of Danzig's difficulties to the cabinet and win the cabinet's unanimous endorsement—without effect. Very clearly the ministries had never co-
ordinated revisionist aims and tactics within their various spheres
of competence. Dirksen observed in 1927 that the ministries
concerned with domestic affairs, while not lacking in understanding for Danzig's problems, believed that they could not
ignore conflicting German interests, especially East Prussia's
objection to continuing concessions to the Free City.[45] The
Foreign Ministry was obliged to plead against what the other
ministries considered German interests of importance, and to
some extent aid for Danzig depended on how persuasively it
could argue that the aims of foreign policy took precedence
over domestic considerations and that Germany's political
designs for Danzig justified an expenditure which economic
common sense found prodigal.

The arguments before the cabinet and in interministerial
meetings maintained that if Danzig did not receive bountiful
aid from Germany, even at the cost of hardship in the Reich,
Poland would gain control and ultimately possession of the city.
German Danzig was the Reich's primary asset in its endeavor
to recover the landbridge to East Prussia. "If we lose this asset,"

44. Memorandum by Wallroth (Foreign Ministry), 21 June 1926,
PA: Wi 1, Danzig Geh., Bd. 2.
45. Memorandum by Dirksen, 3 Oct. 1927, PA: Handakten Direktoren: Dirksen, Minderheiten in Polen.

Dirksen wrote in 1927, "the goals of our entire eastern policy will be seriously endangered." [46] To think that Danzig would require little aid from the Reich because the Germans there were economically secure and their ethnic concentration so dense that Deutschtum could not be undermined, Stresemann argued, was erroneous. If Germany were not to forfeit both the benefit of her past investment and her hopes for future returns, she would be obliged to proffer a comprehensive aid program over an indefinite period. Economic considerations were irrelevant in the light of political necessity. In weighing Danzig's requests, the ministries should adopt the attitude that the city was still, in fact, part of the Reich. "Unless we keep Danzig German, we cannot hope to reclaim the Corridor, and ultimately it will be impossible to retain our sovereignty over East Prussia." [47]

Between 1926 and 1929 Germany gave Danzig more generous, extensive, and systematic aid than ever before. It fell into three broad categories. Direct subvention of the government was the most comprehensive of the programs. The Foreign Ministry agreed to furnish Danzig a regular subsidy to balance its budget, and in December 1927 it placed 2.5 million marks at the Free City's disposal. Of this sum 200,000 marks were earmarked: 150,000 for the Polytechnical Institute, 20,000 for the municipal theater, and 30,000 for a special "cultural fund" of the consulate, to be disbursed by the consul as he saw fit.[48] For the fiscal year 1928 Danzig received 3,250,000 marks, of which about 390,-000 were set aside for specific purposes. The subsidy for the fiscal year 1929 amounted to 4,000,000 marks, of which 515,700 were earmarked. In addition to the Polytechnical Institute, the theater, and the cultural fund, 100,000 were specified to support renovations of the Marienkirche, important to the

46. Ibid.
47. Memorandum by Stresemann, 29 Dec. 1926, BA: R 43 I/548; Kabinettsvorlage, 13 Jan. 1926, PA: Wi 1, Danzig Geh., Bd. 2.
48. Aufzeichnung über das Danziger Zuschussprogramm, 3 Aug. 1927, PA: Handakten Direktoren: Dirksen, Polen, Bd. 11 (5462H/E367947–50); Niederschrift über die Besprechung über das Danziger Zuschussprogramm, 23 Feb. 1928, PA: Fi 3, Danzig Geh., Bd. 1 (K208/K050488–89); Foreign Ministry to Thermann, 17 Dec. 1927, PA: Fi 3, Danzig Geh., Bd. 1 (K208/K050437).

city as a "manifestation of German art and German culture," and another 100,000 for the preservation in the German interest of "nationally endangered economic enterprises." The subvention for 1930 was again 4,000,000 marks, with 534,000 designated for specific purposes.[49]

The Finance Ministry found an ingenious means of accounting for the Danzig subsidy in the German budget, whereby the extra funds for the Free City became at once legal and clandestine. According to the agreement on pensions of January 1924[50] Germany was to pay 60 percent of the civil and military pensions in Danzig. These pensions appeared in the Reich budget under various categories. On 22 December 1927 the competent German ministries, the Foreign Ministry, the Finance Ministry, and the Ministry of Labor, decided that, while they would not alter the agreement to pay 60 percent of the pensions, they would in fact provide Danzig with funds equivalent to 100 percent and more. The excess over 60 percent of the pensions constituted the subsidy to the city.[51] These funds, like all subsequent subsidies, were deposited into the account which the Bank of Danzig held in the Reichs-Kredit-Gesellschaft in Berlin or in its account with the Prussian State Bank. Danzig could thus withdraw the funds without leaving traces of a direct transaction with Berlin.[52]

The Finance Ministry insisted that Danzig exercise the greatest economy. The subsidy was granted and renewed on the condition that the Senate exhaust all other possible sources of income and reduce state expenditure to an absolute minimum. The Free City was required to levy a sales tax and to demand that all state employees renounce part of their salaries (the so-

49. Memorandum by Ministry of Finance, 17 Nov. 1928, PA: Fi 3, Danzig Geh., Bd. 3 (K208/K050673); Ministry of Finance to Sahm, 12 Dec. 1929, PA: ibid., Bd. 4 (K208/K050767–76).

50. It renewed with minor alterations the agreement of 1921; Runderlass by Ministry of Finance, 12 Feb. 1924, BA: R 43 I/375. See above, pp. 50–51.

51. Ministry of Finance to Rechnungshof des deutschen Reiches, 21 July 1930, BA: R 2/19576.

52. Ministry of Finance to Senate, 5 Apr. 1933, PA: Fi 3, Danzig Geh., Bd. 5 (6203H/E468402); memorandum by Reichsbank, 28 July 1933, BA: R 43 I/377.

called *Notopfer*). In 1929 the Finance Ministry obliged Danzig to cut its administrative costs by 10 percent and to reduce the membership of both Volkstag and Senate by constitutional amendment. It dispatched financial and budget experts to inquire into the disposition of funds and suggest means of rationalizing the city's financial affairs. It was not interested in pouring its money into a bottomless pit. The Ministry insisted, however, that Danzig maintain its cultural expenditures—for the Polytechnical Institute, the school system, the Staatsarchiv, propaganda—at full level. Here, clearly, political objectives took precedence over economic considerations. In 1929 Hilferding, then finance minister, acknowledged that the subsidies were granted so that "Danzig's political autonomy" might remain unimpaired and its cultural and social achievements undiminished.[53]

The Senate also received direct subsidies specifically for the support of cultural activities, which would stress the cultural unity with the Reich, boost the morale of the Danzigers, and, not least, make the Free City a showcase of Deutschtum. Prior to 1925, support of the cultural life in the Free City was mostly in local hands. The Senate had pledged itself to preserve the German character of Danzig, and every government saw to it that cultural life flourished. The Deutscher Heimatbund, founded in November 1920, sponsored guided tours, exhibits, and publications on local history and invited prominent Germans to lecture in the city. Each year it promoted the so-called *Deutschkundliche Woche,* at which visitors from Germany and the Corridor joined Danzigers to discuss a particular German theme—historical, literary, or linguistic.

In 1925 the German government replaced its piecemeal aid to Danzig's cultural life with a systematic program. The city was promoted as a town of congresses and athletic events. Each year thousands of Germans streamed into Danzig, taking advantage of reduced train fare for groups and subsidized sea and air travel. The German government financed drama and glee club tours to Danzig and lectures in the Free City. Funds went to the annual Danzig industrial fair and to the support of the

53. Hilferding to Sahm, 12 Dec. 1929, BA: R 2/19576.

municipal theater and the Zoppot Waldoper, which featured an annual Wagner cycle.[54]

The Cultural Department of the Foreign Ministry, which worked in close contact with the Eastern Department, furnished the greater part of the subventions. Money came also from the Deutsche Stiftung, which had been founded in 1920 to distribute secret government funds to the Germans in the lost territories,[55] and which concerned itself particularly with subsidizing the press in Danzig and the local Deutschtum organizations. Contributions were generous. In 1927–28 the Deutsche Stiftung put 60,000 marks at the consul's disposal. For the same year the Cultural Department gave the Danzig consulate 162,000 marks for projects ranging from funds for social clubs for the elderly to German tours for Danzig gymnastic clubs.[56]

The cultural fund granted to the consul in the annual subsidy gave him the opportunity to pursue a policy of the open hand. He spent it on the promotion of varied and usually minor activities whose importance to the German element in the city merited financial assistance: on the maintenance of nurseries and kindergartens, on the construction of a student dormitory, and on libraries, charities, confessional associations, and local celebrations.[57] The educational system in the Free City was of particular importance to Berlin: if it were kept wholly German, Danzig would remain German in perpetuity. The Foreign Ministry and the Deutsche Stiftung gave large sums to the Polytechnical Institute and encouraged it to expand its curriculum beyond the traditional disciplines to history, literature, philosophy, and political economy. The Deutsche Stiftung provided scholarships for German students from both the Reich

54. Dirksen to Foreign Ministry, 5 Oct. 1923, PA: Po 25, Danzig, Bd. 1; Dirksen to Foreign Ministry, 26 Aug. 1924, PA: Po 2, Danzig, Bd. 1; Thermann to Dirksen, 16 July 1927, PA: Handakten Direktoren: Dirksen, Polen, Bd. 11 (5462H/E367930–33).

55. Memorandums, 6 Feb. and 5 Dec. 1929, PA: Staatssekretär, NM, Bd. 2 and 3 (4555H/E147507–11 and E148036–41).

56. Thermann to Foreign Ministry, 10 Mar. 1928, PA: Po 25, Danzig Geh. (L1580/L479935–42); Thermann to Dirksen, 28 Mar. 1928, PA: Fi 3, Danzig Geh., Bd. 2 (K208/K050515–17).

57. Thermann to Foreign Ministry, 13 and 21 Jan. 1928, PA: Fi 3, Danzig Geh., Bd. 1 (K208/K050470–71 and K050473–74).

and the ceded territories, and the Polytechnical Institute became a major educational center in the East.[58]

On a second level, the German government gave direct financial support to Danzig's industry. The most spectacular example was the rehabilitation of the Schichau shipyard. Founded in 1837, this company and its subsidiary in nearby Elbing (East Prussia) had achieved world fame for the construction of luxury liners and warships for the German navy. After the First World War it had changed over to the construction of merchant ships, machinery, and turbines. It was, however, troubled by a lack of contracts and markets: employment dropped from 5,000 in 1914 to 3,400 in 1926, and turnover from 30 to 8.3 million marks. In 1925 Schichau turned to Berlin for contracts and credits.[59]

In March 1925 the cabinet decided, in concert with Prussia, to extend 10 million marks. The government prompted a consortium of private banks to provide a further 5 million, which it guaranteed. Both loans were paid out in June 1926; both fell due in April 1931. In the spring of 1928, when another shortage of funds threatened to curtail production, a further 7.7 million marks was provided by several government and private agencies. No cure was accomplished, and investigation showed the need for 35 million more—18 for the remission of debts, 17 for working capital. An additional 3.5 million was necessary to cover the annual running expenses. At a combined meeting the Reich and Prussian ministries agreed that further credits were economically indefensible and only political reasons justified a continued effort.[60]

Political reasons prevailed. The cabinet decided to have the shipyard transformed into a joint stock corporation, whose shares were to be held by Germany, Prussia, Danzig, and Elbing, and whose chairmanship would be placed in the hands of the

58. Thermann to Foreign Ministry, 24 Nov. 1927, PA: Fi 3, Danzig Geh., Bd. 1 (K208/K050412–15).

59. Memorandum, 3 Mar. 1926, PA: Sch 4, Danzig Geh., Bd. 1 (K215/K055168–72).

60. Memorandum, 19 May 1926, AA: Sch 4, Danzig Geh., Bd. 2 (K215/K055215–22); Denkschrift über die wirtschaftliche Lage der Firma Schichau und über die Notwendigkeit ihrer Sanierung, 12 Nov. 1928, PA: Staatssekretär, Poda, Bd. 2 (4570H/E169487–93).

semiofficial Deutsche Revisions- und Treuhand-Aktiengesell-
schaft in Berlin. In May the Reichstag passed the law which
made Schichau a limited partnership company, paid its debts,
provided working capital, and assured its future.[61]

Concessions to trade were the third category of aid from the
German government. Danzig did not receive full privileges for
the passive finishing trade, but the government did agree to
grant concessions on the basis of individual requests. The city
continued to import the established quotas of items at little or
no duty. The Danzig shipyards were able to accept large Russian orders when a German guarantee of credit up to 12 million marks made it possible for them to convert Soviet promissory notes into working capital, and the Foreign Ministry also
secured contracts for Danzig industry, chiefly from government
but also from private sources.[62]

Though the Finance Ministry declared that the law tied its
hands, the Foreign Ministry persuaded it, over the protests of
the other ministries and especially of the East Prussians, to
interpret Article 108 of the *Reichsabgabenordnung* broadly
and reduce significantly duties on livestock and agricultural
products coming from Danzig. Danzig's impoverished farmers were thus permitted to sell their produce at high German
prices.[63] Finally, in the years 1926 to 1929 the Ossa (founded
in 1926), a government front organization disguised as a
private financing corporation, rehabilitated and reorganized
the Raiffeisenbank and the Landwirtschaftliche Grosshandels-

61. Sitzung des Reichsministeriums am 28. Januar 1929 im Reichskanz-
lerhaus, BA: R 43 I/1435; *Verhandlungen des Reichstags, Stenographische Berichte*, Bd. 424, p. 1972.

62. Erläuterungen zur Kabinettsvorlage, 26 Jan. 1926, PA: Wi 1,
Danzig Geh., Bd. 2; memorandum, 2 Aug. 1929, PA: H 12, Danzig/
Russland; Ministry of Economics to Senate, 26 Mar. 1929, PA: Sch 4,
Danzig Geh., Bd. 4 (K215/K056012–15); Dirksen to Klawitter, 11
Apr. 1928, PA: Po 2, Danzig, Bd. 2.

63. Besprechung im Finanzministerium, 8 Oct. 1927, PA: H 11 Nr. 1,
Danzig, Bd. 3. In 1930–31, for example, a ton of wheat brought 324
gulden in Berlin but only 176.80 in Danzig; a ton of rye sold for 210.60
gulden in Berlin, in Danzig for only 129.60. "Bilanz nach zehn Jahren
Danzig-polnischer Zollgemeinschaft," *Danziger Wirtschaftszeitung* (1932),
p. 10.

bank in Danzig, which supplied loans and working capital to farmers in the Free City and the Corridor.[64]

After 1926 Germany was able to further her interests in Danzig on an entirely new level—at Geneva. At the time of the Locarno Treaties, Stresemann had argued before his nationalist opponents that by joining the League, Germany would "participate in all the important decisions" concerning, among others, "the questions of the Saar, Danzig, and the eastern frontiers." [65] Whereas before 1926 France's patronage of Poland had tended to weigh the scales against the professed desires of the Free City, now Germany was able "to combat all Polish ambitions ruthlessly and uncompromisingly." [66] She insisted that Berlin and Danzig collaborate in the preparation of each appeal of a high commissioner's decision which Danzig submitted to the League. The Germans were thereby assured that Danzig's charges and complaints would never subject them to embarrassment, and the Danzig Senate could depend upon unreserved support from its "attorney at the League." [67] Germany's influence was visible in the international loans for Danzig which the League endorsed in 1927 and 1930, in the

64. Stresemann to Chancellery, 29 Dec. 1926, PA: Staatssekretär, NM, Bd. 1 (4555H/E147468–74); unsigned memorandum, 25 Mar. 1929, BA: R 43 I/547; memorandums, 17 Mar. and 29 Nov. 1928, and memorandum by Thermann, 16 Feb. 1929, PA: Po 25, Danzig Geh., Bd. 1 (K214/K054395–96, K054424–26 and K054497–98).

65. *Vermächtnis, 2,* 88. Before the Reichstag and the public Stresemann also argued that membership in the League would permit Germany to avail herself of Article 19 of the League Covenant, which provided for the peaceful revision of treaties. However, in internal memorandums the Foreign Ministry, and particularly its Legal Department, acknowledged that Article 19 could not be invoked until it had been defined and interpreted. The French steadfastly opposed any attempt at definition, and the German government, as Stresemann must have known, had little real prospect of profiting from the provisions of this article. Memorandum by Bülow, 2 Mar. 1926, PA: Staatssekretär, Po, Bd. 1 (4569H/E168512–18).

66. Memorandum by Bülow, 12 Dec. 1925, PA: Referat Völkerbund: Völkerbund-Deutschland, Bd. 11 (L1837/L532423–38).

67. Sahm as quoted by Thermann to Foreign Ministry, 14 Jan. 1928, PA: Gesandtschaft Warschau, P 15, Danzig, Bd. 3.

resolutions which the Council passed on appeals from Danzig, and in the League's decisions in exercise of its duties as guarantor and protector of the Free City.

The lengths to which Germany went in the promotion of her desires for Danzig and the relative success she enjoyed before and after she joined the League are well illustrated in the case of the candidacy, tenure, and reelection of Joost van Hamel as high commissioner in Danzig for 1926–29. The Foreign Ministry had always shown a marked interest in the appointments of high commissioners. It investigated the backgrounds of the candidates minutely, took soundings in European capitals, and used pressure and propaganda to promote the men of its choosing. It sought for the post a representative of a major power which was friendly toward Germany and tolerant of her plans for the East. The qualifications of a candidate mattered much less than his nationality and political views.

On 29 October 1925, about a year before Germany joined the League, the Secretariat raised the question of a high commissioner to succeed MacDonnell, whose term expired the following February. Two weeks later the German consul in Geneva reported to the Foreign Ministry that Hamel, the director of the legal section of the Secretariat, was under serious consideration.[68] This was bad news. Thermann warned the Foreign Ministry that Hamel was an avowed Germanophobe; he had published atrocity reports in the *Groene Amsterdamer* during the war and was deeply implicated in both the division of Upper Silesia in 1922 and the unfortunate mailbox decision in September 1925. His presence in Danzig would gravely jeopardize the policy of the German government and the Senate.[69] The Foreign Ministry instructed its embassies in London, Paris, and Rome to represent firmly to the respective governments the adverse effect such an appointment would have on Germany's disposition toward membership in the League, which the Allies expressly desired. In Geneva the German consul pressed his case with both the secretary general, Eric Drummond,

68. Aschmann (Geneva) to Foreign Ministry, 12 Nov. 1925, PA: Po 11 Nr. 1, Danzig Geh., Bd. 2 (K213/K053370).

69. Thermann to Foreign Ministry, 12 and 17 Nov. 1925, PA: Po 11 Nr. 1, Danzig Geh., Bd. 2 (K213/K053379–80 and K053391).

and Colban.[70] The German press took up the objections and embellished them to the point of vociferousness. Hamel's appointment on 12 December came as a great blow to Berlin, the more so when, in his first public interview, he spoke of himself as less an arbitrator than a mediator, who would "maintain harmony in preference to equilibrium." [71]

Hamel's tenure in Danzig seemed to justify the Germans' worst fears. They found him outspokenly pro-Polish and reluctant to intercede in Danzig-Polish conflicts, but unnaturally interested in the internal affairs of the city, in expanding his authority, and in having his salary increased. Six months later they seized upon Thermann's reports of local gossip about Hamel and the wife of the police chief, von Heydebreck. When Heydebreck sued for divorce in January 1927, Hamel's role, though never explicitly mentioned, was easily guessed. Sahm immediately urged the Foreign Ministry to exploit the case in the international press; Danzig, he promised, would launch its own press polemic and ostracize the High Commissioner socially.[72] Whatever hopes the Foreign Ministry pinned on such a campaign remained unrealized: neither resignation nor recall followed. The scandal was effective only insofar as it gave Germany more material for complaints in private conversations at Geneva and in the Council of the League, to which she now belonged. The Germans stressed the unpopularity of the High Commissioner in Danzig and castigated his vanity and naïveté, seeking to discredit him intellectually as well as morally.[73]

As the time approached for a new appointment to the Danzig post, the Foreign Ministry canvassed widely for a candidate to

70. Embassy London to Foreign Ministry, 30 Nov. 1925, and Embassy Rome to Foreign Ministry, 23 Nov. 1925, PA: Po 11 Nr. 1, Danzig Geh., Bd. 2 (K213/K053414–15 and K053400); Aschmann (Geneva) to Foreign Ministry, 5 Dec. 1925, PA: ibid. (K213/K053417–21).

71. Aschmann (Geneva) to Foreign Ministry, 17 Dec. 1925, PA: Po 11 Nr. 1, Danzig Geh., Bd. 2 (K213/K053461–62).

72. Thermann to Foreign Ministry, 18 and 22 Jan. 1927, PA: Po 11 Nr. 1, Danzig Geh., Bd. 2 (K213/K053613–15); Thermann to Foreign Ministry, 31 Jan. 1927, PA: Staatssekretär, Poda, Bd. 1 (4570H/E169255).

73. Memorandum, 18 July 1927, PA: Miscellaneous Pieces, Bd. 1 (K462/K132779); Thermann to Foreign Ministry, 24 Jan. 1928, PA: Po 11 Nr. 1, Danzig Geh., Bd. 3 (K213/K053765–67).

its liking, leaving little doubt it would oppose the return of
Hamel. When Hamel requested reappointment, the Germans
presented an Italian candidate. The question was delicate—
though Hamel was not particularly liked in Geneva, he had
after all been a charter member of the Secretariat, and his tenure
in Danzig, when the Senate had refrained from raising issues
which the Poles might refer to the High Commissioner, had
been markedly more peaceful than that of his predecessors. It
was generally assumed that his request would entail, if not another full term, at least a generous extension. In a most acri-
monious Council debate behind closed doors, Germany whittled
a proposed one-year prolongation of Hamel's mandate down
to four months.[74] As Hamel's successor, the German choice,
Count Manfredi Gravina, a grandson of Cosima Wagner, was
appointed. Gravina's first press conference confirmed the Germans in the soundness of their selection—he acknowledged the
importance of cooperation between Danzig and Poland for their
common benefit but pointed out, quoting Mussolini, that no
treaty was eternal. He told Sahm that he expected to be Danzig's penultimate if not its last high commissioner.[75]

From a comparison of the result of deliberations on the
Westerplatte controversy, which came before the Council in
1927, with the outcome of the mailbox incident of 1925 one
can deduce the precise extent to which membership in the
League benefited Germany in the pursuit of her policy toward
Danzig. In 1921, under pressure from the League, Danzig had
conceded to Poland the right to maintain within the Free City
a munitions depot supervised by a small contingent of troops.
In 1924, when negotiations on a site had failed to produce
agreement, the League awarded Poland the Westerplatte, a
promontory at the entrance to the harbor. Convinced that the
Poles would use the 88 officers and men stationed on the Westerplatte to gain a military foothold in the city, the Danzigers
argued that the depot exposed the city to the danger of ex-

74. Schubert (Geneva) to Foreign Ministry, 20 Sept. 1928, PA:
Reichsminister, 55, Bd. 1 (3015H/D597974–75).

75. Molly (Danzig) to Foreign Ministry, 3 July 1929, PA: Po 11
Nr. 1, Danzig Geh., Bd. 5 (K213/K054085–86); Thermann to Foreign
Ministry, 5 Aug. 1929, PA: Reichsminister, 55, Bd. 1 (3015H/D597997–
8000).

plosion and demanded that the Senate be allowed to inspect it periodically. Obviously Danzig was prompted not only by fear, whether of Polish military encroachment or of explosion, but also by the desire to assert its sovereign authority over all installations within the confines of the Free City.

In the summer of 1927 the Senate took its brief, which it had prepared, of course, in collaboration with the German Foreign Ministry, to Geneva. The Germans publicly endorsed and propagated Danzig's argument that, because the Poles enjoyed no extraterritorial privileges on the promontory, the Westerplatte remained subject to Danzig law and would have to be accessible to Danzig authorities.[76] Germany's ambassadors abroad pressed the governments which were represented on the Council, and Albert von Dufour-Feronce, a high German official in the Secretariat, addressed himself privately to Drummond.[77]

In the September session of the Council the Polish representative maintained that the matter was not open to debate because the right to the Westerplatte derived from previous Council resolutions and was therefore unalterable. The rapporteur and members of the Council appeared to agree. Stresemann opposed the argument on the ground that neither a Council decision nor the agreements concluded between the Free City and Poland constituted "irrevocable legal doctrine" if new evidence were produced. He obliged the Council to refer the matter to a committee of jurists.[78]

The report of the committee, which appeared on the agenda in December 1927, confirmed Danzig's contention and vindicated Stresemann's battle. Sahm accepted it, but the Polish representative requested an opinion from the Hague. Stresemann thereupon, before the Council, begged the Polish representative to withdraw his motion because the authority of the League's

76. Thermann to Foreign Ministry, 23 July 1927, PA: Sch 16 Westerplatte, Danzig Geh., Bd. 2 (K218/K057839–41); Dirksen to Thermann, 21 June 1927, ibid., Bd. 1 (K217/K057614–17).

77. Dufour (Geneva) to Dirksen, 16 Aug. 1927, PA: Staatssekretär, Poda, Bd. 1 (4570H/E169370–71).

78. *Vermächtnis, 3,* 216–17; Dirksen (Geneva) to Foreign Ministry, 27 Sept. 1927, PA: Sch 16 Westerplatte, Danzig Geh., Bd. 3 (K218/K058103–04).

committees would suffer a serious setback if doubt were cast upon their decisions. In this plea he found strong support from Austen Chamberlain, while Briand's attempts at mediation were timid. Thus isolated, the Poles accepted the Council's direction that Danzig and Poland reach a solution by direct negotiations "inspired" by the jurists' report.[79] Negotiations resulted in the agreement of 4 August 1928, whereby Poland granted the Danzig police access to the Westerplatte at any time to verify that proper precautions were taken for the safety of the city.[80]

The similarity between this case and the mailbox incident is obvious. In both instances Poland enjoyed legal rights to a certain Polish presence within the boundaries of the Free City. In its deliberations on the mailbox affair, the Court at the Hague had interpreted the Danzig-Polish Convention of 1920 to this effect. In their discussion of the Westerplatte affair, no member of the League Council disputed that Danzig had given the Poles a concession in 1921. But whereas the Poles had emerged the unambiguous victors of the mailbox controversy, the outcome of the Westerplatte dispute impaired their rights in Danzig. The great difference was that, when the Westerplatte affair was submitted to the League, Germany sat on the Council. At the time of the Hague's opinion on Polish rights to postal privileges in the Free City, Stresemann had claimed that, were Germany in the League, the matter would have turned out differently.[81] When the Westerplatte dispute came before the Council, he made good his assertion.

German aid to Danzig in these years bought Germany the right to intervene directly in the internal affairs of the Free City. Late in 1927, in debates on the formation of a new government coalition, the Socialists, who had won a plurality in the Volkstag, demanded that Sahm be removed because of his "failure" in foreign policy. Alarmed, the Foreign Ministry instructed Thermann to inform the coalition parties that it expected to be

79. Dirksen (Geneva) to Foreign Ministry, 8 Dec. 1927, PA: Staatssekretär, Vötag, Bd. 7 (4587H/E183749–50).

80. Thermann to Foreign Ministry, 10 Apr. 1928, PA: Sch 16 Westerplatte, Danzig Geh., Bd. 4 (K218/K058384–90).

81. *Vermächtnis, 2,* 554.

consulted on any contemplated change in Danzig's foreign policy. Dirksen intervened with the leaders of the Center Party, the other major partner in the coalition. Sahm, he declared, was the symbol of Danzig's Deutschtum and his retention in office was of great importance to the city.[82] Sahm was retained and presided over a Socialist Senate during 1928–30. When the Socialist senators began their tenure in January 1928, Thermann, quick to perceive a threat to German policy, made sure, as he put it, that they were "politically and morally" tied to the Reich. He obliged them to take an active role in negotiations for the secret subsidy. Their complicity compromised them and made them vulnerable to German pressure.[83]

It was during the years 1927 to 1929 that Germany's efforts in Danzig proved most effective. The German government was free to address itself to the city's problems and to offer generous and systematic aid, and Germany's presence in the League expedited her objectives beyond the results which aid alone could have accomplished.

The Free City reached a level of prosperity unique in the two decades of its existence. Poland's economic expansion under Pilsudski and Europe's general well-being stimulated trade through Danzig's port, revenues increased, and industry and agriculture revived. Germany's clandestine support kept pace with the deterioration of Danzig's affairs, which the city's refusal to accommodate itself to Poland necessarily entailed. As long as prosperity and international goodwill prevailed, Danzig's basic weaknesses were well disguised.

82. Thermann to Dirksen, 1 Dec. 1927, PA: Handakten Direktoren: Dirksen, Polen, Bd. 10 (5462H/E367997–800); Wallroth (Foreign Ministry) to Thermann, 5 Jan. 1928, PA: Po 5, Danzig Geh., Bd. 1 (6207H/E469112–13); memorandum by Dirksen, 6 Jan. 1928, PA: ibid. (6207H/E469115–19).

83. Vereinbarung mit Danzig, 23 Mar. 1929, PA: Fi 3, Danzig Geh., Bd. 4 (K208/K050756–57). Thermann personally asked Breitscheid, the leader of the German Socialist Party, to influence party members in Danzig and overcome their scruples about the subsidy. Thermann to Foreign Ministry, 14 Apr. 1928, PA: ibid., Bd. 2 (K208/K050520–21).

CHAPTER 5

The Epigones, 1930–1932

When, as one of the concessions accorded Germany for adopting the Young Plan, the Allies evacuated the Rhineland in June 1930, five years ahead of schedule, the public again surmised that the German government would move at last to revise the eastern frontiers. Revisionist propaganda reached new heights of fervor. The radical parties, thriving on despair at the deepening economic depression which proceeded from the European agricultural crisis and the Wall Street crash, lent their voices to revisionist and nationalist agitation. In an attempt to draw off some of their following, the conservative Brüning government, which in March 1930 had succeeded Hermann Müller's Liberal-Socialist coalition, adopted the language and aims of the extremists.

The speeches of Gottfried Treviranus, minister in charge of the relief program for Germany's eastern provinces (*Osthilfe*), appeared to confirm the public surmise. Speaking on 10 August 1930, the tenth anniversary of the plebiscites in East and West Prussia, he grieved over "the open wound" in the East and Danzig's "bastard status." Until the unrest which the unjust boundaries had created between Germany and Poland could be removed, he warned, the future of the Polish state was not ensured.[1] The speech contained nothing which would have been surprising coming from any other German politician, especially in an election year, but since it was delivered by a member of the cabinet it sounded sufficiently ominous to cause a furore in Poland, the more so when the German press seemed to unite in applauding Treviranus' candor about Germany's grievances. The Poles regarded Treviranus as the vanguard of an intensified course of revision. Foreign Minister August Zaleski delivered a personal protest to the German chargé d'affaires in Warsaw, and the entire Polish press condemned the speech,

---

1. *Deutsche Allgemeine Zeitung,* 11 Aug. 1930.

declaring that revision would mean war.[2] Treviranus, at the behest of the cabinet, sought to calm the agitation he had aroused by explaining "that he had in no way contemplated the revision of the eastern frontiers by adventurous and warlike means." He went on, however, to observe that the solution of the eastern question had become urgent and would appear in the next German program on foreign policy.[3] Thus his clarification neither reduced resentment in Warsaw nor calmed anxiety elsewhere.

The German government, however, did not really desire a radicalization of the eastern question. Speaking in the cabinet on 20 August 1930, Julius Curtius, who had become foreign minister after Stresemann's death in October 1929, explained that, while the German public undoubtedly found present conditions in the East untenable, to take bold steps toward the correction of these conditions would be imprudent at the moment. Germany's campaign to win the sympathies of the major powers was meeting with reasonable success. American Ambassador Frederic Sackett, whom he had asked to travel through the East, showed great interest in Germany's problem. The French, whose attitude was perforce of decisive importance, were finally coming to understand the great significance which the Reich attributed to the Corridor. Remarks such as those made by Treviranus were therefore exceedingly improvident. They aroused misgivings in France, Britain, and Italy, raising the danger that the powers would lose their growing faith in the reasonableness of Germany's claims and either resort to an immediate solution, which would necessarily be imperfect, or insist that Germany content herself with her present boundaries. Moreover, if the government spoke immoderately about the Corridor, the German public would set its expectations too high. Inevitably the present government would be a disappointment.[4]

In March 1931 Curtius sent a lengthy memorandum to his most important diplomatic missions. The foreign press, he wrote,

2. Rintelen (Warsaw) to Foreign Ministry, 14 Aug. 1930, PA: Handakten Direktoren: Trautmann, Polen.

3. Rumbold to Henderson, 15 Aug. 1930, DBFP, 2d series, 1, no. 316.

4. Protokoll der Ministerbesprechung am 20. August 1930, BA: R 43 I/124.

concluded from the tenor of certain public speeches in Germany that revision was imminent. This was an error. The time for a formal opening of the question of the eastern borders had not yet arrived. Germany contemplated no departure from established policy: she would persist in her claims and, now that the Rhineland was evacuated, devote much effort to propagating her views to an ever wider audience, but she would take no definitive steps toward realizing her aims. Curtius instructed his diplomats to affirm that Germany was not opposed to an ethnographic Poland. She aspired to neither a new partition nor a restoration of the prewar borders. She claimed solely the "ethnically non-Polish" region north of the Netze River, including Danzig. The fact that the Corridor was now no longer predominantly German, having been reduced from 70 percent in 1910 to 14.4 percent, did not diminish her right to the area, which was "naturally and organically" German. To satisfy Poland's claim to access to the sea, Germany would agree to a reversal of the current corridor procedure, granting Poland the railway lines Warsaw-Mlawa-Danzig, Bromberg-Dirschau-Danzig, and Bromberg-Gdynia and unobstructed rights to transit, including military transports. Poland would also receive her own port at Danzig, a naval base at Gdynia, and free ports in German harbors on the Baltic. Once the land connection with East Prussia had been restored and some minor border corrections made in Upper Silesia, Germany would be prepared to sign an "eastern Locarno" with Poland, and peace would reign in eastern Europe.[5]

Neither Germany's objectives for the East nor the means by which they were to be accomplished had changed since the days of Stresemann. Moreover, indications that in the late 1920s Germany's propaganda had evoked a sympathetic response in high places confirmed the government in its conviction that current tactics were correct. The policy therefore remained unaltered while the situation in which it operated underwent a radical change.

Stresemann's strategy had presupposed that international tension would decline and that Germany would return to the coun-

5. Curtius to Missions, 7 Mar. 1931, PA: Po 2G, Polen, Bd. 2 (L575/L185481–98).

cils of the great powers as a respected and equal member. He had assumed that while he prepared the way and waited for the international situation to ripen, Danzig could be equipped to hold its own in circumstances which did not militate against its economic prosperity. The onset of the Great Depression, however, prompted a decline in international amity and rendered the Free City painfully vulnerable.

In Danzig the depression was catastrophic. The prosperity of the city depended entirely upon international trade. It was obliged to export its manufactures, which far exceeded the capacities of domestic consumption, and to buy abroad products which it did not produce—autarky was out of the question. When international markets began to close in 1930, the value of goods bought and sold by firms in the city diminished at a rate of about 20 percent per year, and Danzig's industries, which, if solvent at all, showed only marginal profits, received the full impact of the recession. The volume of goods handled annually in the port remained constant at approximately eight million tons—but of these, seven were for export, and some six of the seven comprised coal and timber of which more than 98 percent belonged to the Poles. Seven hundred thousand of the one million tons of goods imported were for transit: ores, scrap metal, and fertilizers which were immediately transshipped into Poland.[6] The depression, therefore, brought disaster to the Free City.

In the spring of 1931 the German Finance Ministry delegated one of its officials, Ernst Reichard, to investigate personally the situation in the city. Reichard, an authority on budgetary finance, had been appointed Reich trustee (*Treuhänder*) for Danzig in 1929. In this capacity he assessed Danzig's needs for assistance and sponsored its requests to the German government. He was therefore intimately familiar with the city and its economy. In 1929, after an extended visit to Danzig, Reichard had drawn attention to alarming developments: the local wholesale trade, once the primary occupation of Danzig's merchants, had vanished, leaving only the carrying trade, and the Hanseatic tradition of the city was virtually extinguished; with the excep-

6. Thermann to Foreign Ministry, 16 Mar. 1931, PA: Wi 1 Nr. 1, Danzig, Bd. 2.

tion of the Schichau shipyard, which had become a corporation
managed by the Reich, there was little vigor in industry; agriculture was languishing; and the income of the state treasury
no longer matched expenditure.[7]

Reichard's investigations in 1931 revealed that the situation
had deteriorated drastically since 1929. Customs revenues had
dropped from 19.1 million gulden in 1929 to 12.5 million in
the fiscal year 1930, and higher taxes had increased proceeds
to the state by only 2 million gulden to 16.7; the cumulative
budget deficit was 15.5 million, roughly 13 percent of the total
disbursement of the state. Danzig's commerce suffered because the value of trade through the port was declining, and
because in Poland discriminatory treatment, an unofficial boycott, and a whole array of rules and regulations which favored
domestic commerce had constricted Polish markets. A number
of firms had shut down for lack of raw materials and working
capital; 70 companies had become bankrupt in the past year;
there were 25,000 unemployed in December 1930, who drew
an annual unemployment relief of 13.2 million gulden. The
prices of Danzig's agricultural products had dropped to the
Polish level, while local production costs were still equivalent
to those of the Reich; any number of farms were up for sale.

Reichard feared that, in these straits, Danzig might seek economic relief from the Poles and allow them in return to acquire
property in the Free City and to displace German Danzigers
in the customs administration, the port, and the police—a disastrous prospect. To forestall such developments he urged that
Germany increase and broaden her aid program, but he pointed
out that, if only to maintain local morale, the Danzigers would
have to be encouraged to do their part: pure subvention would
only accelerate the city's debilitation.[8]

Despite a calamitous domestic financial situation, Berlin responded with extensive support. In October 1930 the Finance
Ministry pressed the Bank für deutsche Industrieobligationen
into granting the Free City an emergency loan of 16 million
marks. In May 1931 the bank floated another emergency loan

7. Bemerkungen zur finanziellen Lage der Freien Stadt Danzig, September 1929, PA: Fi 3, Danzig Geh., Bd. 4 (K208/K050831–98).
8. Denkschrift über die Lage Danzigs, 1 May 1931, BA: R 2/19578.

for 6 million, whose discount charges the Finance Ministry absorbed and for which it deposited collateral in the form of Reich treasury bonds. In July another 6 million came from the Reichsbank.[9] The standard subsidies were continued: 4.2 million marks were given in March 1931 and another 4.2 in December. From both funds sums were diverted to the Polytechnical Institute, a rural housing development, the support of "nationally endangered economic enterprises," and the renovation of the Marienkirche.[10] Another subsidy became available in 1930 when Danzig, angered at the Finance Ministry's refusal to honor the city's supplementary requests, threatened to apply to Germans in the Free City a new law whereby the jobs of all foreign workers might be given to unemployed Danzigers. Germany responded by agreeing that the Ministry of Labor would pay Danzig 2 million gulden, ostensibly for the relief of unemployed and impoverished German citizens in the city, though they numbered only 600 among 19,000 unemployed in August 1930. In February 1931, when Danzig's unemployment rolls reached 28,067, of whom 21,943 were on relief, the funds were doubled, and another 4 million gulden were given the city the following year.[11] At the prompting of the Finance Ministry both the Reichspost and the Reichsbahn agreed to pay the whole of their pensions in the city, which had not been affected by the subterfuge of 1926 that raised the Reich's other pension payments from 60 to 100 percent. These payments, which began in 1931, amounted to another 1.3 million marks annually.[12]

Danzig's farmers received liberal customs preferences from Germany, though these represented a sizable financial loss to

9. Memorandum by Meyer (Foreign Ministry), 17 Mar. 1931, PA: Reichsminister, 55, Bd. 2 (3015H/D598121); Ministry of Finance to Reichs-Kredit-Gesellschaft, 20 May 1931, BA: R 2/19578; Ministry of Finance to Senate, 30 July 1931, PA: Fi 3, Danzig Geh., Bd. 5 (6203H/E468265–66).

10. Ministry of Finance to Senate, 20 Mar. and 30 Dec. 1931, BA: R 2/19576 and PA: Po 25, Danzig Geh., Bd. 2 (K214/K054648–49).

11. Memorandum by Thermann, 7 Sept. 1930, and Ministry of Finance to Foreign Ministry, 28 Aug. 1930, PA: So 2, Danzig Geh., Bd. 2; Ministry of Finance to Ministry of Labor, 14 Mar. and 10 Nov. 1931, PA: ibid.

12. Memorandum, February 1931, BA: R 2/19576.

the Reich, itself in straitened circumstances. A memorandum of January 1931 enumerated the products which Danzig exported to Germany at reduced rates of duty in 1930 and 1931:[13]

wheat	20,000 tons	10% of normal duty
wheat flour	1,000 tons	15% of normal wheat duty
rye	2,000 tons	10% of normal duty
seed corn	550 tons	20% of normal duty
sugar beets	700,000 quintals	free of duty
refined sugar	145,000 quintals	.50 marks per quintal
cheese	10,000 quintals	20 marks per quintal
seedlings	9,000	free of duty
horses	400	10% of normal duty
fattened hogs	15,000	22.50 marks each
breeding livestock	3,000	20 marks each

In March 1931 the Finance Ministry agreed to raise the wheat quota by 5,000 tons and the livestock quota by 1,000 head, constituting a loss to the Reich of another 1.5 million marks in customs revenue, and to lower the duty on various items.[14] Industry and commerce continued to receive quotas of German goods at reduced rates of duty, and Danzig retained the privilege of the passive finishing trade.

The Danzigers for their part were expected to adjust the high salaries of the Danzig civil service to German levels, to diminish the number of employees in state service, to reduce unemployment compensation, and in general to economize strictly.[15] In February 1931 the Senate increased income, sales, property, and occupation taxes, and revenues rose from 16.7 million in 1930 to 25.3 million in 1931.[16] In 1930 Danzig had ratified a

13. Leistungen des Reichs an die Freie Stadt Danzig, 20 Jan. 1931, PA: Fi 3, Danzig Geh., Bd. 4 (K208/K051077–80).

14. Memorandum by Noebel (Foreign Ministry), 6 Mar. 1931, PA: H 11 Nr. 1, Danzig Geh., Bd. 1 (K209/K051249–50). Preferences were expanded once more in April and June 1931. Senate to Foreign Ministry, 19 Apr. 1932, PA: H 11 Nr. 1, Danzig Geh., Bd. 1 (K209/K051467–71).

15. Ministry of Finance to Ziehm, 8 June 1931, BA: R 2/19578.

16. Ernst Reichard, Aufzeichnung über die Finanz- und Kassenlage der Freien Stadt Danzig, 19 Nov. 1932, PA: Fi 3, Danzig Geh., Bd. 5 (6203H/E468353–90). Danzig's industrialists and merchants resented the

constitutional amendment which reduced the Volkstag from 120 to 72 deputies and the Senate from 22 to 12.

The extensive German effort and Danzig's own attempts to economize might have done much to tide the city over the depression if the depression had been the only cause of economic distress. But Danzig suffered from a problem which greatly exacerbated the effects of the depression and threatened the very life of the city—the competition of the Polish rival port at Gdynia.

The plan to construct a port on Polish territory—on the narrow strip of seacoast on the Corridor—dated from 1920. In that year Poland's attempts to gain ascendancy in Danzig by means of a favorable Convention had been foiled by the Danzigers, whom the Allies supported. Polish misgivings about a port which Danzig controlled had been confirmed shortly thereafter when the Danzig dockers refused to unload war supplies intended for Poland and the Constituent Assembly attempted to have the city declared neutral territory. Clearly Poland could not rely on the alien population of Danzig; she still enjoyed no free access to the sea on which she could depend in an emergency. The idea implicit in Poland's terms for the Convention —that should Danzig not become Polish, another outlet to the sea would have to be secured—now became explicit. In November 1920 a naval committee was dispatched to investigate the feasibility of a port at the tiny fishing village of Gdynia, about ten miles from Danzig. The committee was satisfied, and under the direction of the Polish Ministry of War construction began forthwith.

The project at Gdynia enjoyed great popularity in Poland, and the port experienced a spectacular rise. Its freight turnover climbed from 414,005 tons in 1926 to 3,628,331 in 1930. Companies wishing to settle in Gdynia received extensive credit at no interest, and the Polish government made it possible for them to construct such facilities as oil presses, rice mills, and capacious refrigerators at low cost. The syndicates which took their traffic to the new port were rewarded with bounties, and the new Polish merchant fleet, which was based at the harbor,

---

sacrifice these new taxes entailed. Thermann to Foreign Ministry, 4 Apr. 1930, PA: Fi 3, Danzig Geh., Bd. 4 (K208/K050970–71).

was given a subsidy. The Polish Emigration Syndicate sent its charges by way of Gdynia. Foreign trade was attracted by means of low harbor fees, reduced customs duties, rebates, and preferential railway tariffs.[17]

At first the Danzigers had scoffed at Poland's ambition to convert a fishing village into an overseas port. After 1926, however, they became worried at the steady climb of import-export figures:[18]

	Imports		Exports	
	(metric tons)			
YEAR	DANZIG	GDYNIA	DANZIG	GDYNIA
1926	640,696	179	5,659,605	413,826
1927	1,517,194	6,702	6,380,420	889,439
1928	1,832,409	190,133	6,783,273	1,767,213
1929	1,792,951	324,298	6,766,700	2,497,893
1930	1,090,632	506,037	7,122,488	3,122,294
1931	754,300	558,548	7,576,205	4,741,564

In March 1928, when Gdynia had become irritating, the Senate had considered an appeal to the high commissioner to the effect that Poland was obliged to make full use of Danzig and had no right to prefer a Polish port. The Foreign Ministry had not been sympathetic. There was nothing in the treaties which gave Danzig a monopoly on Polish traffic or forbade Poland to build another harbor. The Germans could never uphold such a claim at Geneva.[19] On 31 March 1930 Sahm broached the question again. He pointed out to the Foreign Ministry that overseas trade was Danzig's lifeblood and expressed his anxiety for the future. The Free City would have to request from the high commissioner a confirmation of Haking's decision that Poland

17. *Collection of Documents . . . in the Matter of Danzig-Gdingen,* pp. 8–13.

18. Ibid., p. 28; *Danziger Statistisches Taschenbuch 1933* (Danzig, 1932), p. 36.

19. Memorandum by Zechlin (Foreign Ministry), 4 Apr. 1928, PA: Sch 16, Danzig W, Bd. 4.

was obliged "to make full use of the port of Danzig whatever other ports she may open in the future on the Baltic coast." [20]

The Foreign Ministry examined the problem. It was concerned chiefly with the political side of the issue. The complaint on Gdynia would raise the whole question of the Corridor in a most awkward fashion. The very nature of the complaint made it impossible for Germany to introduce a more fundamental issue: whether it was necessary or wise to provide Poland with territorial access to the sea, as foreseen by the Treaty of Versailles. Discussion would be confined to whether established access was to be through Danzig or Gdynia, and any decision on the problem would entail a renewed acknowledgment of the current arrangement. And yet, the Foreign Ministry owned, the development of Gdynia itself jeopardized the possibility of ever broaching the more fundamental question. A flourishing port on the Polish littoral would settle Poland's access to the sea by way of the Corridor once and for all. It was therefore in the Reich's interest to support the Danzigers and combat Gdynia. Certainly—and this was only to be welcomed—the discussion in Geneva would bring the problem of the Corridor before the world in its full seriousness, and Germany would have the opportunity to indicate that she intended never to accept the existing arrangement as final.[21] To Germany's diplomatic missions the talented State Secretary Bernhard von Bülow, who had succeeded Schubert in 1930, admitted that the complaint on Gdynia came at an inopportune moment, since circumstances were not yet ripe for revision. Nonetheless, Germany would support Danzig, for the threat to the Free City was not only economic but also political. The Poles could use the city's economic misery to bring it into dependency and thus deprive the Reich of this enclave of loyal Germans in the severed territory. Germany's most cogent argument in her case for revision of the borders would disappear. It was of great im-

20. Memorandum by Schubert, 31 Mar. 1930, with the provisional draft of the Danzig complaint appended, PA: Reichsminister, 55, Bd. 2 (3015H/D598021–26).

21. Gaus (Foreign Ministry) to Schubert, 19 Apr. 1930, PA: Staatssekretär, Poda, Bd. 2 (4570H/E169545–49).

portance, therefore, that the legal question be settled, and to this end the diplomats were to do their part.[22]

Danzig submitted the Gdynia issue—that all Polish trade not passing the land frontiers should be transshipped in the harbor of Danzig and that Poland must refrain from all measures designed to divert trade to other ports, or, in the words of the complaint, that "Danzig should form the outlet, i.e. Poland's sole outlet to the sea"—to the high commissioner on 9 May 1930. For some two years legal arguments went back and forth. In the Senate's opinion, which it based on its interpretation of the Versailles articles and on numerous Polish and Allied statements to the effect that the Free City had been created solely to provide Poland with an access to the sea, Poland was bound to make use of the port of Danzig to its fullest capacity before she utilized any other outlet. Thus the construction of Gdynia and, worse, the preferences accorded it to attract traffic and commerce were illegal and would have to cease. The Poles disputed Danzig's title to a monopoly of their seaborne trade, asserted that they had rights but no obligations in Danzig, and rejected the matter entirely as an unwarranted intervention in Polish internal affairs, an attempt to curtail the economic autonomy and development of the republic. There was no truth, they maintained, in the allegation that Danzig was of no interest to the Poles; quite the contrary, Danzig was an important factor in Poland's economy. Danzig had blossomed as a free city, and besides, the traffic of a normal economy would fully occupy both ports.

Danzig delivered a rebuttal. The Senate rejected all Polish arguments about the city's prosperity as false and irrelevant and maintained that, while trade through Danzig undoubtedly had grown since the war, nevertheless the port was not being used to its alleged capacity of 15 million tons. The comparison with prewar days was misleading anyway, for at that time Danzig had not been encumbered with the peculiar political character imposed upon it at Versailles. Moreover, the impressive trade statistics did not necessarily spell large profits: most of the loading and unloading in the port was done by inexpensive

22. Bülow to Missions, 8 Aug. 1930, PA: Reichsminister, 55, Bd. 1 (3015H/D598044–50).

mechanical means, and whereas before the war trade and transit had been in the hands of local merchants, now only a tiny fraction of the total was Danzig's own. To become a mere port of transit was fatal for Danzig: the growing unemployment and the rising number of bankruptcies showed how false was any impression that the city was prospering.[23]

Germany backed Danzig's complaint. Foreign Minister Curtius told Drummond on 15 May that, whatever one might think of the political implications of the issue, the fact remained that, given the rate of Gdynia's development, any delay in raising the issue would irreparably prejudice Danzig's rights. One was concerned here, not with the problem *of* the Corridor, but with one of the most important problems *in* the Corridor. The League would lose whatever worth it had if the Council could not discuss and decide a delicate issue on its own merits.[24]

When it became clear that Danzig and Poland could not reconcile their differences, Gravina, on 15 October, requested from the Council the legal opinion of a committee of jurists on whether Haking's decision was juridically binding and applicable. The committee, with one member dissenting, came to the conclusion that the Haking decision had been a deliberate effort to protect Danzig from any eventual competition at Gdynia by extending the Polish rights in Danzig to an obligation and was therefore binding. Gravina adopted this opinion. On 26 October 1931 he announced that, though Danzig held no monopoly on Polish trade, the Poles were obliged to make full use of the Danzig harbor and were not privileged to prefer other installations.[25]

Neither party was pleased with the decision. In December both Warsaw and Danzig appealed to the Council. The Danzigers contended that Gravina had rejected their claim to the full volume of Poland's overseas trade on the grounds that Danzig had no right to a monopoly. They disclaimed any desire for a monopoly on Polish commerce and did not dispute Poland's

23. *Collection of Documents . . . in the Matter of Danzig-Gdingen.*
24. Niederschrift über eine Besprechung mit dem Generalsekretär über die Frage Gdingen, 15 May 1930, PA: Reichsminister, 55, Bd. 1 (3015H/D598030–31).
25. *Entscheidungen . . . 1928–1932* (Danzig, 1933), pp. 14–19.

right to build other ports. However, they wanted the High Commissioner's decision to take into account the extent to which the port at Danzig, which was sufficiently capacious to carry all of Poland's present traffic, was being neglected and to make clear provisions for its legal preeminence. The risk of insufficient utilization should be borne, not by Danzig, but by Poland's other ports. The Poles maintained that the Haking decision had been merely a recommendation and that they retained the right to decide on economic grounds which ports to use.[26]

In January 1932 the Council decided to reappoint the previous committee to examine the new legal points raised by the appeals. The committee, which met in early April, again decided that Poland had a direct obligation to use the port of Danzig to the fullest extent and that this obligation extended to all forms of traffic. It did not, however, recognize Danzig's claim that Polish ports should bear the risk of insufficient commerce or consider the question whether Poland was in fact meeting its obligation to Danzig. On the basis of the committee report the Council resolved in May 1932 to suspend Gravina's decision of the previous October and to return the question to him with the suggestion that he decide how fully, in fact, the port was being used.[27] Ironically, that same month the total traffic in goods through Gdynia surpassed that through Danzig for the first time.[28]

Once again the High Commissioner called upon League experts, to whom he sent Danzig's and Poland's appraisals of the actual extent to which the port was being utilized. The Senate prepared a long statistical survey in which it pointed out that its fears had now been realized and that Danzig's share in Poland's total overseas trade had dropped from 69.4 percent in 1930 to 51.3 percent in 1932. The rest was shipped via Gdynia. The situation was exacerbated by a drop in Poland's total overseas trade in the same period, from 11,838,841 to 10,670,340 tons. Contrary to Polish assurances, Danzig was

26. LN: C.993.1931.I.
27. LN: C.442.1932.I.
28. Thermann to Foreign Ministry, 28 June 1932, PA: Sch 16A, Danzig Geh., Bd. 5 (K219/K059580–81).

becoming a supplementary port. In fact, the Senate was at pains to point out, Gdynia was superfluous. Danzig's capacity of approximately 15 million tons, two-thirds in bulk, would rise to 35 or 40 million tons after the completion of the harbor basins currently under construction.[29]

The Polish memorandum set out to prove statistically Poland's constant efforts to improve the port of Danzig and her intense promotion of her seaborne trade, which increased from 7.4 percent of her total trade in 1922 to over 60 percent in 1932. That Danzig benefited from this, the Poles reasoned, was manifest in the figures of traffic through the harbor. Whereas in 1913 Danzig's total tonnage had been 2,112,101, in 1928 it had risen by 308 percent to total 8,615,682; the current slack in trade was to be attributed entirely to the world depression. Poland affirmed that she included the Free City in her overall trade planning despite the obstacles presented by the local political situation, the Danzigers' refusal to adopt the zloty and adjust to Polish legislation, and their intransigence toward Polish wishes to settle, purchase property, and receive citizenship. If private firms were bypassing Danzig, this was simply a result of the hostile attitude they encountered in the Free City.[30]

The committee submitted its report on 14 September. It concluded that with a few exceptions the harbor at Danzig could deal with the combined traffic of both ports. Poland should not apply administrative measures which benefited Gdynia at the expense of Danzig. Duties and harbor dues in the two ports should be identical, and the overseas trade of the Polish state should go via the port at Danzig to the limit of its capacity. The valuable emigrant traffic through Gdynia should return to Danzig. Otherwise free trade should govern the relations between the two outlets.[31] The Danzigers and the Germans were pleased, for they felt that on the whole the report adopted

29. Ergänzende Bemerkungen der Freien Stadt zu ihrem Schriftsatz in der Angelegenheit der vollen Ausnutzung des Hafens von Danzig durch Polen, 19 May 1932, PA: Sch 16A, Danzig Geh., Bd. 5 (K219/K059599–641).

30. Thermann to Foreign Ministry, 26 July 1932, PA: Sch 16A, Danzig Geh., Bd. 4 (K219/K059663–66 and K059672–92).

31. Thermann to Foreign Ministry, 6 Oct. 1932, PA: Sch 16A, Danzig Geh., Bd. 4 (K219/K059719–24).

Danzig's view. They looked with particular satisfaction on the committee's finding that the competition between two ports depending on the same hinterland was destructive—an implicit rejection of the claim that Poland required two outlets. In December, at the High Commissioner's urging, Danzig and Poland opened negotiations, which were still in progress when the Nazis came to power in the Free City in May 1933.

While the dispute over Gdynia dragged on, Poland harassed Danzig with unique vehemence. According to the German minister in Warsaw, her motive was fear. Germany was freeing herself of the burden of reparations and of restrictions on her armaments and therefore might be able to embark on new departures just when the economic crisis made patent the inadequacies of the Versailles settlement and the need for amendment. Poland was frightened, too, of the political radicalism in Germany and Danzig. The Liberal-Socialist Senate of 1928 was replaced in January 1931 by Nationalists under Ernst Ziehm. A Prussian civil servant like Sahm, whom he succeeded,[32] Ziehm was personally modest, sincere, and possessed of his predecessor's sense of dutiful determination to preserve Danzig's rights against Polish encroachment. His government was supported also by the National Socialists, who, in the November election, had won 12 of a total 72 seats in the Volkstag, about the same percentage the Nazis had captured in the Reichstag in September 1930. There was reason to believe that Nazi pressure might encourage the German government to seek prompt revision. Thus the Polish government was preoccupied with the German-Polish borders, and their security was fast becoming the formative aim of its foreign policy.[33] The Germans were at no pains to attenuate Polish apprehensions. Early in 1931 Chancellor Brüning toured Germany's eastern provinces and, in an effort to win back the disaffected radicals, commiserated with the people, assuring them that Berlin was mindful of their suffering. In the spring of 1932, the German-Polish trade war, now in its seventh year, was intensified when Germany burdened Polish imports

32. Thermann to Foreign Ministry, 17 Jan. 1931, PA: Po 5, Danzig, Bd. 5. Sahm had declined to serve as a parliamentary senator and left the city to become lord mayor of Berlin.

33. Moltke (Warsaw) to Foreign Ministry, 13 Jan. 1932, PA: Po 1, Polen, Bd. 5 (L555/L156261–70).

with new tariffs. That summer German troops held maneuvers near the Polish border, and these exercises were explained as precautionary measures against rumored Polish aggression. The Poles, in turn, concluded that it was the Germans who were about to launch a war. The German minister in Warsaw could characterize Poland's attitude in 1932 as *Revisionspanik*.[34] The Polish government intended to neutralize German revisionist propaganda, which had become rampant during the one presidential and two Reichstag elections of 1932, and to paralyze revisionist policy. The chosen battleground was Danzig.

In March 1932 the Poles launched a campaign against Danzig's economy which brought the Free City close to collapse. It began when Poland, feeling the effects of the depression and wishing to protect her industries, sought safety in high tariffs and complained that Danzig was a gap in her tariff wall. As in the crisis of 1923, controversy arose about the quotas of goods which Danzig, under the Warsaw Agreement of 1921, was allowed to import free of Polish duty. Now the Poles attacked not only the evasions by which Danzig's customs officials enlarged the city's imports beyond the legal limits, but the quota system itself. On 29 February 1932 Poland asked Gravina to decide whether these articles of the Warsaw Agreement should be revised, arguing that the quotas, which Danzig, moreover, abused, were meant merely for a period of transition.[35] Without waiting for the High Commissioner's verdict, the Polish Finance Ministry decreed on 29 March that maximum duties (up to 300 percent of the established rate) would apply to German goods, whether for Danzig or for Poland. These tariffs were applied to the formerly duty-free import quotas, in effect nullifying the advantage of the concessions. At the same time, goods manufactured or processed in the city from material imported under the quotas were to be treated as foreign merchandise in Poland and subjected to prohibitive import duties.[36]

The Danzig Senate lodged a protest with Gravina on 13 April.

34. Moltke (Warsaw) to Foreign Ministry, 25 Jan. 1933, PA: Po 1, Polen, Bd. 5 (9184H/E645813–25).

35. Koester (Danzig) to Foreign Ministry, 17 Mar. 1932, PA: Wi 7, Danzig, Bd. 1.

36. Senate to Commissioner General, 14 May 1932, PA: H 11 Nr. 1, Danzig, Bd. 1 (K209/K051612–13).

On 22 April, Hans von Moltke, the German minister in Warsaw, was instructed to inform the Polish government that its action was inimical to an improvement in German-Polish relations. And on 25 April in Geneva, the German chancellor stressed to Zaleski that the issue was of grave economic and political significance to the Reich.[37] The Poles, however, were not to be dissuaded.

For the Danzig economy the measure was disastrous. Within two months the new tariffs reduced the quantity of goods imported under the quotas by 80 percent and the value of these goods by more than 50 percent. Simultaneously a private boycott in Poland and various official Polish regulations subjected Danzig's merchants to additional hardship. Trade, which the low purchasing power of Poland's depressed economy had made barely profitable, now became almost worthless, and even where the boycott did not apply, traffic was almost insuperably obstructed. The Danzigers were confronted with discriminatory commercial classifications, veterinary requirements, excise taxes, confiscation, limitations, and delays in transportation and financial transactions.[38] Morale and prosperity, therefore, were already at low tide when in June 1932 the Poles decided on a show of strength in the oldest quarrel between Poland and the Free City—the question of a mooring station (*port d'attache*) for Polish warships in Danzig harbor.

In October 1921 the Free City and Poland, after protracted negotiations, had come to a provisional agreement by which Poland obtained the right to anchor and revictual her warships at Danzig without having to comply with the regulations applied to the ships of foreign powers. The issue came up again in 1927 and was brought before the League when Danzig, arguing that Gdynia was sufficiently developed to accommodate Polish warships, sought to cancel the agreement of 1921, and the Poles refused to accede to Danzig's demand that their ships obey

37. Foreign Ministry to Legation Warsaw, 22 Apr. 1932, PA: Handakten Direktoren: Ritter, Polen (5643H/H000118–19); Bülow (Geneva) to Foreign Ministry, 25 Apr. 1932, PA: H 11 Nr. 1, Danzig Geh., Bd. 1 (K219/K051520–22).

38. Thermann to Foreign Ministry, 31 May 1932, PA: H 11 Nr. 1, Danzig Geh., Bd. 2 (6205H/E468659–75); memorandum by Reichard, March 1932, BA: R 2/19580.

international regulations governing foreign warships in Danzig's harbor. The Germans supported Danzig's plea in the Council. In January 1928, however, the Socialists entered the Danzig government and, as a gesture of conciliation, decided in July to prolong the renewed agreement for another three years.[39] In July 1931 the Nationalist Senate, which had meanwhile returned to office, announced that the accord was now invalid. After the Poles protested to the High Commissioner, the Council, on his motion, submitted the dispute to the Permanent Court of International Justice for an advisory opinion. The Court decided in December 1931 that Poland could not claim a position in the port different from that enjoyed by other foreign powers. Thus foiled, the Poles took the extraordinary step of asking the Council in January 1932 to confer the rights which the Court had just denied them. Danzig thereupon decided to capitalize on Poland's loss of face and display a conciliatory spirit. It would extend the agreement of 1921 until April 1932 and in the meantime negotiate with the Poles for certain special facilities they might enjoy in the harbor. The Poles accepted the proposal, and the Council endorsed negotiations. The negotiations failed to produce a settlement by the April deadline, whereupon Danzig, ignoring Poland's objections, announced that the extended agreement had lapsed.[40]

Out of this state of affairs emerged the single most spectacular violation of Danzig's sovereignty. The Poles, frustrated by the dispute, moved for a showdown. In June, on the occasion of an official visit from a British flotilla, the Polish destroyer *Wicher* entered the harbor to pay its respects to Danzig's guests without, however, first notifying the Senate, as the Hague ruling had stipulated.[41] The intrusion passed without incident, but the diplomatic repercussions were extensive. The Danzigers protested to the Polish commissioner general and to the High Commissioner, and Gravina alerted the League. Excitement

39. Memorandum by Dirksen, 13 Aug. 1928, PA: Po 11 Nr. 1, Danzig Geh., Bd. 4 (K213/K053877–84).

40. LNOJ (1932), pp. 488–89; Thermann to Foreign Ministry, 4 Apr. 1932, PA: Sch 16 port d'attache, Danzig Geh., Bd. 3 (K216/K056785–86).

41. Thermann to Foreign Ministry, 15 June 1932, PA: Sch 16 port d'attache A, Danzig Geh., Bd. 1 (K217/K057115–16).

grew at Geneva as the great powers formed a unified front against Poland. In his capacity as rapporteur for Danzig questions, Sir John Simon, the British foreign secretary, requested from Polish Foreign Minister Zaleski an official statement condemning the incident and giving assurances against any recurrence. If Zaleski refused, Simon threatened, a special Council meeting would have to be convened. Prime Minister Herriot of France supported Simon's request. Zaleski, after an initial refusal, gave in under pressure.[42]

The show of force, however, achieved its objective. In August 1932 the Senate agreed to a settlement of the harbor dispute. Poland received privileges beyond those customary under international usage in return for the promise to take steps against the economic boycott—a promise which Poland, incidentally, never kept. Thermann thought that the settlement left little to distinguish the city from a Polish naval base.[43]

A decline in the international status of the Free City paralleled and underscored its economic decline. With impunity Poland encroached upon its sovereignty, slighted its legal rights, and overlooked the League's decisions. Though Germany sat on the League's Council and was ever ready to assert her interest in the status of the city, the protection afforded was nonetheless inadequate in the new climate of relations with Poland. A feeling of growing isolation greatly damaged the city's sense of security.

Gdynia was central here, too. The economic impact of its competition was readily apparent. Its impact on Danzig's spiritual welfare was equally strong. If the Poles were free to confine their trade to their own port at Gdynia, then Danzig, in its most vital capacity—as the port of Poland—had become redundant, and the city was reduced to a place without meaning and purpose. This premonition destroyed the morale which had been so decisive in maintaining resistance against Poland and on which Berlin had counted. Civil unrest—street battles between extremists of the right and left—expressed the malaise which

42. Foreign Ministry to Legation Warsaw, 18 June 1932, PA: Gesandtschaft Warschau, P 15, Flottenbesuch.
43. Thermann to Foreign Ministry, 18 Aug. 1932, PA: Sch 16 port d'attache, Danzig Geh., Bd. 3 (K216/K056938–42).

prevailed in the city. Rumors of an impending Polish or, alternatively, Nazi coup perpetuated civil strife. The growing violence induced the Senate in 1931 to pass an enabling act, and the Foreign Ministry, which feared for its revisionist policy if Danzig lapsed into chaos, admonished the Senate to preserve order by whatever means necessary.[44] The reports from the German consulate in Danzig during 1932 abound with descriptions of "Polish provocations." Danzig railway employees were abruptly dismissed and replaced by Poles, a Polish language test became mandatory for employment with the railroad, and Poles living in Danzig received undisguised military training on the territory of the Free City. Protests in Warsaw and Geneva, Thermann noted, elicited Polish reprisals, which exacerbated Danzig's misery.[45]

Economically the situation had never been so dire. Unemployment figures, which in October 1931 stood at 25,000, rose two months later to 32,956. In March 1932, 36,481 were without work, by the end of the year 40,726—about 20 percent of the labor force. Thermann reported in September 1932 that the unemployment meant a loss of 2 billion gulden per year in the purchasing power of the citizenry and of 2.4 million gulden in taxes. The finance senator calculated that in 1932 the state lost at least 43,439,000 gulden in revenues and that the economic relationship with Poland had cost private enterprise 73,500,000 gulden.[46]

Once more the Germans sought to counteract the Polish onslaught with massive economic aid. Now that the meaning of Danzig's possible bankruptcy had become clear to all, there was little need, despite Germany's own poor finances, for the Foreign Ministry to plead Danzig's case before the other ministries. When a critical shortage in Danzig's supply of cash arose

---

44. Bülow (Foreign Ministry) to Thermann, 29 June 1931, PA: Po 5, Danzig, Bd. 5.

45. Thermann to Foreign Ministry, 31 Jan. 1933, PA: Allg. 3, Danzig W, Bd. 1 (9065H/E366238–41); Thermann to Foreign Ministry, 22 Feb. 1932, PA: Wi 1 Nr. 1, Danzig, Bd. 2.

46. Thermann to Foreign Ministry, 22 Feb. 1932, PA: Wi 1 Nr. 1, Danzig, Bd. 2; Thermann to Foreign Ministry, 1 Sept. 1932, PA: Z, Danzig Geh., Bd. 1 (K222/K060680–83); Finance Senator Hoppenrath to Meyer (Foreign Ministry), 19 Aug. 1932, PA: Z 9, Danzig, Bd. 4.

in March 1932, the Finance Ministry immediately set about securing another (the third) emergency loan. By consigning Reich treasury notes to the Reichs-Kredit-Gesellschaft and accepting the responsibility of amortization should Danzig fail, the Finance Ministry was able to arrange for a credit of 5.5 million marks. The Ministry also paid the discount rate directly so that it would not be deducted from the sum to the Free City. Similarly, on the advice of the Foreign Ministry, the Industriebank in Berlin provided a 6 million mark credit to Danzig's Landwirtschaftliche Bank, enabling it to grant debt conversion credits to needy farmers.[47] When in April 1932 the Senate submitted a request for increased export quotas for agriculture, the Foreign Ministry passed it on with a strong endorsement, urging prompt consideration so that these concessions might enable it to control Danzig's deteriorating political situation.[48] In July the Finance Ministry released its list of newly reduced agricultural customs quotas for Danzig in 1932 and 1933:[49]

wheat	42,000 tons	8% of normal duty
rye	2,000 tons	8% of normal duty
barley	5,000 tons	.80 marks per quintal
cheese	10,000 quintals	20 marks per quintal
seedlings	15,000	23–40 marks per quintal
horses	300	5% of normal duty
breeding livestock	4,000	20 marks each
fattened hogs	20,000	20 marks each

In October and November additional quotas were furnished:[50]

47. Ministry of Finance to Senate, 18 Mar. 1932, BA: R 2/19580; Ministry of Finance to Reichs-Kredit-Gesellschaft, 23 Mar. 1932, BA: ibid.; memorandum, 9 Feb. 1932, PA: Po 25, Danzig Geh., Bd. 2 (K214/K054659–60).

48. Foreign Ministry to Ministry of Finance, 27 Apr. 1932, PA: H 11 Nr. 1, Danzig Geh., Bd. 1 (K209/K051480–1).

49. Ministry of Agriculture to Ministry of Finance, 12 July 1932, and Ministry of Finance to Landesfinanzamt Königsberg, 26 July 1932, PA: H 11 Nr. 1, Danzig Geh., Bd. 2 (6205H/E468739–44 and E468768–69).

50. Ministry of Finance to Landesfinanzamt Königsberg, 24 Oct., 10 and 19 Nov. 1932, PA: H 11 Nr. 1, Danzig Geh., Bd. 2 (6205H/E468847–49, E468862–63, and E468882–83).

wheat flour	10,000 quintals	2.85 marks per quintal
wheat bran	3,350 quintals	8% of normal duty
cheese	6,250 quintals	50% of normal duty
seedlings	15,000	75% of normal duty
peas	2,500 tons	8% of normal duty
breeding hogs	200	17 marks each
breeding livestock	3,500	15 marks each

The Foreign Ministry also went to great lengths to meet individual requests. It arranged further customs preferences and induced other ministries, despite their straitened circumstances, to award contracts to Danzig industry.

Yet all these subsidies, preferences, and quotas could not counterbalance Poland's pressure on the Free City. In November 1932 Reichard presented another report on the financial situation of Danzig: it concluded that, as a result of the general economic crisis, the competition of Gdynia, and the Polish strangulation measures, the city was no longer in a position to help itself. This was a far remove from Reichard's prognostications of the previous year. Despite German aid, the fiscal year 1931 would end with a deficit of 10.7 million gulden, that of 1932 with an estimated deficit of 10.8. The debts of the city and the municipality combined amounted to approximately 100 million gulden, of which 37.5 million derived from the short-term and emergency loans from the Reich. Even the enabling acts which had sought to boost the income and curtail the expenditure of the state had failed to improve the situation, he reported. Customs receipts had decreased from 19,147,295 gulden in 1929 to 9,228,641 in 1931 and an estimated 5,500,000 in 1932; the cost of unemployment relief had risen in the same period from 9,988,238 to an estimated 16,200,000 gulden. Reichard recommended that Germany continue her subsidies and her payment of the unemployment costs, and that she provide a further subsidy of 8.5 million marks *à fonds perdu* to amortize the deficits of 1931–32. "Loans are no longer of any help," he wrote, "for Danzig can neither pay interest on new loans nor can it repay the principal." [51]

51. Ernst Reichard, Aufzeichnung über die Finanz- und Kassenlage der Freien Stadt Danzig, 19 Nov. 1932, PA: Fi 3, Danzig Geh., Bd. 5 (6203H/E368353–90).

It was a period of crisis for Germany's whole eastern policy. The head of the Eastern Department, Richard Meyer, estimated the sum necessary to cover expenditures in all the ceded provinces in the East to be at least eight billion marks. He noted:

> Since it appears questionable that in the next several years we can pursue in the East an active revisionist policy which would lead to an alteration of the territorial borders, we have for the moment no choice but to see to it that in the ceded areas all the strongholds of Deutschtum which are at all salvageable are maintained. We are concerned here in equal measure with political, economic, and cultural strongholds. If this policy is to be pursued—and it seems the only possible means of securing a basis from which a more active revisionist policy can later proceed—we must realize clearly that sums considerably in excess of the means provided heretofore are necessary.

Referring specifically to Danzig, he estimated that in 1933 the Reich would have to advance, in addition to the regular subsidy, the unemployment costs, the agricultural quotas, and the money from the Deutsche Stiftung, a sum of 505,000 marks to cover propaganda, trade unions, and agricultural cooperatives. He requested sums of 3,074,000 marks for the Corridor, 1,070,000 for Memel, 490,000 for Upper Silesia, and 420,000 for Schleswig.[52]

The year 1932 was the *annus terribilis* in the history of the Free City. Danzig had fallen into difficulties which even intensified assistance from Berlin could not relieve. To the Germans it seemed that the Free City's continued decline played into the hands of the Poles; the whole edifice of Weimar's eastern policy was crumbling.

The year had brought Danzig various moral victories, such as the League's decisions on Gdynia and the port d'attache, but these had not been material victories. The Poles demonstrated, most clearly with the *Wicher* incident, that moral victories were without substance unless they could be enforced. The problem

52. Memorandum by Meyer (Foreign Ministry), 15 Nov. 1932, BA: R 43 I/548.

of Gdynia remained uncorrected, and the Senate had been pressed into concluding an unadvantageous agreement on the port d'attache in August. The dispute about the quota system, for which the Warsaw Agreement of 1921 made provisions favorable to Danzig, was settled when the High Commissioner decided in November 1932 that, though quotas should be continued, their quantity should henceforth be determined by a binational commission presided over by a neutral chairman, whom he would appoint. Also in November the High Commissioner decided that Danzig was entitled to market in Poland goods manufactured from material obtained under the quotas.[53] However, while this decision prevented Poland from legally excluding Danzig's goods, she curtailed their quantity by permitting products only from those firms which pledged not to avail themselves of the quota system or to buy from firms which did, and which agreed to permit Polish inspectors to check their premises and their records. Goods from firms which did not forgo the quotas were spurned by companies which had complied with Polish requirements and confiscated if they entered Poland. The boycott, which the Poles had not curtailed despite their assurances in August, but which they had officially lifted in November when the High Commissioner released his decision on the quota system, thus effectively remained in force.[54] As Thermann commented, it was becoming increasingly obvious that Poland felt no obligation to take the League's decisions seriously and that she believed she could coerce the Free City into concessions (in return for economic survival) without fear of retribution.[55] The year 1932 demonstrated that the Free City was "free" in the realm of abstract concept alone.

Reactions in Danzig itself aggravated the issue for Germany. There were some, among them members of the Senate and the Chamber of Commerce, who were discussing the dissolution of the customs union with Poland and economic autonomy for the Free City. Such a measure would, of course, separate Danzig

53. *Entscheidungen* . . . *1928–1932*, pp. 67–73.

54. Polnische Zollkontrollen, February 1933, PA: Z, Danzig Geh., Bd. 1 (K222/K060686–91).

55. Thermann to Foreign Ministry, 18 Nov. 1932, PA: H 11 Nr. 1, Danzig Geh., Bd. 2.

from the Corridor and thus defeat Germany's plan for revision. Others in Danzig, a small but influential minority of merchants and industrialists, advocated political surrender to Poland in return for economic concessions. The August agreement on the port d'attache, which was announced to the German consul only in the last hour, was in part motivated by the Senate's desire to escape these pressures.[56] In April another group of Danzig entrepreneurs had gone to Warsaw to reach a private modus vivendi with Poland. Many accepted the Polish inspection system, and in October these firms formed an organization under the auspices of the commercial counselor of the Polish Commissariat "to promote Danzig-Polish economic relations." They were favored with reduced Polish duties and Polish markets for their goods. In return they employed Poles and promoted Polish schools and other cultural institutions in Danzig.[57] The Senate's fear that it might lose control of the situation began to trouble the Foreign Ministry seriously.[58]

At the end of the year Germany could only concede that she had lost ground. Danzig merchants were clamoring for change; economic and political pressure was driving the city to the edge of surrender; German aid was inadequate. And of course Gdynia, which continued to thrive as Danzig declined, undermined Germany's case for retrocession and cost Danzig its value in the campaign for revision. English and French newspapers were suggesting that Danzig, alone and severed from the Corridor, be returned to the Germans.[59]

56. Thermann to Foreign Ministry, 1 Sept. 1932, PA: Z, Danzig Geh., Bd. 1 (K222/K060680–83).

57. Koester (Danzig) to Foreign Ministry, 18 Apr. 1932, PA: H 11 Nr. 1, Danzig, Bd. 1 (K209/K051500–02); Thermann to Foreign Ministry, 24 Oct. 1932, PA: Gesandtschaft Warschau, P 15, Danzig, Bd. 6.

58. Thermann to Foreign Ministry, 1 Sept. 1932, PA: Z, Danzig Geh., Bd. 1 (K222/K060680–83).

59. Embassy Paris to Foreign Ministry, 13 Jan. 1932, and Embassy London to Foreign Ministry, 28 Apr. 1932, PA: Reichsminister, 55, Bd. 2 (3015H/D598070–74 and D598087).

CHAPTER 6

Hitler

When the National Socialists assumed control of the German government in January 1933, it was not apparent that policy toward Danzig was soon to undergo a fundamental change. The aid program was continued in routine fashion. In response to Reichard's assessment of November 1932 the Finance Ministry authorized on 17 March the annual subsidy of 4.2 million marks, to which it added on 5 April a subsidy of 5 million to cover the deficit in the budget; the Ministry of Labor provided 4 million gulden to offset unemployment costs; credits of 8 million marks went to public works and employment programs.[1] In response to the application of the Senate, the Ministry of Agriculture renewed its customs preferences for Danzig's farm products on a scale commensurate to that of former years; the preference system was expanded to include manufactures, thus offsetting the losses entailed by the closing of Polish markets. Government contracts continued to flow to Danzig concerns.[2]

Internal discussion of foreign policy outlined a tactic which had changed little since Stresemann. Early in February 1933 State Secretary Bülow instructed the German ambassador in Paris not to "broach the revision of the eastern frontier at this

1. Ministry of Finance to Senate, 17 Mar. 1933, *Documents on German Foreign Policy* (DGFP), series C, *1*, no. 96; Ministry of Finance to Senate, 5 Apr. 1933, PA: Fi 3, Danzig Geh., Bd. 5 (6203H/E468402); Ministry of Labor to Ministry of Finance, 17 May 1933, PA: So 2, Danzig Geh., Bd. 4 (8819H/E614009–10); Bank of Danzig to Schacht (Reichsbank), 10 Aug. 1933, PA: Fi 3, Danzig Geh., Bd. 5 (6203H/E468423–31).

2. Ministry of Agriculture to Ministry of Finance, 13 May 1933, PA: H 11 Nr. 1, Danzig Geh., Bd. 2 (6205H/E468957–60); Ministry of Finance to Landesfinanzamt Königsberg, 18 Aug. 1933, PA: ibid. (6205H/E468991–92); Ministry of Finance to Foreign Ministry, 3 Apr. 1933, PA: Wi 6, Danzig Geh., Bd. 1 (K221/K060564–68); Thermann to Foreign Ministry, 18 May 1933, and Reichsbank-Direktorium to Foreign Ministry, 11 Jan. and 13 July 1933, PA: ibid. (K221/K060588–89, K060530, and K060603).

time because the question is not yet ripe for discussion." He
added that the chancellor shared his view. Once Germany had
emerged from the depression, negotiations could be undertaken
with the Poles, for in these circumstances it would be clear to
them "that without our cooperation and without a settlement
of the frontier question they can never achieve economic prosperity." [3] A letter from Konstantin von Neurath, foreign minister
since June 1932, to Vice-Chancellor von Papen ran in much
the same vein. "The campaign to explain to the rest of the
world the meaning and justice of our revisionist demands has
not yet advanced far enough to assure us of sufficiently broad
support." If the eastern borders were to be a subject of negotiation now, Germany would fare badly. [4]

In a cabinet meeting on 7 April, Neurath described Germany's
foreign policy and presented what he considered a realistic
program:

> The aims of German foreign policy are determined by the
> Versailles Treaty. Our desire for revision requires that
> we show great diligence . . . . Territorial border revisions
> can be broached only when Germany has become militarily,
> politically, and financially strong. Until then we must con-
> tent ourselves with effective propaganda on the basis of
> Wilson's points . . . . Our primary objective remains the
> revision of the eastern border. Only a total solution is to
> be considered. Interim and partial solutions are to be re-
> jected . . . . An understanding with Poland is neither pos-
> sible nor desired. The tension with Poland must be main-
> tained if only for the reason that the world will not lose
> interest in a revision of the German-Polish borders . . . .
> The preservation of Deutschtum in Poland is a matter of
> particular concern, for which as for Danzig considerable
> sums must be expended.

Neurath emphasized the importance of good relations with England and the Soviet Union and cooperation with Italy. An understanding with France appeared impossible in the near future—
in the years since Stresemann, Germany had lost much of her

---

3. Bülow to Embassy Paris, 10 Feb. 1933, DGFP, series C, *1,* no. 19.
4. Neurath to Papen, 9 Feb. 1933, DGFP, series C, *1,* no. 18.

accumulated goodwill in Paris—but Neurath thought that the French were "resigned to progress if it were not too precipitate." As for the League, German membership was not particularly satisfactory, but withdrawal would be worse, for Germany would then have no control over decisions taken at Geneva. Neurath concluded with the admonition that international conflicts and "warlike complications" were to be avoided at all cost "until we have completely regained our strength." Given the "front" which had been formed against Germany, it was wise to be cautious. Hitler, who chaired the session, appeared to agree with Neurath's presentation, and the minutes of the meeting record no vocal dissent.[5] Polish initiative was soon to demonstrate that the unanimity was more apparent than real.

The climate of German-Polish relations had deteriorated when Hitler came to power in 1933. In Warsaw, Pilsudski had initially assumed a wait-and-see attitude, arguing that he would rather have an "Austrian" in the chancellery than a "Prussian" and that, moreover, Hitler would be preoccupied for some time with consolidating domestic support. But he was soon convinced that the new government boded no good for Poland.[6] The boisterous and bullying behavior of the storm troops in East Prussia, Silesia, and the Free City alarmed him: it indicated that the National Socialists intended to revise the borders by force. To the noisy campaign for the Reichstag election in March 1933 Hitler contributed bellicose public statements, calling the Corridor a "hideous injustice" and asserting that the territory "would have to be restored" to Germany; Goebbels, minister of propaganda, spoke openly of the "burning frontiers." [7] In February the Polish minister in Berlin, Alfred Wysocki, protested such outrageous pronouncements and assured the Foreign Ministry that the Poles would rather die in battle than retreat one foot from the present borders.[8]

5. Auszug aus der Niederschrift über die Ministerbesprechung vom 7. April 1933, DGFP, series C, *1*, no. 142.

6. Jules Laroche, *La Pologne de Pilsudski* (Paris, 1953), p. 141; Jozef Beck, *Dernier Rapport* (Paris, 1951), p. 24.

7. Max Domarus, ed., *Hitler: Reden und Proklamationen* (Munich, 1962), *1*, 201–02; Hans Leonhardt, *The Nazi Conquest of Danzig* (Chicago, 1942), p. 46.

8. Memorandum by Meyer (Foreign Ministry), 17 Feb. 1933, DGFP, series C, *1*, no. 22.

In Danzig the National Socialist movement had been growing since 1930 in a fashion and at a rate comparable to the gains in the Reich. It could claim loyalties in the civil service, especially among the police, and leading positions in the customs administration. In November 1932 the Nazis in the Volkstag had withdrawn their support from the Nationalist minority government and attacked the Senate for its "weak" policy toward Poland. Negotiations to admit them to the government had foundered on their irresponsible demands, and they began to clamor for elections, which they were confident of winning. There was reason to believe that the new government in Germany would soon find its like in the Free City, and when the *Vorposten,* the organ of Danzig's Nazi Party, announced its goal BACK TO THE REICH in banner headlines, many took it as advance notice of official German policy.[9]

Poland was therefore sharply mistrustful of Germany. Her relations with Danzig were already burdened by a number of unresolved quarrels about "full use" of the harbor and other issues, for which negotiations had failed to produce a solution, when in February 1933 a dispute about the harbor police opened a further conflict. In 1925 Danzig and Poland had concluded an agreement, valid until 1927, whereby the Senate placed a special detachment of police at the disposal of the Harbor Board. The arrangement continued unaltered after the expiration of the agreement until on 15 February 1933 the Senate, suspecting that the Poles were trying to extend the authority of the harbor police beyond the limits agreed upon, announced that it could no longer tolerate a situation for which there were no legal provisions. Henceforth the detachment which policed the harbor would be responsible, not to the Harbor Board, but only to the Free City. Poland suggested a harbor patrol composed of Poles and subordinate to the Board, but Danzig declined to entertain this scheme.[10]

The impasse was Pilsudski's opportunity for what his foreign minister called a "new energetic act" which would "confront the

9. Koester (Danzig) to Foreign Ministry, 23 Feb. 1933, PA: Po 2, Danzig, Bd. 3 (6023H/H044505–06).

10. Memorandum by Meyer (Foreign Ministry), 7 Mar. 1933, PA: Sch 16 Westerplatte A, Danzig Geh., Bd. 1 (6208H/E469325–29).

Senate with a fait accompli" and serve at the same time as "a warning" to the new German chancellor that Poland would not be intimidated by a barrage of hostile propaganda or refrain from resorting to arms in the defense of her interests.[11] Under the pretext that "revolutionary elements" in Danzig jeopardized the security of the Polish munitions depot on the Westerplatte, Pilsudski sent the Polish transport *Wilja* into the harbor before dawn on 6 March, the day after the tumultuous Reichstag election. One hundred twenty men landed to reinforce the guard at the depot and "protect the munitions stores." It was a clear breach of existing agreements. According to the League's decision in 1925, the guard of the depot could be increased only with the prior consent of the high commissioner, whom the Poles had omitted to consult. In an official communiqué published after the landing, the Poles argued that the urgency of this "provisional and temporary" measure of defense justified their precipitate action.[12]

The Senate immediately informed Helmer Rosting, a Danish official of the Secretariat, who had become acting high commissioner after Gravina's sudden death in September 1932, and requested that he require Poland to withdraw her forces without delay. The Polish reply to Rosting's sharp note was a polite refusal. The situation was as menacing as any encountered by a high commissioner. On 7 March, Rosting referred the issue to Geneva, where the Council was in session.

Feelings ran high. In Danzig the police and the civil militia were put on twenty-four-hour alert. The Senate exhorted the populace to remain calm. The Polish press, though apparently taken by surprise, fulminated against the High Commissioner for not intervening against "the armed bands" which endangered Polish interests in the Free City.[13] The Foreign Ministry in Berlin informed its missions of the incident, which it described as another illegal measure by which Poland aimed to undermine Danzig's autonomy. The embassies were instructed to point out

11. Beck, p. 25.
12. Memorandum by Meyer (Foreign Ministry), 7 Mar. 1933, PA: Sch 16 Westerplatte A, Danzig Geh., Bd. 1 (6208H/E469325–29).
13. Moltke to Foreign Ministry, 8 Mar. 1933, PA: Sch 16 Westerplatte A, Danzig Geh., Bd. 1 (6208H/E469372–73).

to their host governments "the danger of complications whose consequences could not be foreseen." [14]

In Geneva "emotions surpassed all expectations." [15] The matter, which was placed on the agenda for 14 March, was construed as a challenge to the prestige of the League. Drummond, the secretary general, took a strong stand. He was, according to Ziehm, very perturbed. He regarded the issue as an attack on the principle of the inviolability of treaties, upon which the League had been founded. If the League defaulted here, it would lose its meaning. Drummond promised Ziehm that he would bring his whole influence to bear.[16] The great powers seemed of one mind. Joseph Paul-Boncour, France's permanent delegate to the League, made private representations to Jozef Beck, who in 1932 had succeeded Zaleski as Polish foreign minister, and Sir John Simon, rapporteur for Danzig questions, was uncompromising in his condemnation. The speech he proposed to deliver to the Council expressed Great Britain's disapproval:

The issue is one of international obligations and of the maintenance of the authority of the League and its High Commissioner. If we admit that Poland was entitled to substitute her own judgement for that of the High Commissioner and so alter the terms of an agreement solemnly entered upon by her under Council auspices, merely because she thought it to be in her interest to do so, then it is clear that the whole statute of Danzig and much else is in serious danger.

I ask you to consider the matter in this light, discarding all extraneous considerations, and you will undoubtedly come to the conclusion that we have no option but to ask the Polish government, respectfully but firmly, to regularize her

14. Neurath to Missions, 7 Mar. 1933, PA: Sch 16 Westerplatte A, Danzig Geh., Bd. 1 (6208H/E469330–31); Neurath to Missions, 8 Mar. 1933, PA: Reichsminister, 55, Bd. 2 (3015H/D598249–50).

15. Beck, p. 26.

16. Aufzeichnung: Besprechung Ziehm/Drummond, 11 Mar. 1933, PA: Sch 16 Westerplatte A, Danzig, Bd. 2 (8841H/E615183–87); Ziehm, pp. 167–69.

position without delay by withdrawing her forces from the Westerplatte in excess of the allotted number.[17]

The German delegation was ready to deliver a carefully prepared denunciation which would have completed Poland's humiliation.[18]

The matter, however, never came to public discussion. Negotiations conducted in the Secretariat produced an agreement that Beck should inform the Council on 14 March that the troops would be withdrawn within two days and the situation restored to normal. He was to add that Poland recognized the legal limitations of her right to the Westerplatte and did not intend to treat this measure as a precedent. Ziehm in his turn consented to restore the detachment of Danzig police to the authority of the Harbor Board.[19]

The smooth conclusion of the episode was almost wrecked by events in Danzig. A few hours after the Council session Beck informed Ziehm that the troops could not depart after all, for the city was "threatened by an insurrection of the Nazis." That morning Thermann, acting on orders from Berlin, had hoisted the swastika on the consular building in the presence of Nazi storm troopers. The local *Gauleiter,* Albert Forster, had used the occasion to celebrate the victory of National Socialism in Germany and to declare that the swastika would soon be flying over the city hall. Ziehm reacted to this "stab in the back" by having the Senate prohibit all public demonstrations and begged Meyer, director of the Eastern Department, who was also present in Geneva, to contact Berlin and have the Foreign Ministry persuade Hitler to call Forster to order. After renewed efforts, Drummond and Rosting were persuaded that the Nazi agitation was not to be taken very seriously and that peace reigned in the

17. Erster Entwurf des Berichts des Rapporteurs in der Westerplattenfrage, der nicht zur Verteilung kam. PA: Sch 16 Westerplatte, Danzig Geh., Bd. 5 (K218/K058497).

18. Deutsche Delegation Genf to Foreign Ministry, 12 Mar. 1933, PA: Reichsminister, 55, Bd. 2 (3015H/D598261–63).

19. Meyer (Geneva) to Foreign Ministry, 14 Mar. 1933, DGFP, series C, *1,* no. 82; LNOJ (1933), pp. 626–29.

Free City. Beck was constrained to honor the agreed schedule.[20]

The Westerplatte incident, meant to warn the Germans, had been a warning to the Poles. It was something of a diplomatic reverse. No records have come to light on the discussion preceding Beck's declaration in the Council, but the Poles cannot have escaped noticing that they faced the undivided opposition of both European diplomacy and European public opinion. The Polish government must have regretted having to defend its actions before the united powers at Geneva. It may have expected to find support from some few among them, especially from the French. Instead it faced the possibility of diplomatic isolation.

Events of the weeks following the Westerplatte compromise confirmed Pilsudski's misgivings. On 16 March British Prime Minister Ramsay MacDonald suggested a disarmament scheme which would have given Germany and France parity in military strength. Two days later Mussolini produced a plan for a directorate of Europe, composed of the four great powers, Britain, France, Germany, and Italy. The Italian proposal affirmed the principle of peaceful revision of treaties, and to the Poles this implied loss of the Corridor.

Warsaw reacted violently. The proposal jeopardized both the prestige and the national security of the Polish state. As at Locarno, peace in the West was being bought at the price of peace in the East. Beck protested to the French ambassador and reiterated Poland's determination to go to war in defense of Polish territory. Pilsudski was confirmed in his suspicion that the French were withdrawing from their commitments toward Poland. With Beck's collaboration he moved away from Poland's established orientation toward France and the League.[21] The new course of Poland's foreign policy, foreshadowed by the Russo-Polish détente of 1932, was nearing its inception. Pilsudski aspired to friendly relations with his eastern and western neighbors, but close attachment to neither.

The Germans, too, had found the Westerplatte affair profoundly disturbing. It had ominous overtones which the *Wicher* incident, a discrete gesture of defiance, had lacked. For it stood

20. Ziehm, pp. 173–75; Deutsche Delegation Genf to Foreign Ministry, 17 Mar. 1933, PA: Reichsminister, 55, Bd. 2 (3015H/D598274).
21. Beck, p. 283; Laroche, p. 123.

in the context, not of an isolated quarrel over matters of prestige, but of the Polish government's attitude to the whole complex of political developments in Germany and Danzig. At the time of the landing on the Westerplatte, reports reached the Foreign Ministry that the Poles were reinforcing their troops at Gdynia, and military concentrations in the Corridor were rumored. To the German military this information suggested that the incident in the Danzig harbor might have been a show of strength preliminary to a much more ambitious undertaking.[22] The Germans were not alone in these speculations. Throughout March and April word came in from Prague, Warsaw, and Danzig that Poland was contemplating a "preventive war." [23] The truth of this allegation has never been established. It has been suggested that Pilsudski planted the rumors to intimidate Hitler and make him amenable to rapprochement with Poland.[24] It is also possible that the Poles planned some kind of police action, a temporary occupation of territory to force the Germans to abide by the Peace Treaty's prescriptions for frontiers and disarmament— sanctions on the model of the Ruhr. Such plans, however, presupposed French support, which, as the deliberations at Geneva had made clear, was not forthcoming. To the Germans, nevertheless, the danger of a Polish military offensive was real.[25]

Hitler was preoccupied with domestic affairs at the time. His grandiose plans for Germany required that he address himself first to internal problems. In the week following his appointment as chancellor he outlined his objectives before a number of high-ranking naval and army officers at the home of General von Hammerstein-Equord, commander in chief of the army. The objective of all his policy, Hitler told his audience, was Germany's

---

22. Hans Roos, *Polen und Europa* (Tübingen, 1957), p. 68.

23. Thermann to Foreign Ministry, 13 Mar. 1933, PA: Sch 16 Wester-platte A, Danzig Geh., Bd. 1 (6208H/E469443); Legation Prague to Foreign Ministry, 25 Apr. 1933, DGFP, series C, *1,* no. 184.

24. Zygmunt Gasiorowski, "Did Pilsudski Attempt To Initiate a Preventive War in 1933?" *Journal of Modern History* (1955), pp. 135–51; Boris Celovsky, "Pilsudskis Präventivkrieg gegen das nationalsozialistische Deutschland," *Welt als Geschichte* (1954), pp. 53–70.

25. Auszug aus der Niederschrift über die Ministerbesprechung vom 7. April 1933, DGFP, series C, *1,* no. 142; Moltke to Foreign Ministry, 23 Apr. 1933, DGFP, series C, *1,* no. 180.

recovery of political strength. To this end, Germany's domestic situation would have to be radically reformed. Marxism, pacifism, and "the cancer of democracy" would be extirpated. The country required the most stringent authoritarian government. The most important prerequisite for the attainment of his great objective was the rebuilding of the armed forces. Once political vitality had been regained it could best be used for the conquest and ruthless germanization of new *Lebensraum* in the East.[26]

Hitler wished first of all to consolidate support at home. He used the powers granted him by the enabling act of March 1933 to coordinate the civil service, the trade unions, and the other political parties with the National Socialist doctrine. Rearmament began that same spring: large appropriations went to all branches of the military, funds for munitions appeared in the budget under a misleading rubric, and the unemployed were put to work in armaments industries.[27] Obviously such an ambitious domestic program could be executed only if Hitler were assured of no untoward interferences from the outside. And these, as the Westerplatte incident had illustrated, were most likely to come from Poland, the more so since Polish reaction to German rearmament, which could not be concealed indefinitely, would be vehement. The Poles would have to be placated.

Hitler could offer the Poles concrete assurances of German amity because the Weimar policy of territorial revision had been subsumed into a larger policy—Lebensraum. Germany, he wrote in 1928, should under no circumstances pursue "a formal border policy." Such a tactic aspired to the restoration of borders which were satisfactory "neither nationally, militarily, nor geopolitically." Germany was destined to extend her territory beyond the borders of 1914 into Russia.[28] Hitler had discarded revisionist claims in favor of territorial expansion. He thought to regain the lost territories by a method which required neither stubborn

26. Thilo Vogelsang, "Neue Dokumente zur Geschichte der Reichswehr 1930–1933," *Vierteljahrshefte für Zeitgeschichte* (1954), pp. 434–35.

27. Karl Dietrich Bracher, Wolfgang Sauer, Gerhard Schulz, *Die nationalsozialistische Machtergreifung* (Cologne, 1960), pp. 796–806.

28. *Hitlers Zweites Buch,* ed. Gerhard Weinberg (Stuttgart, 1961), pp. 113–14; Adolf Hitler, *Mein Kampf* (Munich, 1933), p. 742.

maintenance of Danzig against Polish encroachment nor the cultivation of diplomatic sympathy from the western powers.

It was a happy coincidence of reoriented foreign policies in Germany and Poland. Pilsudski, skeptical of France's friendship, sought other assurances against German invasion. Hitler, eager to free himself of the possibility of Polish interference, was ready to oblige him. On 15 March he informed the cabinet that he had instructed the Danzig Nazis to desist in their rowdy agitation for new elections and "maintain the greatest reserve." [29] When Ziehm returned from Geneva on 22 March, Hitler received him at great length, approved his prohibition of open-air demonstrations in Danzig—directed mainly against the Nazis —and assured him that the local Nazi party had received instructions to heed all decrees promulgated by the Senate.[30] On 23 March he told the Reichstag that he was prepared "to extend his hand in genuine friendship to every nation which is willing finally to make an end of the sad past." [31]

Early in April the German minister in Warsaw, Moltke, more annoyed at than frightened by anti-German demonstrations so vehement that the legation had to be protected by guards, speculated that the Polish government might be encouraging the disturbances in an attempt to gain "direct contact" with Berlin.[32] The German government did not respond, and a second opportunity presented itself later the same month, when the campaign preceding new elections in Danzig became boisterous. The Poles took the initiative.

Apparently because of the tumultuous atmosphere in Danzig after the Westerplatte incident, Hitler had hesitated to approve the elections for which the Danzig Nazi Party was clamoring. Later in March, however, he became persuaded that new elections in the Free City were feasible and even desirable.[33] On

29. Memorandum by Neurath, 16 Mar. 1933, DGFP, series C, *1,* no. 85.

30. Ziehm, pp. 184–86.

31. Norman Baynes, ed., *The Speeches of Adolf Hitler* (London, 1942), p. 1017.

32. Moltke to Foreign Ministry, 19 Apr. 1933, DGFP, series C, *1,* no. 167.

33. Memorandum by Lammers (Chancellery), 1 Apr. 1933, BA: R 43 I/377.

3 April the Foreign Ministry had Thermann instruct Ziehm,
who had no choice but to obey the government upon which his
regime was materially and psychologically dependent, to dissolve
the Volkstag and call for new elections. The following day
Thermann telephoned Berlin that Ziehm had agreed.[34] The campaign began immediately and soon produced such heat that the
Polish commissioner general in Danzig found reason to protest
to the High Commissioner against infringements of Polish rights
which the police could not control. Rosting felt constrained to
tell the Senate that if internal disorder could not be quelled he
would call in Polish troops.[35]

At this point the Poles found an opportunity to approach
Berlin directly. On 20 April the Polish minister in Berlin,
Wysocki, called at the Foreign Ministry with a request to be received by the Chancellor. The interview took place on 2 May.
Wysocki told Hitler that events in Danzig were producing uneasiness in Poland and that his government desired assurances that
Germany had no intention of bringing about a change in the
present status of the Free City. Access to the sea was a vital
Polish interest which Poland would not neglect to defend. Hitler
replied that Germany had more reason for uneasiness than Poland, since she felt herself constantly threatened by Polish troop
movements and such incidents as the Westerplatte. The ill-
considered borders stipulated by the Treaty of Versailles made
peaceful coexistence extremely difficult, but "Germany desired
peace," and "a forceful expropriation of Polish territory was
far from her thoughts." At Wysocki's request, a communiqué
was issued after the visit, in which Hitler "stressed the firm
intention of the German government to keep its attitude and
its conduct strictly within the limits of existing treaties." It "expressed the wish that both countries might review and deal with
their mutual interests dispassionately." [36] It was the first step
toward German-Polish rapprochement.

34. Memorandum by Meyer (Foreign Ministry), 3 Apr. 1933, DGFP,
series C, *1,* no. 131; Telephonische Mitteilung aus Danzig, 4 Apr. 1933,
PA: Reichsminister, 55, Bd. 2 (3015H/D598279).

35. Thermann to Foreign Ministry, 20 Apr. 1933, PA: Po 5, Danzig,
Bd. 6 (9062H/E634808–10); LN: C.386.1933.I.

36. Memorandum by Neurath, 2 May 1933, DGFP, series C, *1,* no.

Hitler reiterated his conciliatory line in a speech before the Reichstag on 17 May—the famous *Friedensrede*—in which he reaffirmed his "respect [for] the national claims of others" and asserted that "Germany is prepared to agree to any solemn pact of nonaggression, for she does not think of attacking but only of acquiring security." After mentioning the "reasonable claims of Poland" and the "natural rights of Germany" in the East, Hitler avowed his willingness "to come to a peaceful agreement with other nations on all difficult questions." [37] In Danzig the Nazis gave High Commissioner Rosting similar assurances.[38]

Such pronouncements brought a favorable response from Warsaw. On 20 May, Beck expressed to Moltke his satisfaction at the "growing relaxation" of tensions and, touching on the situation in Danzig, assured the German minister that Warsaw "considered the elections and the reorganization of the Senate an internal affair of the Free City which did not affect Poland if the elections took a normal course and neither the statute nor the treaties were violated." [39]

Predictably, the Nazis won the elections. They received 50.03 percent of the popular vote (in the Reichstag elections of 5 March the Nazis had won 43.9 percent of the vote) and an absolute majority—38 of 72 seats—in the Volkstag.[40] Danzig's very geography augured for a Nazi victory: the Germans in the border territories had always been more preoccupied with nationalism than the Germans in the Reich, and the Nazi program appealed strongly to frustrated nationalism. Antagonism toward Poland and Danzig's catastrophic economic situation—25 percent of the work force was unemployed—also promoted sympathy for the Nazi Party. The Nazis' campaign, moreover, had gained funds and speakers from the party in the Reich, as well

---

201; *Official Documents Concerning Polish-German Relations . . . 1933–1939* (London, 1939), nos. 1, 2.

37. Baynes, pp. 1047, 1056–57.

38. Thermann to Foreign Ministry, 17 May 1933, PA: Gesandtschaft Warschau, P2i, Bd. 3.

39. Moltke to Foreign Ministry, 20 May 1933, DGFP, series C, *1,* no. 253.

40. The Socialists and Communists together won 18 seats, the Center Party 10, and the Nationalists 4.

as contingents of storm troopers, who rallied support and intimidated the opposition. In a radio broadcast on 27 May, the eve of the election, Hitler told the Danzig electorate of the "internal bond of National Socialism" which would "surmount the frontiers that externally sunder the German people" and exhorted them "to join this inner community of soul and spirit." [41]

If Hitler was to achieve a true détente with Poland—in late May in a conversation with Dirksen, now ambassador to Russia, he expressed his hope of arriving at a pact[42]—the major points of friction between the two countries had to be eliminated. Danzig, which, encouraged by the Weimar government, had been a hotbed of disputes, became his chosen instrument for German-Polish reconciliation. Four days after the victory at the polls, one of the Danzig party leaders recalled, Hitler received the victorious Nazis at the chancellery and outlined his intentions. Germany's aims could not be attained "in a few days or weeks"; therefore it was necessary to be "astute." For the moment it was important to "avoid anything that might give the world cause for suspicion."

> There was a choice between only two kinds of action: one might pretend or one might be quite sincere in one's aims. He himself was determined to make any treaty that would ease the position of Germany. He was determined to get on with Poland, and it was our task to support him in this. The Danzig problem could not be solved by us, only by him, and even by him only if Germany was strong and feared. The more silently and secretly we carried on our struggle for existence, the better for Germany. It was not our task to solve the Danzig problem or that of the Corridor. This we should have to leave to the Reich. But it would be our business, whenever possible, to clear away difficulties from the path of the Reich.[43]

41. Baynes, pp. 1061–62; Leonhardt, pp. 57–60.
42. Herbert von Dirksen, *Moskau, Tokio, London* (Stuttgart, 1949), p. 123.
43. Hermann Rauschning, *Hitler Speaks* (London, 1939), pp. 91–92; Rauschning to Ministry of Finance, 2 June 1933, PA: Wi 7, Danzig Geh., Bd. 1 (6211H/E469610–20).

At the same meeting Hitler endorsed the Senate's request for a subsidy to cope with the economic situation, whereupon the Finance Ministry awarded the city a total of ten million gulden in addition to the regular subventions.[44]

Hermann Rauschning, the new president of the Senate, was pleased with Hitler's plans. Rauschning represented the moderate, bourgeois wing of the party. He was a nationalist and, like his vice-president, Arthur Greiser, came originally from the Corridor. He had been active in the minority movement, had written and published a dissertation on the de-germanization of West Prussia, and had become an agricultural expert after he settled in Danzig in 1926. He was the very opposite of the local Gauleiter, Albert Forster, his superior in the party hierarchy, a crude and extremist Bavarian who styled himself "Julius Streicher's beloved disciple." [45]

To the new president of the Senate, Hitler's desire to seek friendship with Poland could not have been more agreeable. Rauschning advocated permanent cooperation between Danzig and Poland. Instead of perpetuating the tiresome legal disputes before the League and preoccupying himself with fine judicial points of sovereignty and interpretation of the treaties, as Sahm and Ziehm had done, he proposed direct contact with Poland and the removal of all obstacles to harmonious relations. Rauschning saw himself as the protagonist of a Danzig-Polish and thus German-Polish conciliation. Danzig was to become the "proving ground" of German-Polish cooperation, the birthsite of a "new order" in Europe: the "peaceful evolutionary solution of the eastern European problems." Rauschning's ultimate aim is difficult to define. He foresaw a "peaceful expansion" and "a great future" for Germany "if, instead of a rigorous revisionist policy, she were to carry out a policy of peaceful alliances." Occasions for war would be removed by "the abandonment of any claim to hegemony" and by "building up a system of pacts based on the inviolability of boundaries, which would sterilize the frontier problem." Ultimately, central Europe might become "a federa-

---

44. Chancellery to Ministry of Finance, 9 June 1933, PA: Fi 3, Danzig Geh., Bd. 5 (6203H/E468408); Ministry of Finance to Senate, 18 Aug. 1933, PA: ibid. (6203H/E468434–37).

45. Leonhardt, pp. 55–56.

tion of national elements in supranational union." [46] Though Hitler sought to win Poland's confidence for other reasons, for the time being—until Rauschning's resignation from the Senate in November 1934—a relationship was inaugurated between the two which enabled each to use the other for his own ends.

On 23 June, at the first plenary session of the newly elected Volkstag, Rauschning announced his policy. All energies would be dedicated to fostering Danzig's German heritage and preserving the close cultural community between Danzigers and Germans. At the same time the Senate was committed to a policy of peace and would respect existing treaties and agreements. It was prepared, he concluded, to enter directly into discussions with Poland in order to settle all pending questions.[47] Rauschning made his offer in all seriousness. Later he was to admit that at the time the task seemed hopeless and absurd, and the differences between Danzig and Poland loomed very large. How could negotiation alter the geography of two neighboring ports which competed for the same hinterland? How could an economic union be compatible with differing standards of living? Rauschning realized that any settlement would require major concessions from Danzig, but in the interest of a solution which would benefit the city economically and promote his larger plan, he was willing to surrender rights which had hitherto been defended with legal success, if not material effectiveness.[48]

Polish response to Rauschning's declaration was mixed. The semiofficial Iskra News Agency reported that Warsaw would look forward to further and more concrete details about the promised negotiations. The *Gazeta Polska* merely reaffirmed the view that Danzig's cultural bonds with Germany had never been in dispute but that Danzig had been created a free city to serve the Polish economy.[49] The Polish government's response was more cordial. In the first week of July, Rauschning and Vice-

46. Hermann Rauschning, *Die Revolution des Nihilismus* (Zurich, 1938), pp. 398, 400, 411, 414, 418; Rauschning, *Hitler Speaks*, p. 121.

47. *Gesetzblatt der Freien Stadt Danzig,* 26 June 1933.

48. Radowitz (Danzig) to Foreign Ministry, 19 Jan. 1934, PA: Po 1, Danzig, Bd. 7.

49. Moltke to Foreign Ministry, 29 June 1933, PA: Gesandtschaft Warschau, P2i, Bd. 3.

President Greiser paid an official inaugural visit to Warsaw—
the first since Sahm's in 1921—and were received with all the
honors due heads of state. After they had met with the finance
minister, Zawacki, and with Beck, it was agreed that negotiations on a number of outstanding questions should begin immediately, and Rauschning spoke to the press about "normaliza-
tion" and "amicability" between Danzig and Poland. Pilsudski
expressed to the delegation his satisfaction that Danzig sought
reasonable relations.[50]

By mid-July, Danzig and Poland had established binational
commissions to explore the grounds for agreement. There were
many problems. Danzig goods were still subjected to Polish
boycott; the disputes about the passive finishing trade and the
Danzig quota system were awaiting solution; at that very moment some thirty-five cases were on the High Commissioner's
desk. Of particular importance were the conflicts about Gdynia
and about the status of the Polish minority in the Free City.
Competition from Gdynia had not abated. In the first half of
1932 Danzig had still handled 53.5 percent of Poland's total
overseas trade; in the corresponding period in 1933 this percentage had shrunk to 46.2. The decrease, in absolute figures,
was from 2,507,400 tons to 2,257,000.[51] The conflict about
the status of the Polish minority in Danzig, perpetually a point
of friction, dated from 1930. The Polish commissioner general
had submitted a complaint to the high commissioner, requesting
a decision on "the unfavorable treatment [accorded] Polish nationals and other persons of Polish origin or speech in Danzig"
when they sought educational facilities, rights of settlement, acquisition of Danzig citizenship, and freedom to use their own
language. The Senate had rejected the complaint as unfounded
and, in a detailed rebuttal, had compared conditions in Danzig
favorably with those of the German minority in Poland. The
question had been referred to the International Court at the
Hague, which, in February 1932, delivered an advisory opinion
favorable to Danzig. The treatment of Polish nationals in Dan-

50. Legation Warsaw to Foreign Ministry, 5 July 1933, PA: Po 3,
Danzig, Bd. 25 (9081H/E637589–90); Beck, p. 27.
51. Thermann to Foreign Ministry, 19 Aug. 1933, PA: Gesandtschaft
Warschau, P 15, Danzig, Bd. 8.

zig was to be, not equal to that of Danzig citizens, but in accord with the standards set by the minority treaties of 1919, which Poland had signed.[52] The negotiations between Danzig and Warsaw, which sought to settle the dispute on the basis of this ruling, had been abandoned when the election campaign had further provoked public abuse of Danzig's Polish residents.

At the end of July the first outlines of the proposed accord were visible. Danzig had agreed to major concessions on the rights of the Polish minority and the issue had been settled in principle. In return the Poles had offered assurances that the two ports, Danzig and Gdynia, would be used equally, but they had postponed definite arrangements to a later date. On 5 August, Danzig acceded to a draft agreement which guaranteed the Polish minority extensive privileges in return for Poland's promise to see that seaborne traffic through Danzig decrease no further and that Poland's foreign trade be divided equally between Danzig and Gdynia. Talks were to continue without delay, and if neither party resubmitted the questions to High Commissioner Rosting before 15 September, the settlement was to become effective. On 18 September the negotiations culminated in agreement. The Danzigers signed the draft on minority privileges which they had accepted in August. It afforded public elementary schools for Polish-speaking children and private Polish schools for all levels of education, full recognition of Polish diplomas, the abolition of discrimination against Poles at the Polytechnical Institute, and acceptance of the Polish language in all contexts. Poland guaranteed Danzig a minimum of 4.5 million tons of trade yearly (3.5 million were to be in timber and coal), thereby perpetuating on an annual scale the volume of traffic which had passed through Danzig in August 1933, approximately 50 percent of Poland's seaborne trade. The settlement was a far cry from Danzig's demand in 1930 for "full use" of the harbor.[53] Implicitly Danzig acknowledged Poland's contention that she bore no obligation toward the port at Danzig

52. Köpke (Foreign Ministry) to Missions, 31 Mar. 1933, PA: Referat Völkerbund: 66. Ratstagung (L785/L232355–75).

53. Thermann to Foreign Ministry, 5 Aug. 1933, PA: Sch 16A, Danzig Geh., Bd. 5 (9071H/E636733); Koester (Danzig) to Foreign Ministry, 20 Sept. 1933, PA: ibid. (9071H/E636781–803).

and the corollary that the hinterland required the services of two outlets. The provisions for the Polish minority went far beyond any agreement ever previously entertained. For the first time in the history of Danzig-Polish, and thus German-Polish, relations the right to cultural equality and autonomy found official endorsement. The agreement removed a major stumbling block from the relationship of the two states. To affirm Poland's desire to establish harmonious relations, Prime Minister Janusz Jedrzejewicz visited Danzig on 22 September.

Rauschning was delighted with the accord. Early in September, in an article which appeared in the National Socialist *Vorposten,* he had explained his purposes and justified the sacrifices which would be exacted from Danzig. It was difficult, he knew, even for the government, to put aside cherished hopes and abandon the wish for reunification with the fatherland. The Senate, however, adopted a policy of conciliation and relinquished its aims of political revision:

> because we know and acknowledge that there is a higher level of politics in eastern Europe, a level on which the constituent territorial problems such as national entitlement to Danzig will play a relatively minor role. Heretofore the level of political confrontation with Poland afforded Danzig and Germany no other possibility than to demand that the treaties be revised, to which Poland replied with the reciprocal demand for further acquisition of territory. The National Socialist politics of peace, which in Danzig too has set itself new goals, seeks a higher basis for the resolution of questions between the peoples of eastern Europe which formerly seemed unsolvable. To create a lasting new political order here is the purpose of the Danzig Senate's efforts in foreign policy.[54]

Now he hailed Danzig as the "link and intermediary" between Germany and Poland.[55] The first step in his larger plan had been accomplished.

The Foreign Ministry was incensed. Rauschning's trip to War-

54. *Danziger Vorposten,* 6 Sept. 1933.
55. Hermann Rauschning, *Zehn Monate nationalsozialistische Regierung in Danzig* (Danzig, 1934).

saw in early July had annoyed the German diplomats, not least because he had neglected to consult them beforehand. The negotiations which proceeded from this visit had been pursued despite their strong misgivings and repeated admonitions. In the estimation of the Foreign Ministry, Danzig was conceding rights and privileges which it was legally entitled to retain and for which both Danzig and Germany had fought at great cost for more than ten years. To elevate a national minority to virtual equality with the native populace was excessive. The International Court at the Hague, in its ruling of February 1932, had said as much. Furthermore, Danzig was entitled to full use of its port, as the League's committee of jurists had recognized in September 1932, and to settle for less was spendthrift. To have conceded all this in return for promises which the Poles, in all likelihood, had no intention of keeping, to expose oneself so to Polish exploitation, was inconceivable. The entire course of revisionist policy had been compromised by an idealist, as Thermann described Rauschning, who greatly overestimated the significance of Hitler's projected Danzig-Polish détente.[56] For the Foreign Ministry was convinced that Hitler's plans toward Poland represented a tactical and temporary maneuver and did not impinge upon major policy—revisionism as it had been practiced since Stresemann.

It was wrong. At the September session of the League Council, where congratulations were exchanged all around, the German and Polish delegations exhibited the greatest cordiality toward one another. Neurath listened with gratification to Beck's repeated expressions of pleasure at the relaxation of tension during recent months, particularly in Danzig, and brought him together with Josef Goebbels, Hitler's personal representative at the Council meeting. Goebbels assured Beck that Hitler realized "the old German policy was burdened with many errors which were detrimental to the interests of Germany . . . and . . . believed that direct understanding between partners could do more for the détente . . . than any Geneva conventicles."

56. Thermann to Foreign Ministry, 10 Aug. 1933, PA: Sch 16A, Danzig Geh., Bd. 5 (9071H/E636735–39); Niederschrift über die Besprechung am 2. und 3. August in Danzig, 7 Aug. 1933, PA: Po 3, Danzig, Bd. 26 (9081H/E637619–21).

Both agreed—and in this were joined by Neurath—that most of the pending questions between Germany and Poland could best be solved by direct consultation.[57]

In October the divergence between Hitler's plans and the policy pursued by the Foreign Ministry became patent. On 26 September, within a week of the signing of the Danzig-Polish agreements, the president of the Bank of Danzig, with Rauschning's knowledge, proposed to the German government a plan designed to further Rauschning's scheme of reconciliation with the Poles. The plan envisioned a transfer of gold and foreign exchange reserves (some 25 million gulden) from the Bank of Danzig to the Bank Polski in order to shore up the Polish currency, which was at the point of collapse. Such an offer would be very tempting to the Poles, and certain conditions could be attached. It might well be possible to exact extensive economic concessions. The banker admitted that a few months earlier such a plan would have been labeled a "betrayal of the German cause." The times, however, had changed: no longer did Danzig wish to remain "the open wound" in the German body politic, and the possibility of an early solution to the Corridor problem was obviously remote. The Corridor in fact had of late come to be called "the cement" and no longer the wedge between Poland and the Reich. The recent agreements had been only the beginning of a course which would allow Danzig to reenter the Polish economy as in centuries past.[58]

This description of Danzig's new political course came as a great blow to the Foreign Ministry. It signified "a complete departure from the fundamental concepts of Germany's official eastern policy if the Corridor is described as the cement between the Reich and Poland," and if the existing connections between the Reich and East Prussia were considered adequate. Should this concept become "the common property of public opinion in the ceded areas, the defenders of the Versailles eastern system will be provided with a strong argument which practically amounts to our permanent renunciation of the Corridor."

57. Memorandums by Neurath, 25 and 26 Sept. 1933, DGFP, series C, *1*, nos. 449, 451; Beck, pp. 30–31.

58. Reichsbank-Direktorium to Foreign Ministry, 3 Oct. 1933, PA: Fi 4, Danzig Geh., Bd. 1 (6204H/E468587–97).

The projected transaction would promote the detachment of Danzig from its close association with the Reich and its attachment to Poland. And to propose helping "a financially embarrassed Poland with funds provided by the Reich" was the limit of ingratitude.[59]

Objections from Meyer, the director of the Eastern Department, did not deter Rauschning. On 17 October he secured Hitler's approval of the Senate's intentions "to arrive at an understanding with Poland in all fields, insofar as this could possibly be done without imperiling the German character of Danzig and German interests." [60] In Rauschning's opinion, the credit offer did not imperil "German interests." It was the means by which various matters of contention—Rauschning listed some 27 of these for the Foreign Ministry[61]—could be settled. Rauschning listened to the reservations of the Foreign Ministry, which regarded the scheme as foolhardy and really the very last concession Danzig could make; but he declared that, given the broad authorization he had received from Hitler, he would have to reserve the right to a decision on his own responsibility, regardless of what the Foreign Ministry thought.[62] He arranged a visit to Warsaw in the first half of December to see Pilsudski and discuss the Danzig-Polish relationship and also to describe his offer and the expected concessions to Beck and the appropriate ministries. The Foreign Ministry had been outplayed. It was an early instance of what Hitler was to practice henceforth with ever greater success.

Rauschning arrived in Warsaw at a crucial moment in German-Polish relations. When Hitler, in his first major diplomatic move, withdrew from the Disarmament Conference and the League in October, Poland was disconcerted. While Jozef Lipski, the new Polish minister to Berlin, presented his credentials to President Hindenburg four days later, on 18 October, and ex-

59. Memorandum by Hey (Foreign Ministry), 11 Oct. 1933, DGFP, series C, *1*, no. 491.

60. Memorandum by Neurath, 17 Oct. 1933, DGFP, series C, *2*, no. 11.

61. Memorandum by Rauschning, 8 Dec. 1933, PA: Fi 4, Danzig Geh., Bd. 1 (6204H/E468618–24).

62. Memorandum by Meyer (Foreign Ministry), 8 Dec. 1933, PA: Fi 4, Danzig Geh., Bd. 1 (6204H/E468515–17).

pressed his wish to devote himself to the development and perfection of German-Polish relations in accordance with the principles of the May communiqué,[63] Pilsudski inquired in Paris about the state of German armaments and is reported to have inquired in London and Paris about the preparedness of the respective governments to launch an attack on Germany.[64] On 24 October Hitler asserted publicly that Poles and Germans would have "to live side by side and get along together." [65] This pronouncement apparently reassured Warsaw, for on 13 November, the fifteenth anniversary of resurrected Poland, Beck told a radio audience that while Poland would remain loyal to the concept of the League of Nations, the idea of bilateral agreements was by no means obsolete. The regulation of affairs with Germany represented a major problem, and Poland intended to remove all obstacles to good relations.[66]

Two days later Lipski had an audience with the Chancellor. The Polish minister explained that Germany's withdrawal from the League was causing uneasiness in Poland. Poland's security had always been based on one of two foundations: common membership in the League or bilateral treaties. What assurances, he demanded somewhat abruptly, could Germany offer? In reply Hitler declared that he "took for granted the existence of the Polish state," and that "it was nonsense to wage a war over small border revisions." He was prepared, he asserted, "to issue a statement to the effect that the German government had every intention of refraining from a forcible solution of the problems" pending between the two countries.[67]

On 16 November Hitler authorized the Foreign Ministry to draft a declaration renouncing the use of war between Germany

63. Robert Machray, *The Poland of Pilsudski* (London, 1936), p. 337.

64. Richard Breyer, *Das Deutsche Reich und Polen 1932–1937* (Würzburg, 1955), p. 99; Waclaw Jedrzejewicz, "The Polish Plan for a 'Preventive War' against Germany in 1933," *The Polish Review* (1966), p. 86.

65. Baynes, p. 1113.

66. Wolffs Telegraphisches Büro, 14 Nov. 1933, PA: Po 2, Polen, Bd. 41.

67. Foreign Ministry to Legation Warsaw, 15 Nov. 1933, DGFP, series C, *2*, no. 69; *Official Documents Concerning Polish-German Relations . . . ,* nos. 6, 7.

and Poland. The document was to dispense with the legal formulations usual to such accords and avoid any explicit description, and thereby implicit recognition, of the present eastern borders.[68] The Foreign Ministry was unenthusiastic. In its estimation such a declaration eradicated the distinction between the eastern and western frontiers which the Locarno Treaties had so carefully established. The pact would be universally interpreted as a renunciation of Germany's longstanding revisionist claims, and, moreover, it would restrict Germany's "political freedom of action for many years." [69] The officials protested to no avail. On 28 November Moltke delivered the proposed text with the Chancellor's greetings to Pilsudski, in the presence of Beck. Pilsudski approved of the declaration in principle and promised to have it studied and appraised.[70]

Thus Rauschning's visit on 11 and 12 December 1933 came at an opportune moment. On the 11th he was received by Pilsudski in the presence of Beck and Papée, the commissioner general in Danzig. The interview opened with a discussion of Poland's relations with the Free City. Rauschning reiterated his hope that direct discussions could produce full agreement on the remaining conflicts and spoke again of Danzig's readiness to comply with Poland's customs and economic policies as long as its cultural and political autonomy was guaranteed. In return Pilsudski assured him that Danzig's German character, which he found indisputable, had no effect on the city's status as an important commercial port of Poland. The subject then moved to National Socialism in Germany. Rauschning met Pilsudski's misgivings about the new regime with assurances that National Socialism sought direct understanding with all nations. Pilsudski exhibited, Rauschning informed Moltke, strong interest in the ambitious work of the Chancellor and reservations lest the Nazis' internal reforms be more radical and more rapid than the people would tolerate. Rauschning was left with the impression

68. Meyer (Foreign Ministry) to Missions, 16 Nov. 1933, DGFP, series C, *2*, no. 70; memorandum, undated, DGFP, series C, *2*, no. 81.

69. Memorandum, undated, DGFP, series C, *2*, no. 77.

70. Moltke to Foreign Ministry, 28 Nov. 1933, DGFP, series C, *2*, no. 90.

that, despite an obvious desire for closer relations with Germany, the Polish leaders were in no hurry to make decisive moves.[71]

The larger context of this frank exchange gives the conversation a special significance. Unlike Moltke, who was a carryover from the Weimar period, Rauschning in Pilsudski's eyes represented Germany's new line. His policy in Danzig, which Hitler had doubtless authorized, and his genuine interest in conciliation presumably reflected German policy. Pilsudski, who could not have overlooked Rauschning's sincerity, was thus persuaded of the wisdom of friendship with Germany which would enable the Polish government, now estranged from its ally France, to pursue its own independent foreign policy. What Pilsudski did not know was that, beyond a certain similarity in immediately desired effects, Hitler's policy diverged from Rauschning's to an extent that Rauschning himself did not properly understand.

On 16 December discussions of the German draft began. They continued throughout the month. On 9 January Lipski submitted a revised draft to Neurath with the announcement that Poland was ready to sign at any time. By 22 January the Poles and the Legal Department of the Foreign Ministry had agreed on the final version, and two days later Bülow informed the major embassies that signature was imminent. The accord, he reassured them, was essentially nothing more "than an express confirmation of the Kellogg Pact for the relations between Germany and Poland." [72]

The German-Polish Declaration of Nonaggression, signed at Berlin on 26 January, proclaimed that both governments intended "to reach direct understanding" on common disputes and would in no case "proceed to use force in order to settle

71. Moltke to Foreign Ministry, 13 Dec. 1933, PA: Reichsminister, 55, Bd. 2 (3015H/D598307–08); Aufzeichnung über den Besuch Rauschnings in Warschau am 11. und 12. Dezember 1933, PA: Po 3, Danzig Geh., Bd. 5 (6601H/E495071–77); Rauschning, *Die Revolution,* pp. 407–08.

72. Memorandums by Neurath, 16 Dec. 1933 and 9 Jan. 1934, DGFP, series C, *2,* nos. 131, 168; memorandums by Gaus, 16 and 22 Jan. 1934, DGFP, series C, *2,* nos. 186, 203; Bülow to Missions, 24 Jan. 1934, DGFP, series C, *2,* no. 211.

such disputes." A "new phase" would thereby be opened in relations between the two countries.[73]

For diverse reasons Pilsudski, Beck, Hitler, and Rauschning were pleased with the Declaration. It represented the first major victory for Poland's policy of political independence and great-power politics. It released Poland from fear of the Weimar Republic's pro-Russian policy and guaranteed the security of her western frontiers. To Pilsudski it was a coup which sealed good neighborly relations before Germany had become fully re-armed.[74]

For Rauschning the Declaration represented the logical development of his policy of conciliation and the beginning of a permanent détente. Under his auspices Danzig reached further accords with Poland and generally adjusted itself to the interests of the Polish economy. The Poles, for their part, did not interfere with nazification in Danzig. Indeed, Geneva was treated to the unprecedented spectacle of Poland supporting Danzig in disputes about its internal policy before the League Council.

In the German Foreign Ministry the Declaration met with little favor. To be sure, officials of the Ministry had helped draw up the document. But the reorientation of eastern policy, which damaged the cause of revisionism as they understood it, aroused no enthusiasm. Whether after the ten years of German-Polish amity which the agreement foresaw the public and the powers could again be persuaded of the need for revision was a moot question. The Ministry intimated what was indeed the case: the Weimar policy of revision was dead.

For Hitler, German-Polish understanding was a triumph. The accord was a shrewd blow against France's eastern alliance system: Polish rapprochement with Germany was accompanied by *distancement* from France. Though the Franco-Polish agreements did not lapse officially, the Poles and the French had lost confidence in one another. Hitler had achieved his first signal success in foreign policy, removed the danger of unwanted military conflict in the East, and opened the way to

73. Declaration of Non-Aggression and Understanding Between Germany and Poland, DGFP, series C, *2*, no. 219.
74. Laroche, pp. 150–51, 159.

uninterrupted rearmament. An agreement with Poland, he confided to Rauschning early in 1934, would have "a purely temporary significance. I have no intention of maintaining a serious friendship." [75]

75. Rauschning, *Hitler Speaks,* p. 123.

CHAPTER 7

Danzig and German Foreign Policy

The revision of the boundaries which the Versailles Treaty had established in the East was a constant concern of German foreign policy throughout the Weimar period. It was one of the few objectives on which all major political parties agreed. At the very outset of the period the Free City of Danzig was chosen to play a special role in the attempt to gain revision. Geographically, it constituted more than half of the landstrip along the Baltic which connected East Prussia with the Reich; the rest lay in the Corridor. Unique among the ceded areas, Danzig had not been incorporated into Poland and subjected to Polish de-germanization. It remained open to intervention and influence from the Reich and consequently could be maintained indisputably German, and its new status, which had been forced upon it, was generally acknowledged as a transgression of the right of self-determination. The Germans concluded quite correctly that, in their case for the retrocession of the lost areas, they could argue most convincingly for Danzig. And if Danzig were to be returned, they assumed, it would come back with the land that lay within the Corridor, from which the city was economically inseparable. Danzig, therefore, was not an end in itself, but a means by which West Prussia, parts of Posen, and the southern extremity of East Prussia were to be recovered.

The copious support which went to Danzig from the Reich was meant to enable the city to ignore its economic union with Poland and pursue a policy upon which the interests of the Polish state did not impinge. It was meant also to maintain Danzig's irredentism and thus Germany's valid claim to the city and, indirectly, to support the morale of the Germans in the Corridor. "The basic task of everyone who believes in a resurrection of Deutschtum in the East," wrote Dirksen in 1924, "is the firm support of Danzig's Deutschtum." [1] Germany's ma-

---

1. Dirksen to Foreign Ministry, 8 Dec. 1924, PA: Sch 16, Danzig W, Bd. 2.

terial and moral support fostered among the Danzigers a great willingness to endure difficulty and sacrifice in the hope of future restoration to the Reich. To be sure, the Free City was not unanimously desirous of return at all costs. National sentiment clashed with economic interests. Representatives of the commercial world, as the peacemakers had envisioned, labored to achieve cooperation with their Polish neighbor, so that they might profit from Danzig's new position as Poland's outlet to the sea. The Socialists pursued a conciliatory political course. The Nationalist Senate, however, which governed the city for all but two of the years from 1920 to 1933, and by choice acted in proxy of the Reich, saw to it that the advocates of conciliation gained little influence over official policy. Moreover, during the crucial early years before official policy had acquired an unalterable contour, the state of Poland's economy offered little opportunity for profitable trade, and Danzig's populace was made all the more amenable to German subvention and hardline German revisionism. Danzig was "bought" by German aid; it became a German satellite—an "economic colony," as the president of the Bank of Danzig was to say in 1933.[2] Thus were destroyed whatever hopes a small portion of the citizenry might have entertained for a return to Hanseatic particularism and prosperity. When, in 1932–33, Danzig consented to cooperate with Polish policy, the chance had passed: collaboration would no longer assure prosperity; at best it would buy survival.

Weimar revisionism sought to achieve its aims by peaceful means. Removal of the Corridor by war was impossible. Just how the early ministers of the republic envisioned the actual return of the territories is unclear. The Russo-Polish War of 1920 led them to speculate on the consequences of a Polish defeat in such a conflict, and the idea remained alive until 1925,[3] but they seem never to have thought in terms of concrete possibilities upon which a definite plan could be based. Stresemann, however, had a plan. By renouncing Germany's claims to Alsace-Lorraine and Eupen-Malmédy and guaranteeing France

2. Reichsbank-Direktorium to Foreign Ministry, 3 Oct. 1933, PA: Fi 4, Danzig Geh., Bd. 1 (6204H/E468587–97).

3. Memorandums by Stresemann, 30 Sept. and 2 Oct. 1925, PA: Stresemann Nachlass, Bd. 272 (7129H/H147979–98).

and Belgium against German attack, he hoped to make Germany a party to a community of interests shared among all the western powers. His next step was to convince the western powers that they too had a stake in an issue of vital interest to Germany: the revision of the eastern borders. Once the dispute about the borders had been elevated from a German-Polish problem to a European one and the western powers had been persuaded that its solution would ensure European peace, an international conference could bring about a solution favorable to Germany. An opportunity would present itself when the Polish state fell into such dire distress that territorial reorganization would seem a fair price for rehabilitation. In the meantime Germany would invest great effort in propaganda designed to convince the world that her claims were reasonable, she would resist all premature and partial solutions of the problem and she would reject out of hand any French or Polish attempts to induce her to recognize her eastern border.

For about twelve months in 1925–26 it seemed that the time was at hand: Poland's economy was at the point of dissolution. In June 1925 the Germans had refused to renew an agreement, dating from 1922, which had committed Germany to import from Poland duty-free a number of items, notably a monthly quota of 500,000 tons of coal. When, in response, Warsaw decreed restrictions on imports from those countries which restricted the entry of Polish goods, Germany retaliated with prohibitive import tariffs. Thus, without really having planned it, Germany and Poland found themselves in a trade war. In the following months it became manifest that Poland was disintegrating. In 1924 she had sent 43.2 percent of her total exports to Germany; this market could not be closed without repercussions. The Polish economy sank into depression, and unemployment and unrest spread throughout the land. More seriously, the new zloty currency, already sick, fell drastically. Trade talks with Germany dragged on without prospect of settlement. Poland's attempts to float loans in western Europe and the United States met with little success. Control of the situation was visibly slipping from the hands of the parliamentary government.[4]

4. Rauscher (Warsaw) to Foreign Ministry, 30 Dec. 1925, PA: Reichsminister, 69, Bd. 5 (3177H/D689829–33).

Dirksen of the Foreign Ministry's Eastern Department speculated in November 1925 that the deterioration in Poland's
economy might bring her to the brink of revolution. Germany
should promote her decline. It was known that the British were
contemplating the financial stabilization of Poland and that
Germany would be asked to contribute to the loan. Germany
would participate in such a venture only if it entailed territorial
concessions, and at the moment Poland was not yet reduced to
the point that she would be willing to exchange land for rehabilitation.[5] Ulrich Rauscher, the German minister in Warsaw,
dissented. He believed that, given the support which Poland
enjoyed in France, financial pressure, however strong, could
never force her to part with the Corridor. The Reich should
contribute to an international financial rehabilitation even if political questions were excluded. Germany could exact as a
condition that Poland cut her military expenditures and thus
her army. With little army she would be much less attractive
to France. Having been "reduced *politically* at Locarno," she
would be "reduced *militarily*. The third step, the *territorial* reduction, for which the first two were essential preconditions,
must remain for a more distant future." [6]

Dirksen and the Foreign Ministry were unimpressed. "A
financial reconstruction without a political reconstruction is
no reconstruction at all." [7] Stresemann instructed his embassies
in London and Washington to sabotage Poland's appeals for
credit by stressing to the banking houses the risks involved in
aiding a bankrupt country whose eventual stability depended
entirely upon lasting cooperation from Germany.[8]

An unexpected reaction came from Great Britain. Acting
without official instructions, Dufour-Feronce, the counselor of
the German embassy in London, had spoken to Montagu
Norman, governor of the Bank of England, about the possi-

5. Aufzeichnung über Fragen der deutschen Polenpolitik, 16 Nov.
1925, PA: Staatssekretär, Po, Bd. 1 (4569H/E168406–15).
6. Memorandum, 19 Nov. 1925, PA: Staatssekretär, Po, Bd. 1
(4569H/E168398–405).
7. Memorandum by Dirksen, 4 Mar. 1926, PA: Staatssekretär, Po,
Bd. 1 (4569H/E168519–23).
8. Embassy Washington to Foreign Ministry, 29 Dec. 1925, and Embassy London to Foreign Ministry, 2 Jan. 1926, PA: Reichsminister, 10,
Bd. 4 (2945H/E571957–59).

bility of combining a financial rehabilitation of Poland with a territorial settlement. He told Norman that Schacht, president of the Reichsbank, was prepared to proffer German funds if Britain were willing to attach this condition to her offer. Dufour also suggested a conditional loan to Sir William Tyrrell, the permanent undersecretary at the Foreign Office. Tyrrell found that the idea had merits. Of course Poland would have to be provided with access to the sea, but this did not necessarily mean that she would have to retain the present corridor.[9]

In early April, Norman, who meanwhile had been in close touch with Tyrrell, informed Dufour of his efforts to persuade American and British financiers not to extend credit to the Poles "until the time was ripe to discuss seriously the Danzig [sic] Corridor question." He appeared convinced that a combined solution of the financial and the frontier questions was in the interest of Europe. Poland's rehabilitation, Norman believed, should be arranged through the League, which would make aid conditional on a settlement of the pending political differences Poland had with her neighbor. Dufour conveyed this information to Berlin.[10]

Stresemann's response was cautious. While he welcomed the interest of influential British circles in the frontier problem and their appreciation that a "solution . . . was not only the most important task of German policy, but perhaps the most important of European politics in general," he warned against hastiness. A solution satisfactory to Germany could be attained only when "Poland's economic and financial distress had become extreme." Moreover, Germany could not hope to gain her point at an international conclave until her position vis-à-vis the west-

9. Embassy London to Foreign Ministry, 1 Mar. 1926, PA: Staatssekretär, Po, Bd. 1 (4569H/E168585–93); memorandum by Dufour-Feronce, 19 Mar. 1926, PA: ibid. (4569H/E169606–14). Dufour was reproved by the Foreign Ministry for his initiative. He admitted not having received instructions but said in his defense that private conversations with Dirksen had led him to believe he was acting in the interest of the German government. Dufour to Dirksen, 22 Apr. 1926, PA: ibid. (4569H/E168675–76).

10. Embassy London to Foreign Ministry, 25 Mar. 1926, PA: Staatssekretär, Po, Bd. 1 (4569H/E168619); memorandum by Dufour-Feronce, 8 Apr. 1926, PA: ibid. (4569H/E168640–49).

ern powers was considerably improved. At the moment an international rehabilitation scheme, which Stresemann hoped and believed unlikely, could produce only an inadequate solution, which would prejudice the possibilities of a full settlement. Germany therefore should proceed with utmost caution and her representatives should display no initiative, even in private conversation. In the unlikely event that Great Britain should undertake now to rehabilitate Poland, Germany could not withhold assistance. She could not afford to appear as saboteur. But she should use her influence in keeping the loan minimal.[11]

Stresemann's fear that the favor and respect which Germany commanded among the western powers was not sufficient to ensure a cordial reception of her wishes was well-founded. In May the German ambassador in London reported that the British Foreign Office, which, for the sake of German-Polish relations, wanted Germany to contribute to a financial transaction, had made clear that the Germans were not to expect that finance and borders could be linked. Modification of the boundaries would have to be reserved for a later time.[12] Shortly thereafter Montagu Norman changed his position. On 27 May he informed Schacht that the Federal Reserve Bank of New York was seriously considering a loan to Poland and that, after due reflection, he thought no conditions should be attached. Schacht's reply, that Poland could not recuperate as long as she remained at odds with her neighbor, did not alter the decision.[13]

Despite lively German opposition, especially from Schacht, and without German participation, a credit of $62 million plus £2 million was extended to Poland in October 1927. The loan greatly enhanced Polish finances, and it accelerated the improvement in the economy which had begun the previous year when the general strike in Britain opened new markets for Poland's coal and other industrial products. Politics too returned to stability after Pilsudski's coup in May 1926.

11. Stresemann to Embassy London, 19 Apr. 1926, PA: Stresemann Nachlass, Bd. 350 (7414H/H175393–99).
12. Embassy London to Foreign Ministry, 21 May 1926, PA: Po 2, Polen Geh., Bd. 9 (K170/K026285).
13. Memorandum by Schacht, 28 May 1926, PA: Reichsminister, 10, Bd. 5 (2945H/E572263–67).

The opportunity for financial blackmail had passed. Realizing this, Germany abandoned her intransigence about the terms of a new trade agreement with Poland. In December 1926, State Secretary Schubert had remarked to Zaleski, the Polish foreign minister, that relations between their respective countries would not return to normal until the frontier problem had been solved.[14] In the autumn of 1927, however, the Foreign Ministry directed that the trade negotiations be resumed. In March 1930, after Stresemann's death, they concluded in a new agreement, which Curtius initialed. The resumption of trade, Curtius told the Reichstag Committee on Foreign Affairs, did not alter the Reich's policy toward Poland in the least: economic agreements had no effect upon the attempt at revision.[15] It was true. In 1931, when Germany was considering a customs union with Austria, Bülow argued that such an arrangement would isolate Poland and expose "her unstable economic structure . . . to all kinds of dangers: we would have her in a vise, and this sooner or later might put her in a state of mind to consider further the idea of exchanging political concessions for tangible economic benefits." [16]

In abandoning his intransigence toward Poland in 1927, Stresemann introduced a tactical, not a strategic, change in Germany's policy. As soon as it became clear that in this instance Poland could not be reduced to suppliance, he sought to preserve the other precondition of his plan, the favor and respect of the western powers. Germany could not afford to appear hostile eastward and friendly westward; she must seem peaceful and well-intentioned toward all.[17] Because the realization of his plan posited a combination of favorable circumstances which Germany could not altogether control, urgency did not promise success. Revision was a long-term objective.

But even if Stresemann had realized his combination of favor-

14. Memorandum by Schubert, 10 Dec. 1926, PA: Staatssekretär, Po, Bd. 2 (4569H/E168905–09).

15. Stichworte für die Rede des Reichsministers im Auswärtigen Ausschuss zum deutsch-polnischen Wirtschaftsabkommen, 10 July 1930, PA: Reichsminister, 10, Bd. 12 (2945H/E575189–92).

16. Bülow to Legation Prague, 19 Apr. 1931, PA: Staatssekretär, Pol B, Bd. 4 (4620/E199512–15).

17. *Vermächtnis, 3,* 230.

able circumstances, if Poland had fallen into economic and political chaos at a time when Germany enjoyed great prestige
among the western powers, it is questionable that Germany
could have attained her objectives. The British, to be sure, did
not seem opposed to revisionism; they sympathized entirely with Germany's desire to preserve in her treaties a distinction between her eastern and western frontiers. The Americans also exhibited pro-German sentiments, and even in France,
Germany's propaganda and diplomacy had convinced a substantial minority of the injustice and political impossibility of
the eastern settlement. But the German foreign ministers vastly
overestimated the potential of this sentiment if they thought
that by exploiting it they could gain an international conference's approval for actual alteration of the frontiers. The temper
of the United States was more isolationist than interventionist,
and Britain was reluctant to interfere in affairs on the continent.
While she may not have had a stake in the preservation of the
German-Polish borders, neither did she have a vested interest
in their modification. France, as her sharp reaction in 1931 to
the proposed Austro-German customs union showed, was unlikely to become less wary of developments in the East, no matter how ardently the Germans guaranteed her security. In de-
vising her scheme of an international conference Germany had
failed to make due allowance for the very simplest axiom of
all foreign policy: that every power will interpret any relevant
international development primarily in terms of its own interests
and will act in the interest of another party only if the interests
of both countries coincide or complement one another. Unless
Germany convinced the powers that her problems in the East
constituted a real threat to European peace, her grievances, be
they ever so justified, were in the last analysis a matter of no
imminent concern.

And again—even if the Germans had succeeded in bringing
the western powers together at a conference, the Poles in all
likelihood would never have acquiesced in a scheme which
exacted territorial concessions in return for a loan. The Polish
government never even toyed with the possibility of bargaining
with its territory. "It is our deepest conviction," wrote Strasburger, Polish commissioner general in Danzig during 1924–32,

"that the loss of Danzig would not only not be a momentary respite [in revisionism], but would be followed shortly by the loss of Pomerelia and, in consequence, of Poland's independence."[18] Poland considered expropriation a threat to her national security and was prepared to resist with arms, as the *Wicher* episode of June 1932 amply evidenced. The western powers would have been unwilling to urge a settlement which traded a "threat to the peace," as the Germans called the Corridor, for war itself.

Weimar revisionism was indeed in a dilemma. Speaking to the assembled prime ministers of the German *Länder* in November 1925, Chancellor Hans Luther had declared that a peaceable alteration of the frontiers could not be accomplished without cooperation from the Poles.[19] Perhaps unwittingly, he put his finger on the central problem, the disparity between the practice and the realities of German revisionism. But the Foreign Ministry, especially after Stresemann, steadfastly ignored these realities. It refused moreover to acknowledge that the Germans were losing their own argument as they themselves defined it. Dufour-Feronce, who had left his post in London to assume a high office in the Secretariat of the League, expressed his frustration in 1928: "In the Corridor question time works against, not for us. The number of Germans in the Corridor dwindles steadily and the number of Poles increases. If this persists, the Corridor will become entirely Polish and our ethnographic arguments will come to nought."[20] By 1930 ethnic arguments had lost their basis, and when Gdynia was completed and Polish traffic diverted to that port, the Free City had lost its raison d'être. In January 1931 the press in both France and Britain urged that Danzig be restored to the Reich. The very suggestion completely missed the point the Germans hoped to make. The whole clamor about Danzig was meant to imply much more than Danzig alone. The Germans, however, could not admit that they had perforce forfeited this point. In March 1931 Curtius wrote his diplomats that neither the predominance of

18. Henryk Strasburger in *Ostland-Berichte* (1937), p. 15.
19. Quoted in Höltje, p. 181.
20. Dufour-Feronce to Foreign Ministry, 16 July 1928, PA: Referat Völkerbund: Deutschland-Polen-Danzig, Bd. 9.

Poles in the Corridor nor the existence of Gdynia impinged upon Germany's claims.[21] Perhaps not. But they destroyed the argument by which Germany hoped to realize these claims. Danzig and the Corridor were no longer inseparable. The Weimar policy of revision was dead long before the Germans realized it.

It had become a doctrine, as antirevisionism was doctrine to the Poles. Because it was doctrine, to impugn it was heresy. Thus it retained intact all the features which Stresemann had devised at a time when it was not yet patent that the methods of the policy could never attain its end. The firm rejection of any interim or partial solutions, based on the reasoning that such might prejudge the future, blocked all possibility of attenuating present grievances. The foreign ministers and their staffs were content simply to vilify the present arrangement while they speculated about and waited for "the proper economic and political conditions." In time the mere claim for undivided and undiminished title to the eastern territories became more important than the achievement of more modest, and realistic, aims.[22] Incapable of realizing its demands, the Foreign Ministry, by rejecting whatever seemed incompatible with its claims, preserved the pretense that its plan retained real possibilities of fruition.

Ulrich Rauscher, who represented Germany in Warsaw from 1922 to 1930, was as troubled as any patriotic German about the lost territories and as eager for their return. But his experience in Poland led him to recognize the futility of Weimar revisionism. In June 1926, after the financial rehabilitation scheme had broken down, he wrote Berlin that, in his opinion, Poland would never reach a state of impoverishment and need of rehabilitation sufficient to induce her to exchange territory for solvency. The Corridor "will return to the Reich only in consequence of a war and the concomitant political convulsions in Poland, never as an outcome of even the most logical and convincing economic ideas." [23] Dirksen misunderstood these re-

21. Curtius to Missions, 7 Mar. 1931, PA: Po 2G, Polen, Bd. 2 (L575/L185481–98).

22. Broszat, *Polenpolitik*, p. 174.

23. Rauscher to Foreign Ministry, 11 June 1926, PA: Staatssekretär,

marks and reproved Rauscher for advocating a forcible solution.[24] But Rauscher did not wish to suggest that Germany
attack Poland. He meant to imply that only a war, whether
civil or with a foreign power, would produce the chaos necessary
to part Poland from her land. For the moment the prospect for
such a war was remote. Therefore revisionism as Germany
pursued it was senseless—and, by implication, should be discarded—inasmuch as continuing revisionist agitation simply perpetuated German-Polish tensions. Normal relations between the
two countries would be economically advantageous and might
permit Germany to exercise some influence over Poland's internal affairs.[25] But Rauscher, who offered the only reasonable
approach to the problem, was not heeded, and neither were
similar voices from among the Socialist and Center parties.[26]

After 1930 revisionism seriously beclouded Germany's relations with the western powers. Between Locarno and the
depression Germany had found sympathy for her claims abroad
and, encouraged at this response, had intensified her propaganda.
When the depression introduced a serious strain on international
relations, Germany's revisionism came to be regarded as an
unnecessary compounding of more urgent difficulties. In Geneva
the barrage of complaints from Danzig and the German minority
in Poland, a tactic pursued particularly crassly and transparently
after Stresemann's death, succeeded only in inspiring the wish to
banish such questions from the Council. When German-Polish
relations deteriorated after 1930 into overt provocations and
rumors of war, Europe suspected Germany of warmongering.
Thus the western powers not only withdrew their sympathy for
Germany's grievances—they came to resent and to fear the
constant clamor from the Reich.

Finally, doctrinaire revisionism had a grave effect upon Ger-

Po, Bd. 2 (4569H/E168771–78); memorandum by Rauscher, 19 Nov.
1925, PA: Staatssekretär, Po, Bd. 1 (4569H/E168400–04).

24. Dirksen to Rauscher, 15 June 1926, PA: Handakten Direktoren:
Wallroth, Polen, Politik (5265H/E321188–209).

25. Rauscher to Bülow, 13 Aug. 1930, PA: Reichsminister, 10, Bd.
12 (2945H/E575226–29).

26. *Sozialistische Monatshefte* (1930); *Vorwärts,* 11 Jan. 1931; memorandum by Dirksen, 21 Mar. 1927, PA: Staatssekretär, Po, Bd. 3
(4569H/E168975–77).

many herself. The official propaganda for domestic consumption was a double-edged sword. It assured any government that its revisionist policy would command broad strata of support, and this popular response in turn obliged every government to adhere faithfully to revisionism. Any attempt at conciliation in the East would have been a betrayal of the public trust. Even when it sensed that popular expectation had far outpaced the possibilities of gratification, the Foreign Ministry chose to cater to this sentiment rather than to moderate it. In the same internal memorandum it could advise that tension with Poland be eased and direct that the global propaganda campaign about border revision be intensified.[27] While it deliberated on how to forestall "the premature activation" of the Danzig question, it could assure the Danzigers in private and public that their deliverance was not relegated to a remote and unknown future. And it made the Locarno Treaties and Germany's membership in the League acceptable to the public by maintaining, contrary to its own better knowledge, that these were diplomatic maneuvers designed to enable the government to arrive at a direct solution of the problem in the East.[28]

The government's exhortations and pledges gave rise to an eastern border lobby.[29] Having incited it, the government could no longer control and restrain it. The lobby demanded tougher propaganda at home and abroad, intransigence toward Poland, and immediate broaching of the question of the borders. The government could not meet these demands, it seemed in fact to be losing leadership in the matter, and the public in its frustration turned to parties which promised satisfaction. The National Socialists were singularly adept at attracting the loyalties of an angry and thwarted public.

Hitler welcomed the frustrated voters, but he was in no hurry

27. Memorandum, dated 1931, PA: Handakten Direktoren: Dirksen, Minderheiten in Polen.
28. Sahm, *Erinnerungen,* p. 125; memorandum, 20 Dec. 1930, BA: R 43 I/550.
29. Höltje, pp. 127–30; memorandum by Geyl, 15 Jan. 1931, PA: Handakten Direktoren: Trautmann, Danzig, Allgemein (5551H/E388632–33); Denkschrift über die Ostfragen, April 1929, BA: R 43 I/124; Das Korridor Problem, September 1930, PA: Po 2G, Polen, Bd. 2 (L575/L185468–80); Sahm, pp. 157, 169.

to gratify their cravings. Aware that Weimar revisionism automatically evoked Polish hostility and eager to assuage the Poles for his own reasons, he could break, even over the opposition of the Foreign Ministry, a policy with which he was in no way identified. Break it he did, not because he intended to reconcile himself to a situation which the Weimar politicians had not been able to change, but because he intended to change this situation while accomplishing a larger purpose. Having secured peace in the East, he consolidated his power and rearmed. When he turned to the East again he sought expansion. In 1939 Danzig once more became the focal point of European tension. The phenomenon of a German city beyond the boundaries of the Reich was proclaimed intolerable. An outcome of the First World War, the Free City of Danzig constituted the grievance which ostensibly produced the second.

Bibliography

PA = Politisches Archiv, Foreign Ministry, Bonn
BA = Bundesarchiv, Koblenz
LN = Archives of the Secretariat of the League of Nations,
    Library of the European Office of the United Nations, Geneva

Primary Sources
  Archival Sources
    1. Politisches Archiv

Abteilung IA

WK	Der Weltkrieg, vols. 292–97, 1919–22
WK Geh.	Der Weltkrieg, vols. 40–44, 1918–19
WK Nr. 2	Friedensstimmungen und Aktionen zur Vermittlung des Friedens, vols. 85–89, 1918–20
WK Nr. 2 Geh.	Friedensstimmungen und Aktionen zur Vermittlung des Friedens, vols. 63–66, 1918–20
WK Nr. 15	Material zu den Friedensverhandlungen, vol. 29, 1918
WK Nr. 15 Geh.	Material zu den Friedensverhandlungen, vols. 5–6, 1918–19
WK Nr. 20c	Die Zukunft der besetzten Gebiete: Polen, vols. 43–75, 1918–20
WK Nr. 20c Geh.	Die Zukunft der besetzten Gebiete: Polen, vols. 26–27, 1918–20
WK Nr. 30	Waffenstillstands- und Friedensverhandlungen, vols. 1–59, 1918–20
WK Nr. 30 Geh.	Waffenstillstands- und Friedensverhandlungen, 1919
WK Nr. 31	Die Friedenskonferenz von Versailles, vols. 1–12, 1919–20
WK Nr. 31 Geh.	Die Friedenskonferenz von Versailles, 1919
WK Nr. 31 Nr. 1	Zukunft Ost- und Westpreussens, 1919–20

Auswärtiges Amt, Weimar

III.4	Polen, 1919
IV.3	Polnische Frage, 1918–19
IV.13	Ausführung des Friedensvertrages, 1919

Friedensabteilung

F.P. Danzig a	Politische Fragen, Allgemeines, 1919–20
F.P. Danzig b	Räumung, 1919
F.P. Danzig c	Grenzführung, 1919
F.P. Danzig d	Grenzkommission, 1919
F.P. Danzig e	Abstimmung, 1919
F.P. Danzig f	Übergabe von Archiven und Staatseigentum, 1919
F.P. Danzig g	Beamtenfragen, 1919
F.P. Danzig h	Schutz religiöser und anderer deutscher Minoritäten, 1919
F.P. Danzig i	Militär- und Polizeifragen, 1919
F.W. 24	Finanzfragen, Danzig
F.W. 44	Wirtschaftsfragen, Danzig
F.W. 44c	Wirtschaftsabkommen, Danzig
F.W. 57f	Zölle, Danzig
F.R.	Staatseigentum, Danzig

Friedensvertrag

IV Po FV 2 Danzig	Grenzsachen
IV Po FV 3 Danzig	Politische Bestimmungen über Danzig
IV Po FV 8 Nr. 2 Danzig	Wiedergutmachung

Deutsche Friedensdelegation Versailles

Pol 2a	Gesammelte Protokolle der Sitzungen der Friedensdelegation, 1919
Pol 8a	Polen, 1919
Pol 8s	Freistadt Danzig

Deutsche Delegation Danzig

Tätigkeit der Danziger Grenzkommission

Handakten Simons

VI	Regelung der Ostfragen, 1919

Handakten Legationsrat Forster

Danzig, 1919
Grenzgebiete, 1919

Nachlass Brockdorff-Rantzau

Als Aussenminister, 1918–19

Büro Reichsminister

Ic Nr. 1	Aufzeichnungen des Reichsministers, 1929–35
3b	Kabinett-Protokolle
10	Polen, 1920–35
12	Preussen, 1920–24
18	Völkerbund, 1920–35
31	Friedensvertrag 1920–30
55	Danzig, 1920–35
68	Aufzeichnungen über die auswärtige Lage, 1921–22
69	Informatorische Aufzeichnungen, 1921–30
P.A.	Politische Schriftstücke aus dem Nachlass des Reichsministers Stresemann, 1923–29
RM 7	Ausführung des Friedensvertrags, 1920–33
RM 8	Beziehungen zu ausländischen Staaten, 1920–35

Büro Staatssekretär

B Pol	Deutsch-polnische Wirtschaftsverhandlungen, 1927–30
B Pol	Verhandlungen mit Polen über den Abschluss eines Handelsvertrags, 1926–30
NM	Nationale Minderheiten, 1925–29
O	Ostprobleme (Russland, Polen, Danzig), 1924–26
Po	Polnische Angelegenheiten, 1925–30
Poda	Angelegenheiten der Freien Stadt Danzig, 1926–30
Vögen	Völkerbund, 1923–29
Vötag	Völkerbund-Tagungen, 1926–30
Pol A	Briefe in politischen Angelegenheiten, 1930–36
Pol B	Schriftwechsel Staatssekretär mit Beamten des auswärtigen Dienstes, 1930–36

Abteilung IV Politik

Po 1, Polen	Allgemeine auswärtige Politik, 1920–36
Po 2, Polen	Politische Beziehungen Polens zu Deutschland, 1920–34
Po 2G, Polen	Das polnische Grenzproblem, Propaganda, 1927–34
Po 2G Nr. 2, Polen	Revision der Ostgrenzen, Korridorproblem, 1931–33
Po 4, Völkerbund	Zwischenstaatliche aussenpolitische Probleme—Völkerbund, 1920–34
Po 25, Polen	Deutschtum im Ausland, 1920–34
Po 1, Danzig	Allgemeine auswärtige Politik, 1920–35
Po 2, Danzig	Politische Beziehungen Danzigs zu Deutschland, 1920–35
Po 2B, Danzig	Überleitungswesen, 1920–27
Po 3, Danzig	Politische Beziehungen zwischen Danzig und Polen, 1920–34
Po 5, Danzig	Innere Politik, Parlaments- und Parteiwesen, 1920–34
Po 12, Danzig	Pressewesen, 1933–34
Po 25, Danzig	Deutschtum im Ausland, 1920–36
Po 26, Danzig	Politische und kulturelle Propaganda, 1922–34

Abteilung IV Wirtschaft

Allg. 3, Danzig W	Allgemeines, 1929–34
Fi 1, Danzig W	Staatsfinanzen im Allgemeinen, 1920–36
Fi 2, Danzig W	Anleihen, Wertpapiere, 1920–36
H 11, Danzig W	Handelsbeziehungen zu Deutschland, 1920–36
H 11 Nr. 1, Danzig W	Ein- Aus- und Durchfuhr, Allgemeines und Grundsätzliches, 1920–36
H 11 Nr. 3, Danzig W	Austauschgeschäfte, Wirtschaftsabkommen, 1920–23
H 12, Danzig W	Danzig/Russland
I 3, Danzig W	Industrielle Beziehungen Danzigs zu Deutschland, 1922–32
Sch 16, Danzig W	Häfen, 1920–36
Sch 16 Westerplatte, Danzig W	Danzig-polnischer Konflikt wegen Verstärkung der Westerplatte Besatzung, 1933
Wi 2, Danzig W	Abbau der Kriegswirtschaft, 1920–22

Wi 7, Danzig W	Wirtschaftsbeziehungen zwischen Danzig und Polen, 1921–34
Z 9, Danzig W	Zollbeziehungen Danzig/Polen, 1920–34

Abteilung IV Geheim

II FS. 15	Besprechung mit der Marineleitung über Danzig (Studie Ost), 1930–31
H 13, Polen Geh.	Handelsvertragsverhältnis Polens zu Deutschland, 1930
Po 1, Polen Geh.	Allgemeine auswärtige Politik, 1920–33
Po 2, Polen Geh.	Politische Beziehungen Polens zu Deutschland, 1920–35
Po 2E, Polen Geh.	Programm für die deutschen Ostgebiete, 1929–33
Po 2G, Polen Geh.	Das deutsch-polnische Grenzproblem, 1932–33
Po 2H, Polen Geh.	Abkommen mit Polen über den Verzicht auf Anwendung von Gewalt zur Lösung von Streitfragen, 1933–35
Po 25, Polen Geh.	Deutschtum im Ausland, 1920–36
Wi 6, Polen Geh.	Wirtschaftliche Beziehungen Polens zu Deutschland, 1924–34
Fi 1, Danzig Geh.	Staatsfinanzen im Allgemeinen, 1926–35
Fi 2, Danzig Geh.	Anleihen, Wertpapiere, 1920–28
Fi 3, Danzig Geh.	Finanzielle Beziehungen Danzigs zu Deutschland, 1921–36
Fi 4, Danzig Geh.	Finanzielle Beziehungen zwischen Danzig und Polen, 1933–35
H 11 Nr. 1, Danzig Geh.	Handelsbeziehungen zu Deutschland, 1925–34
H 11 Nr. 3, Danzig Geh.	Austauschgeschäfte, Wirtschaftsabkommen, 1922–24
H 13, Danzig Geh.	Handelsverhältnis zu Deutschland, 1924–29
Po 2, Danzig Geh.	Politische Beziehungen Danzigs zu Deutschland, 1923–36
Po 3, Danzig Geh.	Politische Beziehungen zwischen Danzig und Polen, 1922–36
Po 5, Danzig Geh.	Innere Politik Danzigs, 1927–36
Po 11 Nr. 1, Danzig Geh.	Personalien: Oberkommissar, 1920–36
Po 13, Danzig Geh.	Militärangelegenheiten, 1923–33

Po 25, Danzig Geh.   Deutschtum im Ausland, 1926–33
Po 25, Danzig Geh.   Kredite, 1925–36
Sch 4, Danzig Geh.   Schiffbau, 1920–36
Sch 16, Danzig Geh. Häfen, 1920–35
Sch 16 port   Häfen in Danzig, 1926–35
  d'attache,
  Danzig Geh.
Sch 16 port   Häfen in Danzig, 1932–35
  d'attache A,
  Danzig Geh.
Sch 16 Wester-   Häfen in Danzig, 1927–35
  platte,
  Danzig Geh.
Sch 16 Wester-   Danzig-polnischer Konflikt wegen Ver-
  platte A,   stärkung der polnischen militärischen
  Danzig Geh.   Besatzung der Westerplatte, 1933
Sch 16 A,   Benachteiligung Danzigs durch den pol-
  Danzig Geh.   nischen Hafen Gdingen, 1929–36
So 1 Nr. 1,   Sozialversicherung, 1920–36
  Danzig Geh.
So 2, Danzig Geh.   Arbeiterfragen, 1930–36
Wi 1, Danzig Geh.   Allgemeine wirtschaftliche Lage, 1920–
                     36
Wi 1 Nr. 1,   Periodische wirtschaftliche Berichte,
  Danzig Geh.   1928–34
Wi 6, Danzig Geh.   Wirtschaftliche Beziehungen Danzigs zu
                     Deutschland, 1925–35
Wi 7, Danzig Geh.   Wirtschaftsbeziehungen zwischen Danzig
                     und Polen, 1932–34
Z, Danzig Geh.   Zollbeziehungen zwischen Danzig und
                     Polen, 1927–35

Abteilung VI—Kulturpolitik

Deutschtum im   Allgemeines, 1920–34
  Ausland
Deutschtum im   Danzig, 1921–36
  Ausland
Kultur Generalia   Danzig, 1929–37
Minderheiten   Danzig, 1929–38

Referat Deutschland

Po 5n   Ost- und Westpreussen, Danzig, 1920–28
Po 25   Grenzlandsdeutschtum, 1920–33

Referat Völkerbund
Ratstagungen, 1920–34
Deutschland, 1919–33
Polen, 1920–36
Deutschland-Polen-Danzig, 1920–36

Deutsche Delegation in Genf, 1930–32
4/2   Danzig-Gdingen, Ratssitzung, 1932
4/4   Ostpolitik, Allgemeines

Handakten der Direktoren
(a) Vortragender Legationsrat Zechlin
     Generalia, 1919
(b) Ministerialdirektor Wallroth
     Polen, Politik, 1924–28
     Polen, Wirtschaft, 1927–28
     Danzig/Oberschlesien, 1927
(c) Ministerialdirektor Dirksen
     Polen, Propagandamaterial, 1925–26
     Polen, Deutschtum: Allgemeines, 1920–28
     Polen, Deutschtums-Stützung, 1927–28
     Polen, Hilfsaktion Danzig, 1925–26
     Polen, Danzig-Stützung, 1927–28
     Polen, Sahm-Gaus, 1927–28
     Polen, Danzig: Allgemeines, 1927–28
     Polen, Völkerbund, 1927–28
     Polen, Völkerbundsrat und Polen, 1926
     Polen, Korridorgespräche, 1928
     Polen, Korridorpropaganda, 1928
     Polen, Völkerbundssachen Danzig, 1925–28
     Polen, Korridor, 1925–26
     Polen, Schichau, 1928
     Danzig, Klagerecht der Eisenbahner, 1927–28
     Danzig, Westerplatte I, 1922–27
     Danzig, Westerplatte II, 1927
     Danzig, Westerplatte III, 1927
     Danzig, Port d'attache, 1921–27
     Danzig, Generalia I, 1926–27
     Danzig, Generalia II, 1927–28
     Danzig, Spezialfälle, 1924–27
     Geheimsachen, 1927–30
     Politische Aufzeichnungen, 1925–28
     Polen, Minderheiten in Polen, 1922–30

(d) Ministerialdirektor Trautmann
     Danzig, Allgemein, 1931
     Danzig, Material für die Völkerbunds-Ratstagung, 1931
     Danzig, Korridorfrage, 1928–31
     Danzig, Gdingen, 1931
     Ostpreussen, 1926–28
     Ost-Programm, Ost-Kredite, 1930
     Polen, Politik Allgemein, 1928–31
(e) Ministerialdirektor Meyer
     Danzig, 1931
     Danzig, 66. Ratstagung des Völkerbunds, 1932
     Russland, Ukraine, Danzig, Oberschlesien, Polen, 1920–33
     Danzig: Finanzen und Währung, 1932–35
     Danzig: Politisches, 1921–38

Handakten Ritter

Polen, 1930–36

Handakten Eckardt

17   Abkommen über Danzig

Nachlass Edgar Haniel von Haimshausen

Briefe politischen Inhalts, 1920–23
Tagesberichte der Ländergruppen II–VII, 1920
Aufzeichnungen aus Versailles, 1919

Nachlass Stresemann

Allgemeine Akten, 1923–29
Politische Akten, 1923–29
Aus dem Nachlass Stresemann von Konsul Bernhard dem
    Auswärtigen Amt übergebene Schriftstücke, 1923–30

Deutsche Botschaft Paris

III 1 adh. 7   Danzig, 1933–39
III 1 adh. 7a   Handakten Botschafter Koester: Danzig
                      und Ostfragen, 1933

Deutsche Gesandtschaft Warschau

P 2i   Polens Beziehungen zu Danzig, 1929–35
P 15   Danzig, 1920–34
P 15 Flottenbesuch   Deutscher Flottenbesuch in Danzig,
                      1925–32

P 25   Weichsel, Hela, Gdingen, Westerplatte,
                1921–29
P 25a   Danzigs Klage gegen Polen wegen
                Gdingen
P 25b   Gdingen, Hela, Westerplatte, 1927–33
P 25c   Danzig-polnische Vereinbarung über den
                port d'attache, 1925–34

Deutsches Generalkonsulat Danzig

I 2   Danzig-polnische Beziehungen, 1932–34
I   Hoher Kommissar des Völkerbunds in
                Danzig: Helmer Rosting, 1932–34
                Besprechungen mit dem Hohen Kom-
                missar, 1933–34

2. Bundesarchiv

Alte Reichskanzlei

R 43 I/1–7   Friedensverhandlungen, 1919
R 43 I/12–42   Ausführungen des Versailler Vertrags,
                    1919–24
R 43 I/117–26   Polen, 1919–33
R 43 I/161–63   Auswärtige Politik, Allgemein, 1919–33
R 43 I/164–65   Waffenstillstandsverhandlungen, 1919–22
R 43 I/344–48   Gebietsabtretungen, Allgemein, 1919–32
R 43 I/374–77   Gebietsabtretungen, Danzig, 1919–33
R 43 I/378–80   Gebietsabtretungen, Westpreussen und
                    Posen, 1919–34
R 43 I/483–96   Völkerbund, 1919–33
R 43 I/506   Revisionspolitik, 1930–31
R 43 I/542–48   Auslandsdeutschtum, 1919–33
R 43 I/549–51   Deutschtum in den abgetretenen Gebie-
                    ten, 1919–34
R 43 I/1324–26   Kabinettsprotokolle, 1918–19
R 43 I/1348–1477   Protokolle: Reichsministerial- und Ka-
                    binettssitzungen, 1919–38
R 43 I/1795–1813   Heimatschutz Ost: Allgemeine Ost- und
                    Grenzfragen, 1919–33
R 43 I/1822–24   Oststelle bei dem Reichskanzler, 1930–34

Reichsfinanzministerium

R 2/19576–77   Danzig: Reichszuschüsse, 1930–34
R 2/19578–79   Überbrückungskredit II, Danzig, 1930–35

R 2/19580–81   Überbrückungskredit III, Danzig, 1932–
                      35

Preussisches Justizministerium

P 135/1388   Ausführung des Friedensvertrages: Pen-
                      sionszahlungen   im   Freistaat   Danzig,
                      1920–34
P 135/1529–30   Ausführung des Friedensvertrages: Dan-
                      zig, Allgemeines, 1919–21
P 135/1541   Ausführung des Friedensvertrages: Dan-
                      zig, Beamtenabkommen, 1920–23

Preussisches Finanzministerium

P 134/255–56   Grenzlandangelegenheiten: Freistaat
                      Danzig, 1929–36

3. League of Nations

Files of the Administrative Commissions Section

4. Private Papers

The Diary of the Work of Sir James Headlam-Morley at the
Paris Peace Conference, 1919
Memorandum (F.O. 12760) by J. W. Headlam-Morley, 4
April 1925, The Eastern Frontiers of Germany, Section II:
Danzig and the Polish Corridor
Both these sources are in the possession of Professor Agnes
Headlam-Morley, St. Hugh's College, Oxford.

Published Sources

1. Documents

Auswärtiges Amt, Geschäftsstelle für die Friedensverhand-
    lungen, *Denkschrift: Entwurf von Bestimmungen für den
    Friedensvertrag über den Zugang Polens zum Meer. Im
    Auftrage des Magistrats der Stadt Danzig von Heinrich
    Sahm,* Berlin, 1919.
Baker, Ray Stannard, *Woodrow Wilson and World Settlement,*
    3 vols. London, 1923.
Brockdorff-Rantzau, Ulrich von, *Deutschlands auswärtige Poli-
    tik,* Berlin, 1919.
Crusen, Georg, *Der Pariser Vertrag vom 9. November 1920,*
    Danzig, 1936.

Deutsches Reich, *Verhandlungen des Reichstags, Stenographische Berichte,* Berlin, 1918–34.

[Dmowski, Roman], *Problems of Central and Eastern Europe,* London, 1917.

Dmowski, Roman, *La question polonaise,* Paris, 1913.

Documents on British Foreign Policy 1919–1939, 1st and 2d series, London, 1946–67.

Documents on German Foreign Policy, series C, vols. 1, 2, London, 1957, 1959.

Forster, Albert, *Das nationalsozialistische Gewissen in Danzig,* Danzig, 1936.

Freie Stadt Danzig, Senat, *Amtliche Urkunden zum Vertrage zwischen der Freien Stadt Danzig und der Republik Polen vom 9. November 1920,* Danzig, 1920.

——, *Bericht über die Verwaltung der Stadt Danzig während der Kriegszeit,* Danzig, 1922.

——, *Collection of Documents Regarding the Application Submitted by the Government of the Free City of Danzig to the High Commissioner of the League of Nations, Danzig, for a Decision in the Matter of Danzig-Gdingen,* Danzig, 1930.

——, *Collection of Documents Relating to the Dispute Between the Free City of Danzig and the Polish Republic Regarding Article 33 of the Treaty Between Danzig and Poland of November 9th, 1920,* Danzig, 1931.

——, *Danzig vor dem Völkerbund. Verhandlungsberichte und amtliche Schriftstücke betr. Danziger Fragen, die während der Tagung des Rats des Völkerbunds erörtert wurden,* 7 vols. Danzig, 1922–34.

——, *Entscheidungen des Hohen Kommissars des Völkerbunds in der Freien Stadt Danzig,* 7 vols. Danzig, 1921–33.

——, *Gesamtübersicht über die Rechtsfolgen der Entscheidungen des Hohen Kommissars aus den Jahren 1921–1933,* Danzig, 1933.

——, *Zusammenstellung der zwischen der Freien Stadt Danzig und der Republik Polen abgeschlossenen Verträge, Abkommen und Vereinbarungen,* 4 vols. Danzig, 1920–34.

Freie Stadt Danzig, Statistisches Landesamt, *Danziger Statistisches Taschenbuch 1933, 1934,* Danzig, 1932, 1934.

——, *Staatshandbuch der Freien Stadt Danzig,* Danzig, 1926.

Heinemann, B., *Zollhandbuch für Polen und Danzig,* 4th ed. Danzig, 1925.

Hitler, Adolf, *Hitlers Zweites Buch,* ed. Gerhard L. Weinberg, Stuttgart, 1961.

————, *Mein Kampf,* Munich, 1933.

————, *Reden und Proklamationen,* ed. Max Domarus, vol. 1, Munich, 1962.

————, *The Speeches of Adolf Hitler,* ed. Norman H. Baynes, 2 vols. London, 1942.

League of Nations, *Official Journal,* 1920–34.

————, *Treaty Series,* vol. 54, Geneva, 1926.

Lewinski, Hermann, Richard Wagner, and Georg Crusen, *Danziger Staats– und Völkerrecht,* 2 vols. Danzig, 1927, 1935.

Luckau, Alma, *The German Delegation at the Paris Peace Conference,* New York, 1941.

Mantoux, Paul, *Les délibérations du Conseil des Quatre (24 mars–28 juin 1919),* 2 vols. Paris, 1955.

Miller, David Hunter, *My Diary at the Conference of Peace,* 21 vols. New York, 1924–26.

Papers Relating to the Foreign Relations of the United States, 1918, 3 vols. Washington, D.C., 1931–32.

Papers Relating to the Foreign Relations of the United States, 1919, The Peace Conference, 13 vols. Washington, D.C., 1942–47.

Permanent Court of International Justice, *Advisory Opinions,* series A/B, nos. 11 (1925), 43 (1931), 44 (1932).

Poland, Commission polonaise des travaux préparatoires au Congrés de la Paix, *Gdansk and East Prussia,* Paris, 1919.

————, *Questions relatives aux territoires polonais sous la domination prussienne,* Paris, 1919.

————, *Dantzig,* Paris, 1919.

————, Ministry of Foreign Affairs, *Official Documents Concerning Polish-German and Polish-Soviet Relations 1933–1939)* London, 1939.

Rauschning, Hermann, *Deutsche Ostpolitik von Danzig aus gesehen,* Danzig, 1934.

————, *Deutsche und Polen,* Danzig, 1934.

————, *Zehn Monate nationalsozialistische Regierung in Danzig,* Danzig, 1934.

Reiss, Hans, *Die Verfassung der Freien Stadt Danzig in der Fassung der Gesetze vom 4. Juli 1930,* Danzig, 1931.

Reynier, James de, *Le conseil du port et des voies d'eau de Dantzig,* Danzig, 1925.

Rosting, Helmer, and Vladimir Miselj, eds., "Ville Libre de

Dantzig (Manuel des questions dantzikoises, pour l'usage du Secrétariat de la Société des Nations)," Geneva, 1926.

Seymour, Charles, *The Intimate Papers of Colonel House,* 4 vols. New York, 1926–28.

Strasburger, Henryk, et al., *Dantzig et quelques aspects du problème germano-polonais,* Paris, 1932.

Stresemann, Gustav, *Vermächtnis. Der Nachlass in drei Bänden,* ed. Henry Bernhard, Berlin, 1932–33.

Temperley, H. W. V., ed., *A History of the Peace Conference of Paris,* 6 vols. London, 1920.

Treue, Wilhelm, ed., *Deutsche Parteiprogramme, 1864–1951,* Göttingen, 1954.

Turner, Henry A., Jr., ed., "Eine Rede Stresemanns über seine Locarnopolitik," *Vierteljahrshefte für Zeitgeschichte* (1967), pp. 412–36.

2. Memoirs and Diaries

Baden, Max von, *Erinnerungen und Dokumente,* Stuttgart, 1927.

Beck, Jozef, *Beiträge zur europäischen Politik, 1932–1939,* Essen, 1939.

————, *Dernier Rapport. Politique polonaise 1926–1939,* Paris, 1951.

Brockdorff-Rantzau, Ulrich von, *Dokumente und Gedanken um Versailles,* 3d ed. Berlin, 1925.

Curtius, Julius, *Sechs Jahre Minister der deutschen Republik,* Heidelberg, 1948.

D'Abernon, Edgar Vincent, *An Ambassador of Peace, 1920–1926,* 3 vols. London, 1929–30.

Dirksen, Herbert von, *Moskau, Tokio, London,* Stuttgart, 1949.

Gärtner, Margarete, *Botschafterin des guten Willens,* Bonn, 1955.

Hamel, Joost van, *Danzig and the Polish Problem,* New York, 1933.

Kessler, Harry, *Germany and Europe,* New Haven, 1923.

————, *Tagebücher 1918–1937,* Frankfurt am Main, 1961.

Koch-Weser, Erich, *Deutschlands Aussenpolitik in der Nachkriegszeit 1919–1929,* Berlin, 1929.

Laroche, Jules, *La Pologne de Pilsudski. Souvenirs d'une ambassade 1926–1935,* Paris, 1953.

Lloyd George, David, *The Truth About the Peace Treaties,* 2 vols. London, 1938.

Rauschning, Hermann, *Hitler Speaks,* London, 1939.

————, *Makers of Destruction,* London, 1942.

————, *Die Revolution des Nihilismus,* Zurich, 1938.

Rheinbaben, Werner von, *Viermal Deutschland, 1895–1954,* Berlin, 1954.

Sahm, Heinrich, *Erinnerungen aus meinen Danziger Jahren 1919–1930,* Marburg/Lahn, 1958.

Strasburger, Henryk, *Sprawa Gdańska,* Warsaw, 1937 (excerpted and translated in *Ostland-Berichte* [1937], pp. 10–37).

Szembek, Jan, *Journal 1933–1939,* Paris, 1952.

Ziehm, Ernst, *Aus meiner politischen Arbeit in Danzig 1914–1939,* Marburg/Lahn, 1960.

3. Propaganda Material

(a) German

Albert, Ernst, *Polens Kampf gegen den Danziger Hafen,* Danzig, 1933.

————, *Wachsende Konkurrenz Gdingens gegen Danzig,* Danzig, 1930.

Althoff, Hugo, *Polens Wirtschaftspolitik und Danzig,* Danzig, 1931.

Böhmert, Viktor, *Die Rechtsgrundlagen der Beziehungen zwischen Danzig und Polen,* Berlin, 1933.

Brackmann, Albert, ed., *Deutschland und Polen,* Berlin, 1933.

Curtius, Julius, *Germany and the Polish Corridor,* Berlin, 1933.

Donald, Robert, *The Polish Corridor and Its Consequences,* London, 1929.

D'Etchegoyen, O., *Pologne, Pologne,* Paris, 1926.

Fürst, Johann, *Der Widersinn des polnischen Korridors,* Berlin, 1926.

Giere, Gustav, *Danzigs Rechtsstellung unter dem Versailler Diktat,* Berlin, 1935.

Hämmerle, Karl, *Danzig und die deutsche Nation,* Berlin, 1931.

Heiss, Friedrich and A. Hillen Ziegfeld, eds., *Deutschland und der Korridor,* Berlin, 1933.

————, *Kampf um Preussenland,* Berlin, 1931.

Kaufmann, Karl Josef, *Das deutsche Westpreussen,* Berlin, 1926.

————, *Was lehrt die Geschichte über die Verständigungspolitik mit Polen?* Danzig, 1927.

Landsberg, Otto, *Die Freie Stadt Danzig*, Danzig, 1931.

Leers, Johann von, *Polnischer Korridor oder deutsches Weichselland?* Munich, 1932.

Loesch, Karl von, and Max Hildebert Boehm, eds., *Die grenz- und volkspolitischen Folgen des Friedensschlusses*, Berlin, 1930.

Martel, René, *Les frontières orientales de l'Allemagne*, Paris, 1930.

Martin, H., *The Political Status and Economic Importance of the Free City of Danzig*, Danzig, 1926.

Neumann, Rudolf, *Der Danziger Hafen in polnischer Darstellung*, Danzig, 1933.

Peiser, Kurt, *Danzig's Shipping and Foreign Trade*, Danzig, 1930.

———, *Danzig und Gdingen*, Danzig, 1931.

Proeller, A., *Der polnische Korridor, Ostpreussen und der Frieden*, Danzig, 1929.

Rathenau, Fritz, *Deutschlands Ostnot*, Berlin, 1931.

Recke, Walter, *Polens Zugang zum Meer*, Danzig, 1930.

Rudolph, Theodor, *Lehren aus zwölf Jahren der Beziehungen Danzigs zu Polen und zum Völkerbund*, Danzig, 1932.

Tourly, Robert, *Le conflit de demain: Berlin-Varsovie-Dantzig*, Paris, 1928.

Zelle, Arnold, *100 Korridor-Thesen. Eine Auseinandersetzung mit Polen*, Berlin, 1933.

(b) Polish

Askenazy, Szymon, *Poland and Danzig*, London, 1921.

Borowik, Jósef, *Gdynia: Poland's Gateway to the Sea*, Toruń, 1934.

———, *Reply to German Corridor Propaganda*, Toruń, 1930.

Brochwicz, Edouard, *Dix années de relations polono-dantzikoises*, Danzig, 1932.

Dobrzycki, Boguslaw, *Die Entwicklung des Danziger Hafens vor und nach dem Weltkriege*, Danzig, 1933.

Ehrlich, Ludwik, "Poland and Dantzig. The Case of Poland," *The Nineteenth Century and After*, April 1925.

Giannini, Amadeo, *The Problem of Danzig*, Rome, 1932.

Kutrzeba, S., *Dantzig*, Lvov, 1928.

Levesque, Geneviève, *La situation internationale de Dantzig*, Paris, 1924.

Lutman, Roman, *Aperçu historique des relations entre la Pologne et Gdansk*, Warsaw, 1933.

Paderewski, Ignace, "Poland's So-called Corridor," *Foreign Affairs,* April 1933.

Pagès, George, et al., *La Pologne et la Baltique,* Paris, 1931.

Rosinski, Wiktor, *La Pologne et la mer baltique,* Warsaw, 1928.

Siebeneichen, Alfred, *Le port de Dantzig 1919–1928,* Danzig, 1929.

————, *La politique économique de la Pologne et de Dantzig,* Danzig, 1932.

Slawski, Stanislaw, *Poland's Access to the Sea,* London, 1925.

Smogorzewski, Casimir, *Poland, Germany and the Corridor,* London, 1930.

Świątecki, Casimir, *The Development of the Port of Danzig,* Toruń, 1932.

Wagner, J., *Dantzig,* Warsaw, 1933.

Secondary Sources

Anderle, Alfred, *Die deutsche Rapallo-Politik,* [East] Berlin, 1962.

Arens, Paul, *Die Auswirkung des Versailler Vertrags auf das Danziger Wirtschaftsleben,* Frankfurt am Main, 1928.

Bauer, Hanns, and Walter Millack, eds., *Danzigs Handel in Vergangenheit und Gegenwart,* Danzig, 1925.

Bierowski, Thadée, *La ville libre de Dantzig et la guerre polono–bolchévique de 1920,* Danzig, 1932.

"Bilanz nach zehn Jahren Danzig-polnischer Zollgemeinschaft," *Danziger Wirtschaftszeitung,* 1932.

Bloch, Charles, *Hitler und die europäischen Mächte 1933/34: Kontinuität oder Bruch,* Frankfurt am Main, 1966.

Boelitz, Otto, *Das Grenz- und Auslandsdeutschtum,* 2d ed. Berlin, 1930.

Bracher, Karl Dietrich, Wolfgang Sauer, and Gerhard Schulz, *Die nationalsozialistische Machtergreifung,* Cologne, 1960.

Bregman, Alexandre, *La politique de la Pologne dans la Société des Nations,* Paris, 1932.

Bretton, Henry L., *Stresemann and the Revision of Versailles,* Stanford, 1953.

Breyer, Richard, *Das Deutsche Reich und Polen 1932–1937,* Würzburg, 1955.

Brödersdorff, Albert, ed., *Die Entstehung der Freien Stadt Danzig,* Danzig, 1930.

Brönner, W., *Die Revolutionstage in Danzig,* Danzig, 1918.

Broszat, Martin, *200 Jahre deutsche Polenpolitik,* Munich, 1963.

Celovsky, Boris, "Pilsudskis Präventivkrieg gegen das national-sozialistische Deutschland. Entstehung, Verbreitung und Widerlegung einer Legende," *Welt als Geschichte* (1954), pp. 53–70.

Claudon, Louis, "Le problème de Dantzig," *Revue de deux mondes* (1926), pp. 673–703.

Clunet, Edouard, "La 'ville libre' de Dantzig et la Pologne devant le droit international conventionnel," *Journal de droit international privé,* (1920).

Conze, Werner, *Polnische Nation und deutsche Politik im ersten Weltkrieg,* Cologne, 1958.

Craig, Gordon A., and Felix Gilbert, eds., *The Diplomats 1919–1939,* Princeton, 1953.

Crusen, Georg, Waclaw Makowski, and André Tibal, *La question de Dantzig,* Paris, 1933.

Debicki, Roman, *The Foreign Policy of Poland 1919–1939,* London, 1963.

Denne, Ludwig, *Das Danzig-Problem in der deutschen Aussenpolitik 1934–1939,* Bonn, 1959.

Draeger, Hans, *Die deutsche Revisionsbewegung, ihre bisherige Entwicklung und künftige Ziele,* Berlin, 1927.

Erdmann, Karl Dietrich, "Das Problem der Ost- und West-orientierung in der Locarnopolitik Stresemanns," *Geschichte in Wissenschaft und Unterricht* (1955), pp. 133–62.

Eschenburg, Theodor, *Die improvisierte Demokratie,* Munich, 1963.

Flakowski, Gerhard, *Der ökonomische Aspekt des Danzig-Problems,* Heidelberg, 1927.

Foster, Andrew B., "The Free City of Danzig. A Study in Politics and Economics," Unpublished master's thesis, University of Pennsylvania, 1935.

Friedrich, Walter, *Der Hohe Kommissar des Völkerbundes in Danzig,* Jena, 1932.

Fürstenau, Hubert, *Der Ausschuss für den Hafen und die Wasserwege in Danzig,* Münster, 1927.

Gasiorowski, Zygmunt J., "Did Pilsudski Attempt to Initiate a Preventive War in 1933?" *Journal of Modern History* (1955), pp. 135–51.

———, "The German-Polish Non-Aggression Pact of 1934," *Journal of Central European Affairs* (1955), pp. 3–29.

————, "Stresemann and Poland before Locarno," *Journal of Central European Affairs* (1958), pp. 25–47.

————, "Stresemann and Poland after Locarno," *Journal of Central European Affairs* (1958), pp. 292–317.

Gatzke, Hans, *Stresemann and the Rearmament of Germany,* Baltimore, 1954.

Gerson, Louis L., *Woodrow Wilson and the Rebirth of Poland 1914–1920,* New Haven, 1953.

Glamann, Friedrich W., *Die Sanierung der Währung in Danzig,* Königsberg, 1927.

Harder, Hans Adolf, *Danzig, Polen und der Völkerbund,* Berlin, 1928.

Haskins, Charles Homer, and Robert Howard Lord, *Some Problems of the Peace Conference,* Cambridge, Mass., 1920.

Höltje, Christian, *Die Weimarer Republik und das Ostlocarno-Problem 1919–1934,* Würzburg, 1958.

House, Edward M., and Charles Seymour, *What Really Happened at Paris: The Story of the Peace Conference 1918–1919,* New York, 1921.

Jedrzejewicz, Waclaw, "The Polish Plan for a 'Preventive War' Against Germany in 1933," *The Polish Review* (1966), pp. 62–91.

Keyser, Erich, *Danzigs Entwicklung,* Danzig, 1926.

————, *Danzigs Geschichte,* Danzig, 1928.

————, *Geschichte der Stadt Danzig,* Kitzingen am Main, 1951.

Klinkhammer, Reimund, "Die Aussenpolitik der SPD in der Zeit der Weimarer Republik," Unpublished doctoral dissertation, University of Freiburg, 1955.

Komarnicki, Titus, *The Rebirth of the Polish Republic: A Study in the Diplomatic History of Europe 1914–1920,* London, 1957.

Köppen, Kurt, "Triest-Danzig. Ein völkerrechtlicher Vergleich," Unpublished doctoral dissertation, University of Hamburg, 1949.

Korbel, Josef, *Poland Between East and West,* Princeton, 1963.

Kraus, Herbert, "Die Stellung des Völkerbundskommissars in Danzig," *Deutsche Juristenzeitung,* 15 July 1926.

Kruszewski, C., "The German-Polish Tariff War (1925–1934) and Its Aftermath," *Journal of Central European Affairs* (1943), pp. 294–315.

Kunz, Josef, *Die Revision der Pariser Friedensverträge,* Berlin, 1932.

Laeuen, Harald, *Polnische Tragödie,* Stuttgart, 1955.

Leonhardt, Hans Leo, *The Nazi Conquest of Danzig,* Chicago, 1942.

Loening, Otto, "Danzig und Polen," *Zeitschrift für Politik* (1925), pp. 14–38.

————, "Das Danziger- und das Korridorproblem," *Zeitschrift für Politik* (1928), pp. 705–15.

————, *Die Rechtsstellung der Freien Stadt Danzig,* Berlin, 1928.

Maass, Walter, *Der Danzig-polnische Briefkastenstreit bis zur Entscheidung des Völkerbundrates vom 11. Juni 1925,* Göttingen, 1929.

Machray, Robert, *The Poland of Pilsudski,* London, 1936.

Mackiewicz, Stanislaw, *Geschichte Polens vom 11. November 1918 bis 17. September 1939,* Marburg/Lahn, 1956.

Makowski, Juljen, *La caractère étatique de la ville libre de Dantzig,* Warsaw, 1933.

————, *La situation juridique du territoire de la ville libre de Dantzig,* Paris, 1926.

Markert, Werner, ed., *Polen,* Cologne, 1959.

Mason, John Brown, *The Danzig Dilemma: A Study in Peacemaking by Compromise,* Stanford, 1946.

————, "The Status of the Free City of Danzig under International Law," *The Rocky Mountain Law Review* (1933), pp. 85–99.

Morrow, Ian F. D., *The Peace Settlement in the German Polish Borderlands,* London, 1936.

Nelson, Harold I., *Land and Power: British and Allied Policy on Germany's Frontiers 1916–1919,* London, 1963.

Nether, Bernhard, "Die Danzig-Frage in der europäischen Politik 1914–1919," Unpublished doctoral dissertation, University of Hamburg, 1952.

"Die 'Ostforschung'—ein Stosstrupp des deutschen Imperialismus," *Zeitschrift für Geschichtswissenschaft* (1956), pp. 1181–1220.

Peiser, Kurt, *Strukturwandlungen des Danziger Aussenhandels,* Danzig, 1929.

Proeller, A., *Wirtschaftsprobleme der Freien Stadt Danzig,* Danzig, 1929.

Recke, Walter, "Das internationale Statut der Freien Stadt

Danzig: Eine Untersuchung über die Entstehung und Wirksamkeit des internationalen Regimes," Unpublished manuscript, Göttingen, 1952.

——, *Die polnische Frage als Problem der europäischen Politik,* Berlin, 1927.

Rheinbaben, Werner von, "Deutsche Ostpolitik in Locarno," *Aussenpolitik* (1953), pp. 33–40.

Robertson, Esmonde M., *Hitler's Pre-War Policy and Military Plans 1933–1939,* London, 1963.

Roos, Hans, *Geschichte der polnischen Nation 1916–1960,* Stuttgart, 1961

——, *Polen und Europa 1931–1939,* Tübingen, 1957.

——, "Die 'Präventivkriegspläne' Pilsudskis von 1933," *Vierteljahrshefte für Zeitgeschichte* (1955), pp. 344–63.

Rosé, Adam, *La politique polonaise entre les deux guerres,* Neuchâtel, 1945.

Roth, Paul, *Die Entstehung des polnischen Staates,* Berlin, 1926.

Rothschild, Joseph, *Pilsudski's Coup d'Etat,* New York, 1966.

Rudershausen, Jutta, *Die polnische Seehandelspolitik,* Berlin, 1936.

Smogorzewski, Casimir, *Poland's Access to the Sea,* London, 1934.

——, *L'union sacrée polonaise: le gouvernement de Varsovie et le 'gouvernement' polonais de Paris (1918–1919),* Paris, 1929.

Spenz, Jürgen, *Die diplomatische Vorgeschichte des Beitritts Deutschlands zum Völkerbund 1924–1926,* Göttingen, 1966.

Strunk, Hermann, *Kulturpolitik und Kulturleistung in der Freien Stadt Danzig 1920–1930,* Danzig, 1930.

Survey of International Affairs, 1920–1923, 1925, 1932, 1935, ed. Arnold Toynbee, London, 1925–36.

Taylor, Jack, *The Economic Development of Poland, 1919–1950,* Ithaca, N.Y., 1952.

Thimme, Annelise, *Gustav Stresemann: Eine politische Biographie zur Geschichte der Weimarer Republik,* Frankfurt am Main, 1957.

Vogelsang, Thilo, "Neue Dokumente zur Geschichte der Reichswehr, 1930–1933," *Vierteljahrshefte für Zeitgeschichte* (1954), pp. 397–436.

Walters, Francis P., *A History of the League of Nations,* 2 vols. London, 1952.

Wandycz, Piotr S., *France and Her Eastern Allies 1919–1925: French-Czechoslovak-Polish Relations from the Paris Peace Conference to Locarno,* Minneapolis, 1962.

Weck, Nicolas de, *La condition juridique du conseil du port et des voies d'eau de Dantzig,* Paris, 1933.

Wessling, Wolfgang, "Die staatlichen Massnahmen zur Behebung der wirtschaftlichen Notlage Ostpreussens in den Jahren 1920–1930," *Jahrbuch für die Geschichte Mittel- und Ostdeutschlands,* vol. 6, Tübingen, 1957.

Wierutsch, Günther, *Die Eigenart des Danziger Verfassungssystems im Vergleich mit dem deutschen Reichs- und Landesstaatsrecht,* Bonn, 1931.

Wockenfoth, Kurt, *Danzig als Handelshafen seit Errichtung der Freien Stadt Danzig,* Rostock, 1929.

Wolfers, Arnold, *Britain and France Between Two Wars,* New York, 1940.

"Zehn Jahre Danziger Wirtschaft, 1920–1930," *Danziger Wirtschaftszeitung,* January 1930.

Zimmermann, Ludwig, *Deutsche Aussenpolitik in der Ära der Weimarer Republik,* Göttingen, 1958.

Index

Baltic Sea

WEST PRUSSIA

GERMANY

Stettin

Oder

Schneidemühl

Filehne

Netze

Kolmar

Czarnikau

Warthe

Berlin

Warthe

Poznan

Frankfurt

Oder

Guhrau

Breslau

GERMANY'S EASTERN
BORDERS ~ 1919-1939

Former German Terr-
itories, including the
Free City of Danzig

CZECHOSLOVAKIA